# A Cultural History of Gesture

# A Cultural History of Gesture

## From Antiquity to the Present Day

*with an introduction by Sir Keith Thomas*

EDITED BY JAN BREMMER AND
HERMAN ROODENBURG

Polity Press

First published in 1991 by Polity Press
in association with Basil Blackwell

Editorial office:
Polity Press
65 Bridge Street
Cambridge CB2 1UR, UK

Marketing and production:
Basil Blackwell Ltd
108 Cowley Road, Oxford, OX4 1JF, UK

Basil Blackwell, Inc.
3 Cambridge Center
Cambridge, Massachusetts 02142, USA

ISBN 0-7456-0786-1

*British Library Cataloguing in Publication Data*

A CIP catalogue record for this book is available
from the British Library.

Typeset in 11 on 13pt Garamond
by Hope Services (Abingdon) Ltd.
Printed in Great Britain by
T.J. Press, Padstow

This book is printed on acid-free paper

# Contents

# Illustrations

# Contributors

MARIA BOGUCKA is Professor of Modern History at the Polish Academy of Science. Her books include *Nicolaus Copernicus* (1973), *Das alte Polen* (1983), and *Das alte Danzig* (2nd edn 1987).

JAN BREMMER b. 1944, is Professor of History of Religion at the University of Groningen. He is the author of *The Early Greek Concept of the Soul* (1983), co-author of *Roman Myth and Mythography* (1987), and editor of *Interpretations of Greek Mythology* (1987) and *From Sappho to De Sade: Moments in the History of Sexuality* (1989).

PETER BURKE b. 1937, is Fellow of Emmanuel College and Reader in Cultural History at the University of Cambridge. His most recent books are *Vico* (1985), *The Historical Anthropology of Early Modern Italy* (1987), *The Italian Renaissance* (1987), and *The French Historical Revolution: The Annales School, 1929–89* (1990).

HENK DRIESSEN b. 1950, is Associate Professor of Cultural Anthropology at the University of Nijmegen. He is the author of *Agro-Town and Urban Ethos in Andalusia* (1981) and *On the*

*Spanish-Moroccan Frontier: a Study in Power, Ritual and Ethnicity* (forthcoming).

WILLEM FRIJHOFF b. 1942, is Professor of Cultural History at the University of Rotterdam. He is the author of *La société néerlandaise et ses gradués, 1574–1814* (1981) and *Cultuur, mentaliteit: illusies van elites* (1984), co-author of *Prophètes et sorciers dans les Pays-Bas, XVIe–XVIIIe siècle* (1978), and co-editor of *Erasmus of Rotterdam: The Man and the Scholar* (1988).

FRITZ GRAF b. 1944, is Professor of Latin at the University of Basel. He is the author of *Eleusis und die orphische Dichtung Athens* (1974), *Griechische Mythologie* (1985), and *Nordionische Kulte* (1985). He has also published various articles on emblematics.

ROBERT MUCHEMBLED b. 1944, is Professor of Modern History at the University of Paris XIII. He is the author of *Culture populaire et culture des élites dans la France moderne* (1978), *Les derniers bûchers* (1981), *L'invention de l'homme moderne* (1988), and *La violence au village* (1989).

HERMAN ROODENBURG b. 1951, is a Fellow in Cultural History at the P. J. Meertens-Instituut, Department of Folklore, Royal Netherlands Academy of Science, Amsterdam. He is the author of *Onder censuur: de kerkelijke tucht in de gereformeerde gemeente van Amsterdam, 1578–1700* (1990), and co-editor of *Soete Minne en Helsche Boosheit: Seksuele voorstellingen in Nederland, 1300–1850* (1988) and of Aernout van Overbeke's *Anecdota sive historiae jocosae* (1991), a seventeenth-century manuscript containing some 2,500 jokes.

JEAN-CLAUDE SCHMITT b. 1946, is Director of Studies at the École des Hautes Études en Sciences Sociales, Paris. His books include *Mort d'une hérésie* (1978), *The Holy Greyhound* (1983), *Religione, folklore e società nell'Occidente medievale* (1988), and *La raison des gestes dans l'Occident médiéval* (1990).

JOANEATH SPICER b. 1943, is James A. Murnaghan Curator of Renaissance and Baroque Art at the Walters Art Gallery, Baltimore.

She has published a wide range of articles on Dutch and central European art, more recently focusing on pictorial codes, and is completing a monograph on the Dutch artist Roelandt Savery.

KEITH THOMAS b. 1933, is President of Corpus Christi College, Oxford. He is the author of two classic studies: *Religion and the Decline of Magic* (1971) and *Man and the Natural World* (1983). His published lectures include *The Perception of the Past in Early Modern England* (1984) and *History and Literature* (1989).

# Preface

It is only very recently that historians have started to become interested in gestures as a key to the cultural codes and sensibilities of the past. This growing interest seemed a good reason to organize a colloquium on the history of gestures with historians, art historians, philologists, anthropologists and folklorists, in order to explore the possibilities of this promising approach to cultural history. The conference, which was held in Utrecht in the autumn of 1989, was a great success and the resulting volume shows, as Keith Thomas argues in his introduction, that the study of gestures provides us with a fresh and new approach within historical research.

We thank all those who made the event possible. The Royal Netherlands Academy of Science, the Faculty of Letters of the Rijksuniversiteit Utrecht, and the P. J. Meertens-Instituut, Amsterdam supported the conference with generous contributions. Financial support was also received from the Faculty of Theology of the Rijksuniversiteit Groningen. A donation from our friend Jan Gast enabled us to enlarge the number of illustrations in this volume. Peter Burke's advice was most valuable in helping us to define the subject and scope of the conference. We also profited greatly from the encouragement of Professors Jaap van Marle, director of the P. J. Meertens-Instituut, and Douwe Fokkema, director of the Research Institute for History and Culture of the Utrecht Faculty of Letters. Margreet Davidse gave us good advice in the initial stages of the planning, and An van der Linden proved to be of great assistance both before and during the conference. Koos Schell helped us to overcome computer problems in the preparation of this volume, and last but not least, in his characteristically cheerful and helpful way Ken Dowden not only provided us with English versions of some papers for the colloquium at very short notice but also revised the English of most of the contributions to this volume.

Finally, we thank the contributors for their enthusiasm, and for their interest in the colloquium. Without them we would have been unable to offer the reader this volume with its fascinating studies of life in the past, studies which also enable us to take a fresh look at our own gestures which we so often take for granted.

Jan Bremmer
Herman Roodenburg

# Introduction

## KEITH THOMAS

What is gesture? The *Concise Oxford Dictionary* defines it as 'a significant movement of limb or body' or 'use of such movements as expression of feeling or rhetorical device'.[1] In this sense gesture includes any kind of bodily movement or posture (including facial expression) which transmits a message to the observer. The message can be deliberately intended and expressed in some accepted code, as when the sender winks, smiles, nods or points; it can also be inadvertent and expressed symptomatically, as when he or she blushes, grimaces with pain, or twitches with embarrassment. Some of these gestures are intended to accompany speech. Others, like the sign languages of the deaf and dumb or 'emblematic' gestures like thumbing one's nose, are substitutes for it.

The body can also transmit messages without any movement at all. To refrain from gesture, for example by stifling symptoms of grief, could be as demonstrative an act as bursting into tears. The body is not neutral until its owner makes an involuntary movement or decides to send out a signal – for faces, hands, and limbs can be as significant in repose as in motion. There is no attribute of the human body, whether size, shape, height or colour, which does not convey some social meaning to the observer. A few years ago a correspondent in *The Listener* claimed that, 'by the

time he is forty, I can . . . more often than not, read a man's class by
the signature it has left in the lines and folds of his face'.[2] The
assertion was exaggerated, but we know what he meant, for
differences of health, occupation, education, and sensibility usually
leave their mark. As David Hume remarked in the eighteenth
century, 'The skin, pores, muscles and nerves of a day-labourer are
different from those of a man of quality . . . The different stations
of life influence the whole fabric.'[3] The human body, in short, is as
much a historical document as a charter or a diary or a parish
register (though unfortunately one which is a good deal harder to
preserve) and it deserves to be studied accordingly.[4]

The essays in this book are all concerned with the history of
gesture in one form or another, but, in response to its open-ended
nature, they interpret the topic loosely. Sometimes they are
concerned with the physical expression of emotion or the mimicry
of human activities. Sometimes they analyse the deliberate use of
coded signals, like the 'manual rhetoric' of the classical Roman
orator or the figure-language of sexual insult. At other times they
discuss the whole carriage and deportment of the body. This was
indeed the original meaning of the term, for when a fifteenth-
century author described a knight as 'comely of gesture', he did
not mean that he could wink or nod in a pleasing fashion. He
meant that the knight moved and held himself in a graceful
manner. 'Gesture' was the general carriage of the body. Only later
did the term come to be exclusively used in the narrower sense
indicated by the *Concise Oxford Dictionary*.[5]

There is nothing new about the study of gesture. Since the
Renaissance there have been many physiognomists, like G. B. della
Porta, Charles Le Brun, and J. C. Lavater, who have attempted to
codify the facial expressions of emotion and character.[6] In the
seventeenth century Francis Bacon observed that gestures were 'as
transitory hieroglyphics', 'a kind of emblems', and the investigations
of Giovanni Bonifacio and John Bulwer were conducted on the
assumption that there was a universal, natural language of gesture
which was understood by all nations and could be used to facilitate
the conduct of international trade between Europeans and native
peoples.[7] In the nineteenth century Charles Darwin's *The Expression
of the Emotions in Man and Animals* gave new support to the view
that physical expressions might be biologically inherited. Modern

ethologists stress the similarities between the bodily movements which humans and animals employ to express hostility, dominance, or territoriality; and they point to the near-universality of some facial expressions of emotion which, like laughing, weeping, yawning or blushing, seem to cross linguistic and national boundaries.

But most modern writing on the subject starts from the assumption that gesture is not a universal language, but is the product of social and cultural differences. There are many languages of gesture and many dialects. This was the belief of Andrea de Jorio, who in the early nineteenth century attempted to reconstruct the mimic code of classical antiquity on the basis of the Neapolitan gestures of its own day. It was given classic expression in 1936 by the anthropologist Marcel Mauss in his essay on 'The Techniques of the Body', in which he pointed out that the most elementary dimensions of physical behaviour – the way people stand, sit, walk, use their hands, eat or sleep – vary greatly from society to society. The British have only to watch a Japanese film to see that facial expressions are not always intelligible to those raised in another culture; and they need travel no further than Italy to discover that the local gesture indicating 'Come here quickly!' is their sign for 'Go away at once!' Mauss's observations have inspired some notable cross-cultural surveys of bodily expression and facial gesture, while the cultural variability of human gesture has nowhere been more effectively demonstrated than in David Efron's analysis of how immigrant Italians and Eastern European Jews changed their gestural habits as they became assimilated into the life of the United States.[8]

Nowadays the study of gesture is primarily the business of anthropologists, linguists, and social psychologists. They are concerned with gesture as a form of non-verbal communication and they have a word, kinesics, for the study of communicative body movements. Kinesics is a highly developed subject with a variety of subdivisions, ranging from proxemics (the study of the distance which people keep from each other when talking), to haptics (the study of the way in which they touch each other during the conversation).[9] Linguists have regarded gesture as a form of language, possibly even the predecessor of language. They have compiled guides to the sign languages of Cistercian monks,

Australian Aborigines, and the deaf, along with dictionaries of gestures in various contemporary contexts. The recent guide to French gesture, Calbris and Montredon's *Des gestes et des mots pour le dire*, is an entertaining example. The difficulty about such dictionaries, of course, is that gestures tend to be polysemous and their meaning can be determined only by the context. In an admirably lucid survey, Desmond Morris and his collaborators have described and mapped out the European distribution of twenty major symbolic gestures, with historical notes on their likely origins.[10]

More ambitious writers have not been content to record and classify these cultural differences. They have advanced large-scale theories as to why variations in bodily behaviour take the forms they do. Some fifty years ago the sociologist Norbert Elias argued that early modern Europe saw an increasing inhibition of bodily impulses, a growing sense of shame about physical functions, and an enhanced concern to restrain the expression of emotion. In his view these changes reflected changes in the structure of society, notably the imposition by the state of greater restraint and the lengthening of the chains of social interdependence. Belatedly translated from the German, his views have had great influence in recent decades, particularly in the Netherlands, where the conference from which the present volume originated was held. Also influential has been the theory advanced by the anthropologist Mary Douglas that the body is a symbol of social relations and that the control of bodily expression will be more or less strict according to the degree of group pressure upon the individual.

Such large-scale models have received relatively little serious historical scrutiny because it is much harder to study the history of gesture and bodily comportment than to observe their present-day manifestations. It is true that art historians have given much attention to the symbolic meaning of deportment and gesture in painting and sculpture, for they have to master the language before they can decode the picture.[11] Similarly, those who study sermons or plays have examined the oratorical gestures of preachers and actors.[12] Using the evidence of excavated skeletons, some archaeologists have even offered generalizations about the body habits of the past, for example by suggesting that medieval French peasants were more accustomed to squatting than sitting.[13] Historians of the ancient world have long been accustomed to studying the gestures of classical art and oratory.[14] Innumerable literary critics have taken account of the physical expression of meanings and emotions as revealed in poetry, drama, and the novel. Yet most modern historians have shied away from what they regard as a highly elusive and intractable subject. The essays contained in this book are therefore to be warmly welcomed as pioneering ventures into what is still relatively uncharted territory. The contributors are of different nationalities and their subjects range from classical Greece to twentieth-century Andalusia. But though they differ in their preoccupations they are united in regarding the history of gesture as a topic which is both capable of serious study and non-trivial in its implications.

That it is capable of study can hardly be disputed. Historians cannot observe the bodies of the past in motion, but the sources from which inferences can be made are surprisingly rich. There are the published accounts of sign languages, the formal codes compiled for orators, actors, dancers, and monks. There are the incidental descriptions to be found in legal depositions and contemporary accounts of events. There is the huge volume of prescriptive writing on manners, telling children and adults how to control their bodily movements. Finally, there is the whole of European imaginative literature. For it is a feature of the history of gesture, as of so many of the most absorbing topics in modern social history, that there is no single cache of source material to be worked through; rather, the evidence lies scattered throughout the literary remains and material artifacts of the past.

Gesture, then, can be studied historically. But is it worth studying? Is it not too trivial in its implications to engage the attention of those who should be devoting themselves to understanding larger themes? Does it matter whether the Greeks and Romans thought it bad manners to pick their noses or just what James I's brother-in-law, the King of Denmark, did with his fingers when in 1606 he chose to insult the aged Earl of Nottingham, who had recently married a young wife?[15]

There are two reasons why the study of gesture is of more than purely antiquarian interest. The first is that gesture formed an indispensable element in the social interaction of the past. The second is that it can offer a key to some of the fundamental values and assumptions underlying any particular society; as the French historians would say, it illuminates *mentalité*.

In the first place, gesture is an inseparable accompaniment of any spoken language. The difference between a face-to-face encounter and a telephone conversation is a reminder of the extent to which facial expression and bodily movements can amplify, modify, confirm, or subvert verbal utterance. Sorrow or happiness, deference or insult, are conveyed as effectively by gesture as by word. Non-verbal 'leakage' – a shifty look or a momentary hesitation – will undermine the whole effect of an overtly honest declaration. Different languages involve different facial movements and have different bodily connotations. As they said of Mayor La Guardia of New York, one could switch the sound off the television and still know from his gestures whether he was speaking English, Italian, or Yiddish. We all recall the story of the Italian who had to remain silent because it was too cold to take his hands out of his pockets. In many formal contexts, liturgical, legal, or ceremonial, the speaker's posture and bodily movement may be more important than the words uttered. 'Some foolishly imagine that praier is made either better or worse by the jesture of our bodyes,' remarks a sixteenth-century Protestant commentator.[16]

The historian who wants to study the past until he can hear the people talking must therefore also be able to visualize them as they conversed. This involves establishing not just the performative gestures of stylized ceremonial or worship, but also the non-verbal language of daily conversation. That was a language no less complex than the literary language of the time, but there are no grammars or dictionaries setting it out, for one of the defining features of informal gesture is that no one ever teaches it (save those parts which fall under the rules of courtesy and politeness). Anthropologically-minded historians have to establish this grammar of gesture for themselves. The work is part of that larger, inescapable task of reconstructing all the codes and conventions which create the context for meaningful behaviour in the society under study. For all the efforts of the art historians, a recent student of medieval misericords has remarked ruefully that 'the iconography of historical gesture is still in its infancy'.[17] The same could be said of the study of that rich repertoire of non-verbal insult and mockery which no period of history has been without.

The second reason for studying gesture historically is that it has always been an important ingredient in social differentiation. Like all other languages, the language of gesture can separate as well as unite. Aspiring groups have long used distinctive modes of bodily comportment as a means of setting themselves apart from their inferiors. In the first essay in this volume Jan Bremmer shows how in the fourth century BC the Greek upper classes cultivated an upright posture and an unhurried gait; the strict control of emotion and the maintenance of dignity became essential to their authority. Similarly, Maria Bogucka suggests in another chapter that in early modern Poland the nobility marked themselves out by carefully learned posture and bodily comportment; for the Poles, differences in gesture became the outward expression of social hierarchy. The same we know to have been true of early modern England. One Tudor author remarks that a person who came into the company of two people, one brought up in the countryside, the other at Court or in London, could at once tell which was which, partly by their speech, but also by their 'gesture and behaviour'.[18] In the eighteenth century it was accepted that one of the attributes which distinguished ladies and gentlemen was their way of moving.[19] 'You may read their birth on their faces,' wrote William Darrell in the early eighteenth century (anticipating our correspondent to *The Listener*), 'their gait and mien tell their quality.'[20] Adam Smith wrote of the young nobleman that

His air, his manner, his deportment, all mark that elegant and graceful sense of his own superiority which those who are born to inferior stations can hardly ever arrive at. These are the arts by which he proposes to make mankind more easily submit to his authority and to govern their inclinations according to his own pleasure; and in this he is seldom disappointed. These arts, supported by rank and pre-eminence, are, upon ordinary occasions, sufficient to govern the world.[21]

Conversely, the lower classes were normally perceived as rough and ungainly. Adam Smith contrasted 'the most polite persons', who 'preserve the same composure' throughout a public entertainment, with 'the rabble', who 'express all the various passions by their gesture and behaviour'.[22] 'English boys,' according to one

early twentieth-century Oxford don, 'regard displays of anger and
passion as characteristics of the socially inferior.'[23] No student of
social differentiation can afford to neglect the part played by
differences in physical comportment in separating social groups
from each other and arousing feelings of mutual hostility. For if
the superior classes have tended to regard their inferiors as coarse
and heavy-handed, the lower classes have frequently responded by
despising their superiors as pretentious and affected. In his chapter
Robert Muchembled describes the early modern period as one of
'cultural bipolarization'; and it seems probable that it was a time
when such social differences in physical comportment became
more marked, even if their many nuances and gradations make it
hard to squeeze them into a simple polar model.

   Gesture reflected differences of gender as well as of class. At all
periods of history the prescriptions for the physical behaviour of
women have been different from those of men. Characteristically,
women have been encouraged to look modestly downwards, to
walk with small steps, to eat smaller portions of food and, when
handkerchiefs arrived, to blow their noses in smaller ones. An
eighteenth-century aesthetic theorist commented on 'the painful
sentiments we feel when female features assume the expression of
man or those of men assume that of woman'.[24] Any gesture
implying female assertiveness was forbidden; in her chapter on
'The Renaissance Elbow' Joaneath Spicer comments on how
inappropriate it was thought for ordinary women of that period to
stand with arms akimbo, an aggressive posture fitting only for
males or Amazonian women rulers. Conversely Henk Driessen
shows how in rural Andalusia today masculine domination is
upheld by the contentious gesticulation which plays a central role
in what he calls the 'choreography of male sociability'.

   Behind the long history of pedagogic instruction in gesture and
deportment lay not just a concern to reinforce the differences of
gender and rank. There was also an aesthetic-cum-moral conviction
that external bodily behaviour manifested the inner life of the soul.
Bodily control exemplified internal harmony and the superiority
of the mind to the body. Physiognomy betrayed the character.
This was one of the reasons why so little tolerance was normally
displayed to those who employed a different gestural language.
Inappropriate or excessive gesture was either condemned as a

clumsy lack of co-ordination or disparaged as 'gesticulation'. Jean-Claude Schmitt has shown that the distinction between virtuous *gestus* and unpleasant *gesticulatio* was a medieval one.[25] One of the themes running through this volume is that of the distaste of northern Europeans for the gesticulating southerners, particularly the French and Italians. '[Do not] shrug or wrygg thy shoulders as we see in many Italians,' runs an injunction in the first English translation of Erasmus's *De civilitate morum puerilium*.[26]

The origins of this difference between north and south remain obscure, though it is worth recalling that De Jorio interpreted South Italian gesture as a cultural legacy of the Romans. In the early modern period it was very conspicuous. Peter Burke notes that the Italians perceived the Spaniards as gesturing too little, whereas the English and Germans perceived the southerners as gesturing too much. Herman Roodenburg tells us that the Dutch *Groot ceremonie-boeck der beschaafde zeeden* condemned the Italians as uncivil because they 'speak with their head, arms, feet and the whole body'. A few years later Adam Smith commented that 'Foreigners observe that there is no nation in the world which use[s] so little gesticulation in their conversation as the English. A Frenchman, in telling a story that is not of the least consequence to him or to anyone else, will use a thousand gestures and contortions of his face, whereas a wellbred Englishman will tell you one wherein his life and fortune are concerned without altering a muscle.'[27] That quintessential Englishman, Dr Samuel Johnson, was so hostile to gesticulation that 'when another gentleman thought he was giving additional force to what he uttered, by expressive movements of his hands, Johnson fairly seized them and held them down'.[28] As one late Victorian writer proudly declared, 'We English . . . use gesture-language less than almost any nation upon earth.'[29]

Only in the later twentieth century has the British self-definition of themselves as a non-gesticulating people begun to dwindle. Those who attend academic seminars or watch discussion programmes on television will have noticed a growing tendency for earnest intellectual discourse to be accompanied by much waving and flailing of hands. As for the idea of southern Europeans as inveterate gesticulators, there are clearly regional and social distinctions to be drawn. Fritz Graf reminds us that among the ancient Romans gesticulation was thought to be more characteristic of slaves than freemen, while a recent acccount of gesture in France states that its use as an accompaniment of conversation is much more extensive among the working classes than among the bourgeoisie.[30]

Those who study the past usually find themselves arriving at two contradictory conclusions. The first is that the past was very different from the present. The second is that it was very much the same. These essays on the history of gesture produce this same ambivalent effect. For on the one hand it seems that the meaning of many gestures and postures has remained constant. To walk with head erect still signifies authority, dignity, and detachment. To cower and cringe indicates abasement. Gravity and impassivity are evidence of self-control, usually associated with rule and superiority (though not always, if we think of the guardsman on parade or the butler standing behind the host at the dinner-table). To lower one's eyes remains a gesture of modesty and submission. Obtrusive elbows are as much an assertion of territoriality and self-regard today as they were for Joaneath Spicer's Renaissance painters or for the medieval Bakers' Company of London when it fined one of its members 'for lieing on his elboe when the Master and some of the ancients were in the room'.[31]

Yet on the other hand it is clear that the meaning of gesture has changed over time and place. We no longer speak the body language of the past and much of it has to be painstakingly reconstructed. We cannot intuitively know that when Charlemagne pulled his beard he was expressing grief or that for Quintilian the slapping of the thigh meant not exhilaration but anger. In their excavations of the gestural language of the past the contributors to this volume advance our understanding of bygone patterns of communication. They also reveal that changing gestural codes offer a key to changing social relationships. The emergence of the handshake as the normal symbol of greeting is shown by Herman Roodenburg to have been part of the move to a more egalitarian, less deferential, ethic, for the handshake superseded the habit of bowing, kneeling, or curtsying. Perhaps that is why in modern France colleagues will shake hands daily, whereas in Japan the survival of hierarchical attitudes has held back the handshake, just as it has in the more conservative segments of modern Britain. De Tocqueville explained the reserved attitude of the British to the body in terms of the ambiguities of their social structure: 'everybody lives in constant dread lest advantage should be taken of his familiarity. Unable to judge at once of the social position of those he meets, an Englishman prudently avoids all contact with them.'[32]

Several of the contributors recognize in the early modern period that suppression of gesture and growth of bodily control which Norbert Elias saw as part of the civilizing process. But though they confirm his view that this was a key period in the definition of civility as involving a strict curb upon physical impulses, they also demonstrate that he gave a misleadingly unilinear character to what was not a single, unfolding development but one which expanded and contracted with changes in ideology and social context. Jan Bremmer reveals the presence in fourth-century BC Athens of most of the ideals of bodily restraint which Elias associated with a much later period. It was the humanist rediscovery of classical ideals of deportment, transmitted via Cicero and St Ambrose, which underpinned the manuals of civility in the early modern era. Indeed an attempt to reintroduce the refinement and urbanity of the ancient senatorial aristocracy had already been made in the imperial courts of the early middle ages.[33]

Conversely, the late twentieth century displays a gradual rejection of some of these classical restraints. The middle-class youth of western Europe and America have no apparent inhibition about eating in the street, exposing their bodies, gesticulating, shouting, or expressing their emotions in a physical form. The casual kiss on meeting, which Erasmus noted in 1499 to have been a normal English practice, is, as Willem Frijhoff observes, now returning to northern Europe after centuries of repression. The decline of external forms of deference, like the growing cult of informality and 'friendliness', suggests that we are moving into a new era of gestural history, and one appropriate to a more democratic era. Contemporary experience thus confirms the moral which is to be drawn from these studies of the past: namely, that behind the apparently most trivial differences of gesture and comportment there lie fundamental differences of social relationship and attitude. To interpret and account for a gesture is to unlock the whole social and cultural system of which it is a part.

## NOTES

1 For an excellent brief survey of the problems of defining gesture, see Adam Kendon, 'Introduction' to Adam Kendon (ed.), *Nonverbal Communication: Interaction and Gesture* (The Hague, 1981), pp. 28–40.
2 Timothy Poston in *The Listener*, 98 (1 September 1977), p. 276.
3 David Hume, *A Treatise of Human Nature* (Everyman's Library; 2 vols, London, 1911), vol. 1, pp. 115–16 (Bk 2, pt 3, sect. 1).
4 Though not in as indiscriminate a fashion as is suggested by the diverse contributions to Michael Feher (ed.), *Fragments for a History of the Human Body* (3 vols, New York, 1989), where the subject is vaguely defined as 'the area where life and thought intersect'.
5 See *Oxford English Dictionary*, s.v. 'gesture: 1a'.
6 For these authors and those cited below see the Bibliography appended by the editors to this volume. Another bibliographical survey, with a helpfully analytic commentary, is Jean-Claude Schmitt, 'Introduction and general bibliography', *History and Anthropology*, 1 (1984), pp. 1–28.
7 J. Spedding, R. L. Ellis and D. D. Heath (eds), *The Works of Francis Bacon* (14 vols, London, 1857–74), vol. 3, p. 400; vol. 4, p. 440; John Bulwer, *Chirologia: or the Naturall Language of the Hand . . . Whereunto is added Chironomia: or the Art of Manuall Rhetoricke* (2 vols, London, 1644); idem, *Anthropometamorphosis: Man Transform'd: or the Artificial Changling* (London, 1653); Giovanni Bonifacio, *L'arte de' cenni* (Vicenza, 1616); James Knowlson, *Universal Language Schemes in England and France, 1600–1800* (Toronto, 1975), appendix A; Dilwyn Knox, 'Ideas on gesture and universal language, c.1550–1650', in John Henry and Sara Hutton (eds), *New Perspectives on Renaissance Thought* (London, 1990), pp. 101–36.
8 David Efron, *Gesture, Race and Culture* (The Hague, 1972; 1st published, New York, 1941). Cf. Weston La Barre, 'The cultural basis of emotions and gestures', *Journal of Personality*, 16 (1947–8), pp. 49–68, and Gordon W. Hewes, 'World distribution of certain postural habits', *American Anthropologist*, 57 (1955), pp. 231–44.
9 Ray L. Birdwhistell, *Kinesics and Context: Essays on Body-Motion Communication* (Philadelphia, 1970); Michael Watson, *Proxemic Behaviour* (The Hague, 1970).
10 Desmond Morris, Peter Collett, Peter Marsh and Marie O'Shaughnessy, *Gestures: Their Origins and Distribution* (London, 1979).
11 For example, Moshe Barasch, *Giotto and the Language of Gesture*

(Cambridge, 1987); Michael Baxandall, *Painting and Experience in Fifteenth-Century Italy*, 2nd edn (Oxford, 1988), pp. 56–81; François Garnier, *Le langage de l'image au Moyen Age. Signification et Symbolique* (2 vols, Paris, 1982–9); E. H. Gombrich, 'Ritualized gesture and expression in art', *Philosophical Transactions of the Royal Society*, Series B, 251 (1966), pp. 393–401, repr. in Gombrich, *The Image and the Eye* (Oxford, 1982), pp. 63–77.

12  For example, B. L. Joseph, *Elizabethan Acting* (London, 1951); David Bevington, *Action is Eloquence: Shakespeare's Language of Gesture* (Cambridge, Mass., 1984); Alastair Smart, 'Dramatic gesture and expression in the age of Hogarth and Reynolds', *Apollo*, 82 (1965), pp. 90–7.

13  Françoise Piponnier and Richard Bucaille, 'La belle ou la bête? Remarques sur l'apparence corporelle de la paysannerie médiévale', *Ethnologie Française*, 6 (1976), pp. 227–32, esp. p. 229.

14  Andrea de Jorio, *La mimica degli antichi investigata nel gestire Napoletano* (Napoli, 1832); Carl Sittl, *Die Gebärden der Griechen und Römer* (Leipzig, 1890); Richard Brilliant, *Gesture and Rank in Roman Art* (New Haven, 1963); Gerhard Neumann, *Gesten und Gebärden in der griechischen Kunst* (Berlin, 1965); Elizabeth C. Evans, 'Physiognomics in the Ancient World', *Transactions of the American Philosophical Society*, New Series, 59, pt 5 (Philadelphia, 1969), pp. 3–101; Graf, chapter 2 of this volume.

15  William Harris, *An Historical and Critical Account of the Life and Writings of James the First* (London, 1753), pp. 67n–68n.

16  John Marbeck, *A Book of Notes and Common Places* (London, 1581), p. 852.

17  Malcolm Jones, 'Folklore motifs in late medieval art, I', *Folklore*, 100 (1989), pp. 201–17, esp. p. 206.

18  *Cyvile and Uncyvile Life* (London, 1579), sig. Miii$^v$.

19  [James Burnett, Lord Monboddo], *Of the Origin and Progress of Language* (6 vols, Edinburgh, 1773–92), vol. 4, p. 295.

20  William Darrell, *The Gentleman Instructed in the Conduct of a Virtuous and Happy Life*, 9th edn (Dublin, 1727), p. 7.

21  Adam Smith, *The Theory of Moral Sentiments*, eds D. D. Raphael and A. L. Macfie (Oxford, 1976), p. 54.

22  Adam Smith, *Lectures on Rhetoric and Belles Lettres*, ed. J. C. Bryce (Oxford, 1983), p. 198.

23  G. B. Grundy, *Fifty-Five Years at Oxford* (London, 1945), p. 44. He adds, 'That is why the French teachers of a former age were most of them such hopeless disciplinary failures in English schools.'

24 Archibald Alison, *Essays on the Nature and Principles of Taste*, 4th edn (2 vols, Edinburgh, 1815), vol. 2, p. 292.

25 Schmitt, 'Introduction and general bibliography'.

26 Des. Erasmus, *De civilitate morum puerilium*, transl. Robert Whitinton (London, 1540) sig. C7ᵛ. The reference to 'Italians' is the translator's; Erasmus had written *'quod in nonnullis videmus'*.

27 Smith, *Lectures on Rhetoric and Belles Lettres*, pp. 191–2. (I am grateful to Mr J. B. Bamborough, who many years ago pointed out to me the interest of this subject and gave me some valuable references.)

28 *Boswell's Life of Johnson*, ed. George Birkbeck Hill, revd L. F. Powell (6 vols, Oxford, 1934–50), vol. 4, pp. 322–3.

29 J. G. Wood, *Man and Beast Here and Hereafter*, 3rd edn (London, 1876), p. 112. David Efron (*Gesture, Race and Culture*, pp. 53, 59) has suggested that French gesticulation was the result of late sixteenth-century Italian influence and that at least some eighteenth-century English people were less restrained than Johnson and Smith would have liked.

30 Graf, chapter 2 in this volume; Laurence Wylie, *Beaux Gestes. A Guide to French Body Talk* (Cambridge, Mass., 1977), pp. viii–ix.

31 Sylvia Thrupp, *A Short History of the Worshipful Company of Bakers of London* (London, n.d.), pp. 87–8.

32 Alexis de Tocqueville, *Democracy in America*, transl. Henry Reeve, revd Francis Bowen, ed. Phillips Bradley (2 vols, New York, 1945), vol. 2, p. 179.

33 C. Stephen Jaeger, *The Origins of Courtliness: Civilizing Trends and the Formation of Courtly Ideals, 939–1210* (Philadelphia, 1985).

# 1

# Walking, standing, and sitting in ancient Greek culture

## JAN BREMMER

In his pioneering article on the techniques of the body (see Thomas, p. 3 of this volume) Marcel Mauss also paid attention to ways of moving, while drawing upon his own experience.[1] In the First World War he had noted differences in marching between the French and the English, and after observing nurses during a stay in a New York hospital he realized the influence of the American cinema on the way French girls walked. If he had lived today he would surely have noted the curious way in which models have started to move on the catwalk in recent years and the abolishment of the goose step by the East German Ministry of Defence in the summer of 1990, only months before the German reunification. Admittedly, in his interest in ways of walking Mauss had been pre-empted by Balzac, who, like other nineteenth-century authors, was fascinated by the physiognomical theories of Lavater (1741–1801). In 1833, he published an entertaining treatise, *Théorie de la démarche* ('Theory of walking'), which contains many perceptive comments which are still valuable.[2] Balzac's contribution, though, has largely been forgotten and Mauss's investigations have hardly received the attention they deserve; indeed, in most of the subjects he enumerated research has still to begin. In this chapter I would like to follow up this interest in ways of moving and concentrate both on the manner in which the ancient Greeks walked, stood, and sat and upon the values they attached to these body techniques.[3]

## WALKING

The subject of walking is less strange than would appear at first sight. Homer had already noted the hero's stride, and the gait of males attracted interest all through antiquity until the times of the anonymous late Latin physiognomist and Ambrose, who succinctly formulated the importance of physiognomical interest: *habitus mentis enim in corporis statu cernitur.*[4] Unfortunately, the interest of our sources is limited to the upper classes and their public *personae*. Nowhere do we even get an inkling as to how males and females moved in private. As is so often the case, this aspect of ancient private life belongs to a world which is irretrievably lost.

Let us start our analysis with some passages from Homer, our oldest literary source. When Paris challenges the Greeks to a duel in order to decide whether he can keep the beautiful Helen, he arrives on the battlefield armed to the teeth with a bow, sword, and two spears. Menelaus, Helen's deceived husband, sees him approaching 'with long strides (*makra bibas*) in front of the throng' (*Iliad* 3.22). The poet clearly draws the picture of an impressive warrior whose gait denotes powerful movement in order to impress the enemy. In other words, Paris' gait belongs to that category of behaviour that modern ethologists call *Imponierverhalten*.

Despite his being heavily armed and showing off, Paris immediately loses courage when he faces Menelaus and is only saved from death by the intervention of his protectress Aphrodite. When his brother Hector in turn challenges the Greeks, he is confronted by the huge, terrifying Ajax who rushes forward 'with a smile on his grim face, and with his feet below he went with long strides, brandishing his far-shadowing lance. And the Greeks rejoiced when they saw him' (7.211–4). In this passage too the long strides belong to the picture of the impressive warrior whose arrival on the battlefield heartens his comrades.

We find similar gaits in the battle for the ships of the Greeks.

After Achilles had withdrawn into his tent in anger, the situation became critical for the Greeks, as 'the Trojans pressed forward together and Hector led them on with long strides.' The Trojan hero is preceded by Apollo who is even more impressive, waving the terrible aegis 'which Hephaestus gave Zeus to carry to terrify men' (15.306–10). In this case also, Hector and Apollo are pictured as being frightening leaders and warriors whom it would be extremely hard to resist. On the Greek side, Ajax remains as a kind of last bulwark 'going about the many decks of the fast ships with long strides, and his voice reached to heaven' (15.676, 686). Somewhat later in the same battle, Homer even seems to use the expression 'with long strides' as a kind of shorthand depiction of impressive behaviour when he says: 'Ajax was the first to challenge him taking long strides' (13.809; similarly 16.534).

In the *Odyssey* the expression occurs twice. After Polyphemus has been blinded by Odysseus, he carefully searches among his sheep in order to prevent Odysseus and his comrades from escaping. When he notices that his favourite ram is the last one to come out he wonders what has happened as it was always 'the first to graze on the fresh flowers of the meadows with long strides' (9.449–50): the ram as the perfect commander. Our final example is Achilles. When Odysseus had finished speaking to him in the underworld, 'the soul of Achilles went away with long strides' (11.539). It is a fine poetic detail that the last glimpse of Greece's greatest hero shows him in all his might and glory.

In Homer, then, walking with long strides was the sign of the great commander who wanted to assert himself on the battlefield. In the later part of the Archaic age (*c.*800–500 BC), Greek battle tactics were completely transformed by the introduction of the phalanx, a formation in which the troops had to stay together in one line. In this disposition there was no longer room for heroes asserting themselves by striding ahead. So it can hardly be chance that in the Classical period (*c.*500–300 BC) virtually nothing more is heard concerning this gait of males. The only time it is still mentioned is in Aristophanes' *Birds* where the cock 'parades with big strides like the Persian king' (486). The Persian king was considered to be larger than life and was evidently supposed to walk accordingly.[5] Yet this particular gait was not completely forgotten, as in the early Hellenistic pseudo-Aristotelian *Physiognomy* the most

perfect male type, the leonine type, moves slowly (cf. *below*)
'with a long stride' (809a), and the *makrobamon*, or 'the man with
the long stride', is seen as an effective operator (813a). This quality
recurs in the second-century AD Smyrnaean sophist Polemon,
whose physiognomic work only survives in an Arabic version –
and that accessible only in a Latin translation! According to him,
the *amplitudo gressus* denotes *fides, sinceritas, magna efficacia,
animus elatus* ('noble mind') *et irae absentia*. These moral qualities
are far removed from the heroic world, but the origin of the
explanation can still be seen, albeit through a glass darkly.[6]

If the heroes of the Archaic age were not on the battlefield, were
they still asserting themselves through their gait? We can probably
give a positive answer to this question, as the seventh-century poet
Archilochus (fr.114) sings: 'I don't like the great general, walking
with wide strides,[7] / boasting with his locks, his moustache
shaven.' Evidently, in peacetime the 'big men' walked in a way
nowadays perhaps best paralleled in the macho way of walking of
the hero in the Western. And like so many other valued qualities,
this gait found its reflection in early Greek onomastics as well,
since males could be called Eurybatos, or 'He who walks with
wide steps', the best known example being the traitor who caused
the defeat of the famous Lydian king Croesus against the Persians
in the middle of the sixth century.[8]

In fifth-century Athens, the leading cultural centre of Greece, the
development into a democracy had marginalized the political position
of the aristocracy. It is hardly surprising, therefore, that walking
with wide strides disappeared into the background although it did
not disappear completely. When in Aristophanes' *Wasps* (422 BC)
a son tries to teach his father to walk in an upper-class manner, he
still advises him 'to swagger luxuriously, with legs apart' (1169).
Yet most aristocrats must have felt the pressure for less ostentatious
behaviour and therefore chose to distinguish themselves in a
different way.[9] It is now the ability to walk quietly and slowly
which comes to the fore, although Athenian comedy (Phrynichus
fr. 10 K.–A.) ridiculed a timid walk. When in Plato's *Charmides*
(159A,B) Socrates asks Charmides, Plato's maternal uncle and a
member of the Athenian elite, to define *sophrosyne* or 'temperance
and chastity', he answers that he thought it was 'doing all things in
an orderly and quiet fashion – for example, walking in the street.'

Naturally, Plato could be importing contemporary standards in his picture of his uncle, who died in 403 BC, but Plutarch in his biography of Pericles (5.1) also praises the *praotes*, or 'gentleness, unhurriedness', of the politician's gait, and a character in Sophocles' *Thyestes* (fr. 257) says: 'Come on, let's go quickly. For just haste never shall be the subject of reproach.' Moreover, it seems not impossible that this quiet way of walking went along with more quiet gestures in general. From the late sixth century onwards, Athenian aristocracy had been developing a growing control of emotions and refinement of manners. And just as ancient Egyptian art contrasts Egyptian self-control with foreign lack of restraint and in sixteenth-century Europe northerners start to mock southerners for their exhuberant gesturing (Burke, Ch. 4 in this volume), so fifth-century tragedy contrasts Greek self-restraint with foreign abandonment. It is therefore hard to believe that this development had no influence on gestures in general.[10]

The slow gait of the Athenian aristocrat must have struck a happy medium, as Athenian comedy consistently mocked those males who used to walk around in long tunics as being effeminates or passive homosexuals: apparently, they walked too slowly.[11] On the other hand, the fourth-century orator Demosthenes (37.52, 55; 45.77) surely did not intend to praise his opponents by mentioning that they always walked fast. These Demosthenic orations (32 and 45) are particularly interesting because they concern the walks of people who have good reason to be conscious of prejudice against them and to fear that others will use their personal habits as grounds for increasing hostility against them. In both cases, the persons attacked fall short of the Athenian ideal of the leisured, open, and friendly citizen; it is only an arrogant man, according to Theophrastus' *Characters* (24.8), who has no time for conversation when he is walking in the street. Understandably, then, Aristotle (*Ethica Nicomachea* 4.3.34) states that to walk slowly is the sign of the *megalopsychos*, or 'great-souled' man. The words of Alexis (fr. 263 Kock, tr. C. B. Gulick), the most productive fourth-century author of comedies, sum up well the importance of the proper gait in Athens:

This is one trait which I regard worthy of no gentleman – to walk in the streets with careless gait when one may do it gracefully. For this nobody exacts any toll from us, and one need not bestow any honour in order to receive it again from others. Rather, to them who walk with dignity comes full meed of honour, while they who see it have pleasure, and life has its grace. What man who pretends to have any sense would not win for himself such a reward?

The idea recurs in the physiognomists where the *kosmios*, or 'honest, orderly', citizen is slow in his movements (Pseudo-Aristotle, *Physiognomy* 807b; Adamantius, p. 413 Foerster). In fact, in late antiquity an orderly (*kosmion*), quiet (*hemeron*, *hesychon*) and leisurely (*scholaion*) but not sluggish gait is the cultural ideal of pagans and Christians alike. Ambrose put it well in his handbook on the duty of the clergy, *De officiis* (1.18.74f), 'I do not think that it is becoming to walk hurriedly . . . [but] a commendable gait is where there is the appearance of authority, the assurance of weight and the mark of dignity, and one which has a calm, collected bearing.' It is this calm, unhurried gait, which will be the mark of the gentleman in Rome (see Graf, p. 47 of this volume), the middle ages and early modern Europe (see Burke, p. 77, and Roodenburg, p. 159, in this volume).[12]

Let us now for a moment move to the gait of women. In contrast to the male way of moving, women in the Archaic age apparently walked with very small steps (see Thomas, p. 8 of this volume). At least, when the goddesses Hera and Athena appeared before Troy to help the Greeks, they 'resembled in their steps the timorous doves' – exactly the opposite of the striding heroes.[13] As women in ancient Greece were so often contrasted with men, and as socially disapproved behaviour could be termed 'womanish' by the Greek males,[14] we can probably discover further features of proper male walking by paying attention to similarities between females and effeminate males.

A number of females in good spirits are said to have a *habros* foot or walk in a *habros* way; the same expression is used of the Persians, Lydians, and young Ganymede, the wine-pourer of Zeus. Only once, in Euripides' *Medea* (829–30), is the word used of adult male Athenians when they are said to walk *habros* through the air, but it is never found in relationship to individual adults. The word is usually translated with 'dainty, delicate, luxurious', but late Byzantine lexica explain it as 'light'. Even though the latter explanation is inspired by semantical rather than phonological knowledge – *habros* as *a-baroas*, or 'without weight' – it seems to point in the right direction.[15] The word is clearly used for people who are, or should be, in extremely happy circumstances: Lydians and Persians were notorious for their life of luxury. Apparently, they did not have to put down a masculine step but could, so to speak, tiptoe through life.[16] On the other hand, the Greek ideal appears from names such as Iobates, or 'He with the powerful step', and Deinobates, or 'He who walks with impressive step'. The Church fathers also stressed that the proper Christian male step had to be powerful and steadfast. In the Classical age such admonitions would surely have been superfluous.[17]

Some women not only walked on their toes but also wiggled their hips. In the sex-segregated society of ancient Greece it was of course inconceivable that individual decent women would parade on the streets in such a way, so it comes as no surprise that the sixth-century poet Anacreon used the expression 'walking in a wiggling manner' of courtesans (fr. 458) and also called the female followers of Dionysos 'the hip-swaying Bassarids' (fr. 461) – the sexual behaviour of these followers being rather suspect as Euripides' *Bacchae* clearly illustrates.[18] Apparently, some wealthy Athenians also moved along in such a way, as we learn from Aristophanes that a wiggling of the behind – the term used, *sauloproktiao*, contains the word for lizard, an animal that flicks its tail – was considered to be 'the gait of the rich'; perhaps similarly, the Chinese mandarins used to waddle along.[19] Now in Greece it was only a small step from effeminacy to the accusation of passive homosexuality – the ultimate in effeminate behaviour – and this step was indeed taken. Rather surprisingly, 'wiggling' is also used of the satyrs who were sometimes pictured as engaging in homosexual behaviour, just as the *kinaidos*, the 'passive homosexual' but also the 'wagtail'(!), could be recognized by his 'hip-swaying' according to Hellenistic physiognomists.[20]

Mauss, in his essay on the techniques of the body, related that he could recognize a girl from a convent as she would walk with her fists closed. And he could still remember his teacher shouting at him: 'Idiot! why do you walk around the whole time with your hands flapping wide open.' How did the Greek male walk in this respect? We can only approach this aspect in a circumspect way as we have no direct sources, but a passage in Aeschylus' *Prometheus*, where the protagonist of the play defiantly speaks to Zeus' messenger, will help us on the way: 'never think that through terror at Zeus' will I shall become womanish and shall entreat my greatly hated enemy with hands upturned in a woman's way to release me from these bonds' (1002–6). Why would it be womanish to be with hands upturned?

The answer must probably be looked for in the period before Aeschylus when to be with hands upturned would have denoted a man without weapons, that is a man who had symbolically abdicated his manhood. It is in line with this interpretation that the passive homosexual carried his hands upturned and flabbily according to Hellenistic physiognomics,[21] and the orator Dio Chrysostom (*c*.40–115) inveighs against certain citizens of dubiously sexual reputation that they converse 'with upturned palms' (*Orationes* 33.52). The notion of a symbolic abdication of manhood may also explain why the Greeks stretched their arms to heaven with their palms turned toward heaven when they prayed: a diminution of status is a universal feature of prayer,[22] the modern(?) gesture of raising the hands when faced with an armed opponent stands in the same tradition. Although none of these testimonies helps us to understand precisely how the Greek male carried his hands while walking, they all point to the weight attached to a proper bearing regarding this aspect. In this respect, it is also noteworthy that Spartan youths, like their Athenian contemporaries, were obliged to keep their hands within their garments. In Greece, the hand was considered *the* organ for action and therefore could only be shown by real males.[23]

We are left with two more important aspects of walking. First, where and how did the walker look? The question may seem odd to us but evidently not to the ancient Greeks, as gaze was subject to social norms. In public, Spartan youths were only allowed to look towards the ground, and Diogenes the Cynic did not permit the sons of his master to look about them in the streets; similarly, younger Japanese were (still?) not supposed to look higher than the breastbone of the elder. The gaze of a modest maiden should be downcast, as is the case with the modern Greek Sarakatsani, but it is typically the manly Amazon who carries the name Antiope, or 'She who looks straight into the face.' And as the lowering of the eyes seems to be a universal sign of submission, it is unsurprising that ashamed males also lowered the eyes.[24] Moreover, as rolling eyes denoted the madman and those in despair, squinting eyes treacherous persons, and looking around the passive homosexual, we may safely assume that a 'proper' male looked steadfastly at the world.[25]

Finally, the head. According to the sixth-century(?) poet Theognis (535–6) the heads of slaves were never straight but always crooked and their necks oblique, the terms 'straight' and 'crooked' being not only used in a physical but also, as is so often the case, in a moral sense. The downcast eyes of youths and maidens also suggest that they did not carry their heads upright and the same applied, apparently, to adult women. By contrast, therefore, free males must have kept their heads erect, as is also shown by the fact that it was noted when males hung their head in shame, despair, or mourning. And just as some rich citizens did not walk correctly (see p. 21), some did not keep their heads upright but let them incline to the side – according to the physiognomists a sign of passive homosexuality and androgyny.[26]

In classical and later times, then, the proper male behaviour in public walking required a leisurely but not sluggish gait, with steps that were not too small, with the hands firmly held and not upturned, the head erect and stable, the eyes openly, steadfastly, and firmly fixed on the world.

## STANDING

In general, we may suppose that the requirements for walking also applied to standing, but unfortunately, in this area preliminary studies are totally lacking. It is significant, however, that in Homer falling heroes are sometimes compared to trees being felled. As parallels in ancient Celtic and Russian poetry show, the comparison implies that the heroes stood firmly and proudly on the battlefield. The idea was still alive at the beginning of the fifth century, as the following anecdote by Herodotus (9.74) illustrates. During the battle of the Greeks against the Persians at Plataeae (479 BC) the Athenian veteran Sophanes carried an anchor fastened to his belt with a bronze chain. Whenever he came into contact with the enemy, he would anchor himself in order to prevent their attacks forcing him back. According to another, and perhaps more credible, version of the story he only bore the device of an anchor on his shield, which he kept continually spinning round and round. The same insistence on standing firmly occurs in the poem of Archilochus on the great commander, whose beginning we have already quoted; it continues: 'but I would like to have a short one and bow-legged to behold, [but] firmly standing on his feet, full of heart.' The poem also teaches us that the legs should be straight. Comedy mocked those Athenians who had misshapen calves. Bow-legged people were dim-witted according to Aristotle (in Anonymus Latinus 86), whereas according to Anacreon (fr. 473) 'knock-kneed' males were cowards and according to the physiognomists passive homosexuals.[27]

With another aspect of standing we move onto firmer ground. When we look at early Greek statues we cannot but be struck by the fact that before the end of the seventh century statues portraying gods (with the exception of Zeus) or heroes seated are rare, whereas sitting goddesses are perfectly ordinary; yet Homer very often describes meals at which the adults were sitting at the table, or assemblies in which the heroes sat down to confer. Sitting in itself, then, did not carry any stigma, but evidently it was the standing position alone which portrayed the hero in all his glory. Moreover, the heroes, when portrayed, only wear short tunics or hardly any clothes at all. Evidently, they were very keen to show themselves in their full physical power.[28]

Was there any difference in the way in which men and women stood? In modern Western society, when standing, men in general take up more space than women by, for example, keeping their legs further apart. As Greek women walked with smaller steps, they probably also took up less space when standing. However, the only women Greek males would observe standing were the cheaper prostitutes, who had to pose in front of their brothels. In present-day Algeria prostitutes break the rule of space for their gender by assuming masculine poses, such as spreading their arms out or standing with the legs wide. Would the same have been the case in ancient Greece?[29]

The importance of standing started to decline in the later

Archaic age, around 600 BC, as we now find an increasing number of statues of sitting gods. At the same time the aristocrats started to recline at dinner and allowed themselves to be pictured in this position while dressed in long tunics – the first signs of the gradual abandonment of the old warrior ethos. The custom of reclining, which had been taken over from the Orient, also meant a devaluation of the posture of sitting at the symposium, as now females and youths were allowed to sit next to reclining males.[30] In all these cases, though, sitting took place on proper seats. Sitting on the ground was a rather different matter, as we will try to show next.

## SITTING

Let us start with the beggar. The Greek word for hare, a cowering animal, is *ptox*, a word closely related to that for beggar, *ptochos*, which literally means someone who crouches or cringes. Although the Greek beggar often sat on the ground, as of course beggars do all over the world, his low position was intensified, so to speak, by cringing as well. In this case, sitting suggests a posture of self-abasement, which aims at evoking feelings of pity.[31]

We find similar postures of inferiority in supplication, a ritual which frequently occurred in war-torn Greece. Already in Homer we can clearly see the features which suggest a total self-abasement. The suppliant comes forward with his hands empty and outstretched (cf. 'Walking', this chapter), throws away his weapons, and crouches or kneels before the supplicated. Suppliants could even approach their opponents' wives – a sign of symbolic abandonment of manhood. In other cases, though, the suppliant did not enter into an immediate face-to-face relationship but sat down by a place which guaranteed his safety, such as an altar of a god.[32] Another possibility would be the hearth of a house or that of a city, which in Greece was its sacred centre symbolizing the solidarity of the community. Sitting by the hearth as suppliant, then, suggested an appeal for integration into a new group but, as with the beggar, such a wish could only be fulfilled in a manner which, as the best modern student of Greek supplication has expressed it, 'inhibits aggressive reaction by a ritualised act of self-humiliation'.[33]

Like suppliants, slaves and brides were also incorporated into their new households by a ritual which involved sitting near the hearth, though these categories may not have cringed. A similar symbolism could be found in Greek mysteries, where the candidate had to sit on a fleece, with veiled head and in complete silence. In all these cases an important transition was dramatized by the assumption of a humble posture before being raised to a new status.[34]

Our final example of ritual sitting concerns mourning. In the *Iliad* (19.344f), after Hector has killed Patroclus, Achilles 'keeps sitting in front of the ships with upright horns mourning his dear friend'. But when he hears this terrible news for the first time, his reaction is more violent. He pours ashes over his head, scratches his face, puts ashes over his clothes, pulls out his hair and rolls in the dust (18.23–7). And when Iris, the messenger of the gods, finds Priam after the death of Hector, he is rolling on the ground with manure on his head and neck (24.161–3). Ajax, too, in grief after his madness, 'sits quietly without food, without drink' (Sophocles, *Ajax* 324f). As in our other examples – begging, supplication, rites of integration, and initiation – sitting or lying on the ground is part of a complex of gestures which all aim at a total self-abasement of the subject. It is therefore not surprising that when satyrs are portrayed masturbating – an activity typical of slaves and rustics who cannot afford to pay for nice girls – they are often sitting.[35]

The presentation of the self in public, then, was often acted out according to the contrast of high (upright carriage) and low (sitting, prostration); the positive side of 'upright' in this contrast is also shown by the fact that the Greek word *orthos* ('upright') and its cognates frequently carry the meaning 'prosperity', 'uprightness', or 'restoration'. The opposition high–low is of course indicative of a society with strong hierarchies. In a democratic world, both high (thrones, higher seats for directors, etc.) and low (bowing, curtsying) are becoming less and less acceptable.[36]

## CONCLUSION

1   In ancient Greek culture the body served as an important location for self-identification and demonstration of authority. By its gait, the Greek upper-class not only distinguished itself from supposedly effeminate peoples such as Persians and Lydians, but also expressed its dominance over weaker sections of society such as youths and women. And although I have found no literary evidence that slaves could not display an upright carriage either, it seems important to note that on vases and reliefs they are regularly portrayed as sitting in a squatting position or as being of a smaller stature; significantly, on the vases their position is sometimes occupied by dwarfs. The passive homosexual also played an increasingly important role in this process of Greek male self-identification, as time and again we have seen that those males who did not comply with the rules of the proper gait were designated as effeminates and passive homosexuals.[37] The same preoccupation was prevalent in ancient Rome, where the accusation of an effeminate gait belonged to the stock-in-trade of everyday invective against political opponents or religious deviants, such as the followers of the Phrygian Magna Mater. This aspect, although not completely absent, is a major difference from modern Greek concepts of honour and masculinity, which are much more preoccupied with heterosexuality and a possible domination by women. It is undoubtedly the existence of institutionalized pederasty in the Classical period and its gradual disintegration which is the cause of this difference.[38]

2   The origin of the particular Greek gait probably lies before the Archaic age when every free male carried arms and continually had to be prepared to fight for himself in order to preserve his reputation and possessions. In such a society it is of cardinal importance not only to be physically strong but also to look like a real man. Such a situation explains, I suggest, the upright carriage, the steadfast look – also important in battle – and the long stride. Similarly, among the modern Greek Sarakatsani whose value system originated in times when they were not yet dominated by a central authority, the ideal youth is handsome, manly, narrow-

hipped, and nimble, and at public occasions such as weddings he will be noticed because of his upright carriage.[39]

3  In the course of the Archaic age important changes took place in Greek society. Many communities became urbanized and the aristocracy lost its prominent position on the battlefield. Both developments will have contributed to the refinement of manners and control of emotions I have already signalled. By their open display of self-control the elite distinguished itself once again from the masses, but now in the public sphere of the city. And it can hardly be chance that we first hear of an unhurried gait in the case of Pericles, the leading politician in Athens from 460 to 430 BC, since he seems to have been particularly attentive to his public image: Plutarch relates in his biography of Pericles (7.2) that he withdrew from weddings precisely at the moment that the real festivities started, as he considered them beneath his dignity. The fact that war was professionalized in Greece in the fourth century and permanently removed from the hands of the urban elite may explain why the unhurried gait remained the ideal all through antiquity: constructing and maintaining a public body was one of the means by which the elite upheld its superiority. The rise of Christianity meant no significant break in this respect, as important Church fathers, such as Clement of Alexandria and John Chrysostom, were steeped in the Greek cultural tradition and followed upper-class pagan Greek ideals in their prescriptions of the proper Christian gait.[40]

4  We come to our final point. In March 1530 Desiderius Erasmus published a small treatise, *De civilitate morum puerilium libellus*, in which he proposed a new ideal of comportment for children by raising the threshold of modesty. His book was an enormous success, and in the sixteenth century alone it passed through eighty Latin editions. Regarding the gait, Erasmus stated that it should be steady but not hasty (1.28: *incessus sit non fractus nec praeceps*). The chapter on gait, though, is only one of a series of prescriptions regarding parts of the body, such as the head, the arms, and the voice. What they all have in common is that they aim at controlling bodily expressions and, not surprisingly, frequently correspond with the rules we have discovered.[41] Erasmus's prescriptions fitted the early modern civilizing process but were hardly invented by him. As he knew the Classics by heart and had

edited Ambrose's *De officiis* in 1527, we may safely assume that many of his rules came straight from antiquity. Ambrose's observations on the proper gait derive from Cicero's *De officiis* (1.131), who in turn derives his material largely from the Stoic Greek philosopher Panaetius, the Stoics being known for their orderly gait.[42] In short, it seems very likely that Erasmus's prescriptions on gait and much else ultimately derive from Classical and Hellenistic Greece!

## NOTES

For information and comments I am most grateful to Nick Fisher and Professors Adolf Köhnken and Simon R. Slings.

1  M. Mauss, 'Les techniques du corps', *Journal de psychologie normale et pathologique*, 39 (1935), pp. 271–93, reprinted in his *Sociologie et anthropologie* (Paris, 1950), pp. 365–86 ~ *Sociology and Psychology* (London, 1979), pp. 97–123. But note also the caustic remark of the late Erving Goffman, quoted in Y. Winkin, 'Entretien avec Erving Goffman', *Actes de la recherche en sciences sociales*, no. 54 (1984, 85–7), p. 85: 'A côté de ses observations, il n'y a rien dans l'article de Mauss'. On Mauss see R. di Donato (ed.), *Gli uomini, la società, la civiltà. Uno studio intorno all' opera di Marcel Mauss* (Pisa, 1985). Abolishment: *Frankfurter Allgemeine Zeitung*, 9 August 1990.

2  *Oeuvres complets de Honoré de Balzac* (40 vols, Paris, 1912–40), vol. 39, 613–43 (I owe this reference to Benjo Maso). Physiognomical interest: M. Dumont, 'Le succès mondain d'une fausse science: la physiognomie de Johann Kaspar Lavater', *Actes de la recherche en sciences sociales*, no. 54 (1984), pp. 2–30, esp. pp. 29f.

3  As regards the archaic and classical Greek material I am much indebted to B. Fehr, *Bewegungsweisen und Verhaltensideal* (Bad Bramstedt, 1979), a pioneering study unduly neglected by the classical world, even though my approach is different and covers a much longer period.

4  Ambrose, *De officiis* 1.18.71, probably remembered by the early medieval Othlo de Saint-Emmeran, *Liber proverbiorum*, Patrologia Latina (ed. Migne) (PL) 146.312C: *Gestu corporis habitus demonstretur mentis.* I quote the Anonymus Latinus and Ambrose from the

following new editions: J. André, *Anonyme Latin. Traité de Physiognomie* (Paris, 1981), and M. Testard, *Saint Ambrose. Les dévoirs*, vol. 1 (Paris, 1984), who notes that the conventional, longer title of the book, *De officiis ministrorum*, is not based on any manuscript tradition (pp. 49–52).

5 Persian king: E. Hall, *Inventing the Barbarian. Greek Self-Definition through Tragedy* (Oxford, 1989), pp. 95–6. It may also be significant that Herodotus transcribed the Persian name Bagapata as Megabates, or 'He with the big step', whereas Ctesias (29.9) gives the more correct form Bagapates; cf. R. Schmitt, 'Medisches und persisches Sprachgut bei Herodot', *Zeitschrift des Deutschen Morgenländischen Gesellschaft*, 117 (1967), pp. 119–45, esp. pp. 130, 142–3.

6 Polemon, in R. Foerster, *Scriptores physiognomonici* (2 vols, Leipzig, 1893), vol. 1, pp. 260–2; similarly the fourth-century Adamantius (ibid. p. 398) and Anonymus Latinus 75, in André, *Anonyme Latin*, who both drew on Polemon. For the reception of the classical physiognomical treatises in the Middle Ages see J.-C. Schmitt, *La raison des gestes dans l'Occident médiéval* (Paris, 1990), pp. 233–4.

7 In my interpretation of this term, *diapepligmenon*, I follow V. Pisani, 'Sulla radice *PLIX-*', *Annuaire de l'Institut de philologie et d'histoires orientales et slaves*, 6 (1938), pp. 181–92.

8 Eurybatos (– as / es): D. Amyx, *Corinthian Vase-Painting of the Archaic Period* (Berkeley, Calif., and London, 1988), p. 575, no. 71; Herodotus 6.92, 9.75 (an early fifth-century Aeginetan); Thucydides 1.47.1 (a fifth-century Corcyrean); Demosthenes 18.24 and H. Wankel ad loc. (the betrayer of Croesus). For the name see A. Heubeck, '*Iolaos* und Verwandtes', *Münchener Studien zur Sprachwissenschaft*, 48 (1987), pp. 149–66, esp. p. 159, but note that Homer (*Iliad* 1.320, 2.184, 11.127; *Odyssey* 19.247) uses the name exclusively for heralds and evidently interpreted it as 'Broad-ranger'. Typically, the name no longer occurs after the second century BC.

9 Cf. P. Bourdieu, *La distinction* (Paris, 1979); note also the popular and perceptive R. Girtler, *Die feinen Leute* (Frankfurt and New York, 1989).

10 For the growth in self-control, as yet uncharted by Greek historiography, see the preliminary observations in my 'Adolescents, *Symposion*, and Pederasty', in O. Murray (ed.), *Sympotica* (Oxford, 1990), pp. 135–48, esp. pp. 143–4. Egypt: W. Helck, 'Die Ägypter und die Fremden', *Saeculum*, 15 (1964), pp. 103–14, esp. p. 105. Tragedy: Hall, *Inventing the Barbarian*, pp. 130–3.

11 Cf. Plutarch, *Moralia* 317C, who contrasts the *praon* gait of Virtue with the hurried step of Fate; the same expression recurs in Plutarch's

(*Fabius* 17.7) description of the Roman statesman Fabius after the Roman defeat at Cannae, and in Diogenes Laertius' life of the fourth-century philosopher Heraclides (5.86). Long tunics: Eupolis fr. 104, R. Kassel and C. Austin, *Poetae comici Graeci* (Berlin and New York, 1983ff), hereafter 'K.-A.'; Archippus fr. 45, T. Kock, *Comicorum Atticorum fragmenta* (Leipzig, 1880–8), hereafter 'Kock'; Ephippus fr. 19 K.-A.; Anaxilas fr. 18 Kock; note also Demosthenes 19.314.

12 Pagans: Galen, *Pro puero epileptico consilium*, p. 5.18, ed. Keil, Lucian, *Timarion* 54.5; Philostratus, *Life of Apollonius of Tyana* 6.10. Christians: Clement of Alexandria, *Paedagogus* 3.11.73.4; Basil, *De ieiunio* 1.9 (Patrologia Graeca (ed. Migne) (PG) 31.177); Gregory Nazianzen, *Adversos Eunomianos* 5.24, *Orationes* 22.4 (PG 35.1137); John Chrysostom, PG 52.772, PG 59.677. Not sluggish: Basil, *Epistulae* 2.6, *Sermones* 20.1 (PG 32.1353); Pseudo-Macarius, *Sermones* 1.3.3, ed Berthold. Middle ages: Schmitt *La raison des gestes*, p. 94; add Dante, *Purgatorio* 3.10–11, *Inferno* 4.112, 15.121–4, 16.17–18 (with thanks to Robert Parker).

13 *Iliad* 5.778, largely repeated in the *Homeric Hymn to Apollo* 114 for the goddesses Iris and Eileithuia. Achilles, when residing in women's clothes at the court of King Lycomedes of Scyros 'walks like a maiden' (Bion 2.19f); also the close friends whom Theseus took along to Crete 'in drag' had learned to walk like maidens (Plutarch, *Theseus* 23).

14 'Womanish': H. Herter, 'Effeminatus', in *Reallexicon für Antike und Christentum* (1959), vol. 4, pp. 619–50.

15 Females: Euripides, *Medea* 1164, *Trojan Women* 506, *Helen* 1528, *Iphigeneia at Aulis* 614; note also Clement of Alexandria, *Paedagogus* 3.11.68.1. Ganymede: Euripides, *Trojan Women* 820. Persians: Aeschylus, *Persians* 1073; Bacchylides 3.48. Lydians: Aeschylus fr. 60; Herodotus 1.55. Lexica: Orion 3.11 (ed. Sturz); *Etymologicum Magnum Auctum* and *Symeonis Etymologicum* (ed. Lasserre and Livrada) *s.v. habros*.

16 Luxurious Lydians: D. Curiazi, *Museum Criticum*, 19–20 (1984–5), pp. 137, 154f. Persians: H. Sancisi-Weerdenburg, 'Decadence in the empire or decadence in the sources', in *Achaemenid History*, ed. eadem (Leiden, 1987), vol. 1, pp. 33–45; Hall, *Inventing the Barbarian*, pp. 126–9; P. Briant, 'Histoire et idéologie. Les grecs et la "décadence perse"', *Mélanges Pierre Lévêque*, ed. M.-M. Mactoux and E. Geny (3 vols, Paris, 1988–9), vol. 2, pp. 34–47. Note that the term is also used by Telecleides (fr. 25 K.-A.) to characterize the happy life in Athens in the earlier part of the fifth century.

17 Iobates: Hesiod fr. 43 (a).88, cf. Heubeck, '*Iolaos* und Verwandtes'. Deinobates: *Inscriptiones Graecae* II.2516. Church fathers: Gregory Nazianzen, *Orationes* 6.2 (PG 35.724), 22.4 (PG 35.1137).

18 Cf. E. R. Dodds on Euripides, *Bacchae* 222–3; H. S. Versnel, *Inconsistencies in Greek and Roman Religion* (2 vols, Leiden, 1990–1), vol. 1, pp. 159–60.

19 Aristophanes, *Wasps* 1169, 1171–3 and Scholion ad loc.; for related terms see *diasauloumenon* (fr. 635 K.-A.; *Etymologicum Magnum*, 270.38) and *saikonisai* (fr. 882 K.-A.; note also Hermippus fr. 5 West); Hesychius s.v. *diasalakonison, diasauloumenon*; Suda s.v. *diasalakonisai*; Eupolis fr. 176 K.-A. may imply the same hip-swaying. Mandarins: C. Thubron, *Behind the Wall. A Journey through China*, 2nd edn (Harmondsworth, 1988), p. 49.

20 Satyrs: Euripides, *Cyclops* 40; for satyrs as passive homosexuals see F. Lissarrague, 'The sexual life of satyrs', in *Before Sexuality. The Construction of Erotic Experience in the Ancient Greek World*, ed. D. M. Halperin et al. (Princeton, 1990), pp. 53–81, esp. pp. 64–5. *Kinaidoi*: J. J. Winkler, *The Constraints of Desire* (London, 1990), pp. 45–70. 'Hip-swaying': Pseudo-Aristotle, *Physiognomonica* 808a. For the physiognomists and homosexuals, see M. W. Gleason, 'The semiotics of gender: physiognomy and self-fashioning in the second century C.E.', in *Before Sexuality*, pp. 389–415. For dancing like a wagtail see F. Naerebout, *The Dance in Ancient Greece. Three Studies* (Diss. Leiden, 1991).

21 Pseudo-Aristotle, *Physiognomonica* 808a; note also that according to the Anonymus Latinus (98), in André, *Anonyme Latin*, the androgynous man *resupinatas plerumque manus praemovet*; similarly Adamantius, in Foerster, *Scriptores physiognomonici*, p. 416.

22 Greek prayer: *Iliad* 5.174, 6.257, 7.130, 24.301; *Odyssey* 9.294, 13.355; Aeschylus, *Seven against Thebes* 172; Bacchylides 11.100, 13.138, 15.45; Herodotus 9.61; Euripides, *Helen* 1095; G. Neumann, *Gesten und Gebärden in der griechischen Kunst* (Berlin, 1965), pp. 78–81; F. T. van Straten, 'Did the Greeks kneel before their Gods?', *Bulletin Antieke Beschaving*, 49 (1974), pp. 159–89, esp. p. 161.

23 Spartan youths: Xenophon, *Lakedaimonion politeia* 3.4. Athens: K. Polaschek, *Untersuchungen zu griechischen Mantelstatuen* (Diss. Berlin, 1969), pp. 16f. Hand: E. Fraenkel on Aeschylus, *Agamemnon* 1357.

24 Youths: Xenophon, *Lakedaimonion politeia* 3.4; Diogenes Laertius 6.27 (Diogenes). Japan: M. Argyle and M. Cook, *Gaze and Mutual Gaze* (Cambridge, 1976), p. 77. Maidens: F. Bömer on Ovid, *Metamorphoses* 4.681. Sarakatsani: J. K. Campbell, *Honour, Family and Patronage* (Oxford, 1964), p. 287. Universal sign: Argyle and Cook, *Gaze and Mutual Gaze*, p. 30. Antiope: *Lexicon Iconographicum Mythologiae Classicae* (Munich and Zurich, Lower-

ing the eyes Sappho fr. 137; Sophocles, *Oedipus Rex* 528, 1385; Euripides, *Heracles* 1199, *Orestes* 460f. 1981), vol. 1 s.v. Antiope II (literary and iconographic evidence).

25 Rolling eyes: J. Kamerbeek on Sophocles, *Ajax* 447; D. Page on Euripides, *Medea* 1174; add Euripides, *Orestes* 837, cf. L. Koenen and P. J. Sijpesteijn, 'Euripides, *Orestes* 835–46 (P. Mich. Inv. 3735)', *Zeitschrift für Papyrologie und Epigraphik*, 77 (1989), pp. 261–6. Squinting: Eustathius on *Iliad* 2.217. Passive homosexual: Pseudo-Aristotle, *Physiognomonica* 808a; Adamantius, in Foerster, *Scriptores physiognomonici*, p. 415; Anonymus Latinus 98, in André, *Anonyme Latin*. The physiognomists pay much attention to the eyes (Anonymus Latinus 20, in André: *Nunc de oculis disputandum est, ubi summa omnis physiognomoniae constituta est*), cf. Pseudo-Aristotle, *Physiognomonica* 811b; Polemon, in Foerster, *Scriptores physiognomonici*, pp. 106–70; Adamantius, in Foerster, pp. 305–47; Anonymus Latinus, in André, 20–43.

26 Adult women: Xenophon, *Memorabilia*, 2.1.22. Despair, mourning, shame: Euripides *Ion* 582; Aristophanes, *Birds* 1609; Pausanias 10.30.3 and 31.5; Neumann, *Gesten und Gebärden*, pp. 135f, 140. Rich: Archippos fr. 45 Kock; Dio Chrysostom 4.112. Passive homosexuals: an unknown comedian quoted by Clement of Alexandria, *Paedagogus* 3.11.69.1; Pseudo-Aristotle, *Physiognomonica* 808a; Polemon, in Foerster, *Scriptores physiognomonici*, p. 276; Adamantius, in Foerster, *Scriptores physiognomonici*, p. 416; Anonymus Latinus 98, in André, *Anonyme Latin*.

27 Heroes as trees: H. Fränkel, *Die homerischen Gleichnisse* (Göttingen, 1921), pp. 36ff. Celtic: E. Campanile, *Ricerche di cultura poetica indoeuropea* (Pisa, 1977), p. 119. Russian: M. L. West, 'The rise of the Greek epic', *Journal of Hellenic Studies*, 108 (1988), pp. 151–72, esp. p. 154. Comedy: Eupolis fr. 107 and K.-A. ad loc.; note also on the Greek vocabulary of words like 'bow-legged' W. Meid, *Das Problem von indogermanisch /b/* (Innsbruck, 1989). Passive homosexuals: Pseudo-Aristotle, *Physiognomonica* 810a; Polemon, in Foerster, *Scriptores physiognomonici*, pp. 204–6; Adamantius, in Foerster, *Scriptores physiognomonici*, p. 359; Anonymus Latinus 70, in André, *Anonyme Latin*.

28 So, persuasively, argues the inspiring study by H. Jung, *Thronende und sitzende Götter* (Bonn, 1982); on statues of sitting divine females add F. Graf, *Nordionische Kulte* (Rome, 1985), p. 44; R. Özgan, 'Ein neues archaisches Sitzbild aus Knidos' in *Festschrift für Nikolaus Himmelmann*, ed. H.-U. Cain et al. (Mainz, 1989), pp. 47–51.

29 Western society: E. Goffman, *Gender Advertisements* (London, 1970). Greek prostitutes: H. Herter, 'Die Soziologie der Antiken Prostitution im Lichte des heidnischen und Christlichen Schrifttums', *Jahrbuch für Antike und Christentum*, 3 (1960), pp. 70–111, esp. p. 87. Algerian prostitutes: see the fine analysis by Willy Jansen, *Women without Men: Gender and Marginality in an Algerian Town* (Leiden, 1987), pp. 175–89.

30 For these developments and their implications see Jung, *Thronende und sitzende Götter*, pp. 132–8; Bremmer, in Murray, *Sympotica*, p. 139.

31 Crouching beggar: J. Gould, 'Hiketeia', *Journal of Hellenic Studies*, 93 (1973), pp. 74–103, esp. p. 94 n.104; for sitting beggars see Euripides fr. 960; Antiphanes fr. 248 Kock.

32 Here I follow closely the fine analysis of Gould, 'Hiketeia', pp. 94–101. Suppliants and wives: Bremmer, *Mnemosyne*, IV 33 (1980), pp. 366f. Suppliants sitting at or on altars: K. Latte, *Heiliges Recht* (Tübingen, 1920), p. 106, n. 17; add Herodotus 6.108; Sophocles, *Oedipus Rex* 32; Euripides fr. 554; Andocides, *On the Mysteries* 44; Lysias 13.24, 52; Aeschines 1.60 (as a kind of protest); Menander, *Sicyonius* 190; Van Straten, 'Did the Greeks Kneel before their Gods?', p. 183 219n; C. Aellen et al. (eds), *Le peintre de Darius et son milieu* (Geneva, 1986), pp. 71–86.

33 Hearth of person: *Odyssey* 7.153; Euripides, *Heracles* 715; Thucydides 1.36.3; Apollonius Rhodius 4.662–71 and Scholion. Hearth of city: Andocides, *On his Return* 15; Parthenius 18. Note also the sitting suppliant in the Cyrene cathartic law: R. Parker, *Miasma* (Oxford, 1983), p. 350. Best student: Gould, 'Hiketeia', p. 89.

34 Slaves: Scholion on Aristophanes, *Plutus* 768. Brides: Bremmer, *Birth, Maturity and Death in Ancient Greece* (London, 1992), ch. V. Sitting initiates: Parker, *Miasma*, p. 285.

35 For more examples of sitting in mourning see N. J. Richardson, *The Homeric Hymn to Demeter* (Oxford, 1974), p. 218f. Satyrs: Lissarrague, 'The sexual life of satyrs', pp. 57 and 70. Masturbation: K. J. Dover, *Greek Homosexuality* (London, 1978), pp. 96–7.

36 For sitting and prostration in cross-cultural perspective see also the interesting study by R. Firth, 'Postures and gestures of respect', in *Echanges et communications. Mélanges Claude Lévi-Strauss* (2 vols, The Hague and Paris, 1970), vol. 1, pp. 188–209.

37 Slaves: N. Himmelman, *Archäologisches zum Problem der griechischen Sklaverei* (Mainz, 1971); C. Bérard, 'Pénalité et religion à Athènes: un témoignage de l'imagerie', *Revue Archéologique* (1982), pp. 137–50, esp. 144–6; V. Dasen, 'Dwarfs in Athens', *Oxford Journal of*

*Archaeology* 9 (1990), pp. 191–207. Political opponents; Sallust, *Catiline* 15 (the gait of the notorious Cataline was 'sometimes fast, sometimes sluggish'); Cicero, *Orationes* fr. A xiii.22; Tacitus, *Historiae* 1.30.1. Religious deviants: Juvenal 2.17; Apuleius, *Metamorphoses* 11.8; Augustine, *De civitate dei* 7.26.

38 Modern Greece: M. Herzfeld, *The Poetics of Manhood* (Princeton, 1985); D. Gilmore (ed.), *Honor, and Shame and the Unity of the Mediterranean* (Washington, 1987). Institutionalized pederasty: see my 'Greek pederasty and modern homosexuality', in *From Sappho to De Sade. Moments in the History of Sexuality*, ed. Jan Bremmer (London, 1989), pp. 1–14.

39 For the display of virility in an acephalous society see A. Blok, 'Rams and billy-goats: a key to the Mediterranean code of honour', *Man*, 16 (1981), pp. 427–40. Sarakatsani: Campbell, *Honour, Family and Patronage*, p. 279. Fierce look: J.-P. Vernant, *La mort dans les yeux* (Paris, 1985), pp. 39–40; add Euripides, *Heracles* 163.

40 On Clement, John, and Christian deportment, see now Peter Brown, *The Body and Society* (New York, 1988), pp. 122–39 and 305–22, respectively.

41 Erasmus: the best study of Erasmus's treatise is H. de la Fontaine Verwey, 'The first "book of etiquette" for children: Erasmus' *De civilitate morum puerilium*', *Quaerendo*, 1 (1971), pp. 19–30, reprinted in his *Uit de wereld van het boek* (3 vols, Amsterdam, 1975–6), vol. 1, pp. 41–50; see also F. Bierlaire, 'Erasmus at school: the *De civilitate morum puerilium libellus*', in *Essays on the Works of Erasmus*, ed. R. L. DeMolen (New Haven and London, 1978), pp. 239–51; R. Chartier, *The Cultural Uses of Print in Early Modern France* (Princeton, 1987), pp. 76–9.

42 Civilizing process: N. Elias, *Über den Prozess der Zivilisation* (2 vols, Basel, 1939); H. Pleij, *De sneeuwpoppen van 1511* (Amsterdam, 1988); R. Muchembled, *L'Invention de l'homme moderne* (Paris, 1988). Ambrose's source: Testard: *Saint Ambrose. Les dévoirs*, pp. 22–6. Cicero's source: M. Testard, *Ciceron. Les dévoirs* (2 vols, Paris, 1965–70), vol. 1, pp. 25–49. Stoics: Lucian, *Hermotimus* 18.

# 2

# Gestures and conventions: the gestures of Roman actors and orators

## FRITZ GRAF

We all gesticulate – that is, accompany our speech by more or less elaborate movements of arms, hands, and fingers. Northerners gesticulate less, the stereotype says, Mediterranean people more; in 1832, the learned author of a book on Neapolitan gestures (see Thomas, p. 3 of this volume) even asserted that among the inhabitants of northern Europe (that is, presumably, all of Europe north of the Alps) gesticulation did not exist – the cold climate having made them less fiery than the Italians.[1] This exaggerated opinion shows how gesticulation is generally viewed – as something natural and spontaneous, dependent upon factors of climate or character.

But in a way, the learned Neapolitan contradicts himself, since he also speaks about the language of gestures (*il linguaggio dei gesti*), even of its dialects – in Naples, there existed gestures different from those of Apulia or Sicily.[2] Language is nothing natural, it is highly conventional and tied to a specific culture; differences in language mark differences in culture. The metaphor of the language of gestures implies the same conventionality and cultural determination for gestures. The metaphor, incidentally, is quite old: already in the fifties BC, Cicero wrote about *sermo corporis*, 'language of the body', and *eloquentia corporis*, 'eloquence of the body' – albeit in a slightly different way: he meant the entire delivery of a speech, both the voice (as an emanation of the body) and the gesticulation accompanying it.[3]

The metaphor answers a problem which seems (as far as a non-specialist may judge) not yet definitely answered by modern research: just how conventional are gestures?[4] The discussion goes back to antiquity, to Roman rhetorical theory, and it owes its existence to the fact that in rhetorical training not only invention, composition, and style were taught, but also *actio* or *hupokrisis* – delivery of the speech, including the appropriate gestures. The orator had to have not only the qualities of a lawyer, philosopher, and a poet, but had to come close to being a theatrical performer as well[5] – how close he came will be one of the questions discussed in this contribution. Its subject is rather a byway of classical philology: from the sixteenth to the eighteenth centuries, when Europe still had a very lively rhetorical culture, the Roman texts on the subject were often read, discussed and used, though they virtually disappeared from sight in the nineteenth century when classical philology established itself as an academic discipline.[6]

## QUINTILIAN'S ACCOUNT

When reading ancient text books on rhetoric, one gets the impression that their main concern was with the writing of a speech: in a way, they look like courses in better writing. But at least in part, this is the fault of the transmission of ancient texts: attention to the way a public speech should be delivered to be effective is nearly as old as rhetorical theory. The first (though entirely lost) treatise comes from a fifth-century sophist, Thrasymachos; Aristotle and his pupils Theophrastos and Demetrios of Phaleron wrote about it, so did Cicero.[7] Gesticulation is a part of delivery – to put it into the formalized dichotomies of the rhetorical schools delivery, *hupokrisis* or *actio*, consists of two parts, voice (*vox*) and *gestus*, which is both posture (the static way of presenting oneself) and gesticulation (the dynamic way).[8] Circumstantial information about when to use which gestures and which to avoid comes, of course, from a professor (albeit an influential one), Marcus Fabius Quintilianus. Born in Spain in about AD 35, he had been the first public professor of rhetoric in Rome and a teacher of the sons and nephews of the emperor Domitian; after his retirement he wrote a lengthy and very influential compendium 'The Formation of a Public Speaker', *Institutio oratoria*, in twelve books. Its eleventh book is concerned – at least in two of its three parts – with what should happen after one has written a speech; it concerns *memoria*, memory (Greek and Roman orators used to memorize their written texts and to speak without them) and *pronuntiatio* or *actio*, the delivery.

Quintilian's chapter is the only preserved Roman (or for that matter, ancient) text which gives detailed information about rhetorical body language in the Roman sense; some additional information from Cicero's rhetorical writings and from later authors corroborates or qualifies Quintilian's account. After a general introduction and a discussion of voice and pronunciation (paragraphs 14–65), Quintilian dwells on *gestus*, both posture and gesticulation (65–197). He prescribes all the movements which help, and points out those which damage the performance, systematically passing from the head to the feet, via eyes, nose (you should never make gestures with your nose), arms, hands, and body (69–137), with a long section on gesticulation proper: the movements of the hand and the fingers which accompany the spoken word (85–121); he adds advice about how to make use of the orator's garment, the toga, to help create the desired impression on the audience (138–49), and ends with miscellaneous advice.[9]

A number of points catch the modern reader's attention. First, many gestures are meticulously detailed, especially in the section on gesticulation, which sometimes reminds one of the report of a modern anthropological field-worker; others, well-known to his audience, are just hinted at. Often, he explains the significance of the gesture he describes, especially in the section on finger signs; obviously, these signs were either not familiar to the average Roman or they had one meaning in the rhetorical system but another in daily conversation.

Second, the categorization he offers is very rudimentary. Gestures in general are not categorized; in gesticulation – gestures taking place simultaneously with speech – he distinguishes between gestures 'which proceed naturally from us' and 'others which indicate things by means of mimicry' (88).[10] The categorization does not greatly affect his description, but to a certain extent it anticipates the more elaborate categories of hand gestures as proposed by modern theorists, especially David Efron, Paul Ekman and Wallace V. Friesen.[11] They distinguish between four classes: ideographs, pointers, pictorial gestures, and batons. Batons are gestures which beat time to the rhythm of the speech: Quintilian does not mention them, Cicero explicitly forbids them[12] – and since they would have looked rather clumsy, Quintilian certainly would have agreed. Pointers or 'indexical gestures' point at the objects of the words; Quintilian knows some and mentions the admiration Cicero felt for how Crassus used his index finger. Ideographs 'diagram the logical structure of what is said' (in Kendon's words): if we say 'the logical and emotional structure' this category contains most of the gestures Quintilian approves of; the only gesture which is strictly 'logical' in his list is the one accompanying a question, 'the turn of the hand, the arrangement of the fingers being indifferent' (101). These three categories would more or less correspond to his natural gestures. Pictorial gestures, finally, depict what is spoken about: as the name suggests they are the gestures of the mime artist. They correspond more or less to Quintilian's gestures 'which indicate by mimicry'; he very much disapproves of them.

Third (and not unconnected with the second observation), Quintilian demarcates the gestures he is teaching from other gestures – from spontaneous gestures, from the gestures of daily life and common people, from the gestures of foreigners, especially Greeks. But most insistent is the opposition between rhetorical and theatrical gesticulation. Quintilian (and before him Cicero) is at pains to impose a strict demarcation between the two – it seems to be the cardinal vice of a Roman orator to give the impression of being an actor.[13] This is all the more surprising as both thought it worth while to learn from actors – Cicero was familiar with the famous Roscius, and we are told that he used to challenge him privately in declamation and gesticulation; his ideal orator has to have, among other things, the voice of a tragic actor and the delivery of a very good stage professional.[14] Quintilian thought it advisable for a future orator to have had, as a boy, lessons in enunciation, gesticulation, and miming from a professional actor and a training in body movements from a good gym instructor.[15]

To understand the system of Roman rhetorical *gestus* and its peculiarities, it is important to have a clear idea of its aim. Quintilian is outspoken about what it is all about; the gestural language together with the rest of the performance is directed towards the emotions, not the reason, of the audience: 'all emotional appeals will inevitably fall flat, unless they are given the fire that voice, look, and the whole comportment of the body can give them' (2). The body signs of the orator demonstrate his own emotions which in turn excite similar emotions in the audience.

Thus, gestures serve the overall aim of ancient rhetoric, *psychagogia*, 'winning of men's souls', as Plato deprecatingly called it[16] – a goal attained by aiming mainly at the emotions, not the intellect of the audience, especially when addressing huge crowds of fellow citizens or judges. It was these occasions – the address to the democratic assembly or to the large juries in fifth century BC Athens, to the Senate and the People in late Republican Rome – which had called for the development of rhetorical training based on a science of rhetoric. But this direct attack on the emotions is only one side. The theorists analyse the aim of rhetoric as threefold: not only to persuade and move the audience's minds (the direct emotional approach), but also to recommend the orator to his audience.[17] This is done by the orator's creating a favourable impression on his public – by general outward signs and in particular by gestures. We all tend to believe (and often try to overcome it as a prejudice) what to ancient man and especially to ancient theorists was a stated fact: that the outward appearance of a person is an image of the inward personality and character – dress, gestures, walking, any motion, are significant of interior man.[18] 'Gesticulation obeys our mind', says Quintilian (65); Cicero, with his philosophical training, gives an elaborate explication: 'Every motion of the soul has its natural appearance, voice and gesture; and the entire body of a man, all his facial and vocal expressions, like the strings of a harp, sound just as the soul's motion strikes them.'[19]

To a certain extent, the role of gestures in the rhetorical system comes close to the dichotomy between word and gesture which the anthropologist Gregory Bateson had established in 1968: 'Our iconic communication serves functions totally different from those of language and, indeed, performs functions which verbal language is unsuited to perform . . . It seems that the discourse of nonverbal communication is precisely concerned with matters of relationship – love, hate, respect, fear, dependency etc. – between self and vis-à-vis or between self and environment.' There is one very important difference, though: in rhetoric, gestures do not perform a function totally different from language, they underline and amplify the message of language by stressing the emotional, non-rational elements – exactly the modification made by more recent research to Bateson's position.[20]

Among the gestures Quintilian describes, some are clear and unequivocal expressions of emotion. Certain head movements show shame, doubt, admiration, or indignation he says (71); it is a pity that he doesn't describe them: they are too well known – though not to us. With hand signs he often is more circumstantial, not least because, as he writes, 'they are almost as expressive as words' (86). 'Wonder', *admiratio* (both surprise and admiration) – to give some examples – is best expressed as follows: 'the right hand turns slightly upwards and the fingers are brought in to the palm, one after the other, beginning with the little finger; the hand is then reopened and turned round by a reversal of this motion'; regret or anger is indicated by the clenched fist, pressed to the breast.[21]

I cited these two gestures also to show how Quintilian's descriptions combine gestures of different origin: they differ in the way they express their meaning. The gesture for wonder has nothing to do with the feeling it expresses, it is a purely arbitrary and conventional sign, like the sounds of speech or the digits in digital code. Pressing the fist to the breast as a sign for remorse or anger, however, to a certain extent pictures the feelings involved: the clenched fist is a means of aggression, the breast the seat of intense emotions. The emotion thus is indicated in broad outline only; the precise meaning has to be learned for it is a combination of a natural pictorial sign and conventionality.

These clear signs for emotions belong to single sentences, sometimes even words. Gesticulation has another, more general function, as Quintilian explains; it brings home the emotional properties of the structural features of the speech, of its single parts. This is especially true of the hand signs.

A good instance is the hand gesture Quintilian calls 'the most common of all': it 'consists in placing the middle finger against the thumb, and extending the remaining three ... the hand being moved forward with an easy motion a little distance both to the right and the left, while the head and shoulders gradually follow the direction of the gesture' – a splendid instance, by the way, of the lengths Quintilian can go to when describing a gesture.[22] This slow movement, he continues, is most useful in the introductory section of a speech; it also expresses firmness when stating the facts of a case during the narration – but here, the arm moves a little further forward; it finally demonstrates aggressiveness when accusing or refuting adversaries – again with the arm moving even further away from the body and more freely to the left and the right (92).

Here, Quintilian correlates gestures with the main divisions of a forensic speech, the *exordium* or beginning, the *narratio* (where the orator states the facts – or rather what he wishes his audience to believe are the facts), and the *argumentatio* (where he argues his own position and attacks his opponent's): while the basic gesture – both the position of the fingers and the direction of the arm movement – remains basically identical, its speed and amplitude are different for each section. This quantitative variation depends not upon the specific content of the section, but on the general impression: the *argumentatio* has to demonstrate the aggressiveness of the orator, the *narratio* his firmness – qualities of character and personality, not of the specific arguments.

This variation, according to the section of the speech, is a very basic feature. Accordingly, finger figures which express urgency or aggressiveness – like the variation of the described figure where 'the middle and third fingers are turned under the thumb' (93) or the gesture where 'three fingers are doubled under the thumb and the index is extended' (94) – are recommended for the *argumentatio* only, the former being 'more forcible', the latter useful in denunciation and indication and, when pointed toward the ground, demonstrating insistence. On the other hand, parts which have to be slow or without much force – like the *exordium* or the digressions during *narratio* and *argumentatio* – contain only slow gesticulation (164).

Thus the speech has its characteristic crescendo, each division being more forceful and dynamic than the preceding one, as Quintilian explicitly states (161–74); growing intensity of multi-functional gestures or the use of more powerful specific signals underline and amplify this.

A further sign language used to express this crescendo movement is the way the orator presents his garment. Quintilian advises the same pattern of speeding up – the toga 'sitting well upon the shoulders' during the *exordium* (161) is 'allowed to slip back' in the *narratio* (145); in the *argumentatio*, the toga may be thrown back from the shoulder and 'begins to assume something of a combative pose' (144f.) – no wonder that, towards the end of the speech, 'we may . . . let our dress fall in careless disorder and the toga slip loose from us on every side' (147).

The use of gesticulation to underline the emotional properties of the main sections of a speech accounts for the prominence of ideographs among Quintilian's favourite gestures: ideographs, we saw, diagram the logical and emotional structure of what is being said. It also explains why he heartily disapproves of pictorial gestures: 'As for the gesture of demanding a cup, threatening a flogging or indicating the number 500 by crooking the thumb . . . I have never seen them employed even by uneducated rustics' (117); and, more generally, 'gestures which indicate things by means of mimicry . . . should be rigorously avoided in pleading' (88f.). He gives two reasons: the orator should never seem to be a mime artist (*saltator*), and the gesture should follow the thoughts rather than the words of the speech; already Cicero had made the same distinction between 'a theatrical gesture which expresses single words' (which he disapproved of) and the rhetorical gesture 'which explains the entire topic and meaning by signifying, not by demonstrating'.[23] Avoiding the appearance of a mime artist or an actor is fundamental for maintaining the decorum inherent in Roman pleading, but it is not a sufficient explanation for the avoidance of pictorial gesture. Gesticulation following 'thoughts' is gesticulation in the sense of ideographic gestures, diagramming the logical and emotional content; rhetorical *psychagogia* is more effective when the orator only signals general emotional and logical contents instead of freezing attention on single actions by displaying them mimetically.

*Gestus* – gesticulation and posture – not only brings about persuasion by underlining and amplifying the emotional and logical flow of the speech. The correct gestures and appropriate outward appearance are important in creating a favourable impression of the orator with his audience. With the help of the appropriate *gestus*, the orator impersonates what the Roman society regarded as the ideal orator – and since oratory is the main, if not the only way a member of the Roman upper class appeared in public, the orator has to show himself as the ideal Roman aristocrat – in the case of Quintilian's textbook addressed to students of the art, as the ideal young aristocrat. Quintilian never says so explicitly, but his advice is clear.

Let us begin with simple and trivial cases. At the end of his speech, Quintilian says, the orator may show not only his dishevelled dress but may also sweat profusely and show all signs of exhaustion. He has to overtly signal that he did not spare his strength in the interest of his client; even if he does not feel exhausted, at least he has to look it – as, earlier on, Quintilian had advised him to let the toga slip *velut sponte*, as though it were of its own accord, if it didn't do so by itself (147). Obviously, this final impression is important; the orator (at least in ideology) is not a professional acting for a fee, but a Roman nobleman, helping his *cliens*, his follower, in the capacity of *patronus*, protector, and thus fulfilling what his social position demands and legitimizing the social prerogatives of a Roman nobleman. The more exhausted he is (or looks), the better he has fulfilled this obligation.

This may seem far-fetched, at least at first glance, so let us look at what happens at the beginning of a speech. Before he can start to speak, the orator must again make a particular impression; since he cannot do it with words he does it with *gestus*; again Quintilian is very circumstantial. His dress must be immaculate, lacking all extravagance as well as all sloppiness: several paragraphs on dress are summed up by the advice that the dress 'should be distinguished and manly (*virilis*), as, indeed, it ought to be with all men of position (*honesti*)' (137). 'Manliness' is a quality which is demanded of an orator with a particular insistence – already in the second century BC, Cato defined the orator as 'a good man with experience in talking' (*vir bonus dicendi peritus*); Cicero demands, both in *De oratore* (1. 231) and the later *Orator* (59), that the orator performs 'with manly bend of the body' (*virili laterum flexione*). The younger Seneca gives the deeper reason; he regards a 'strong, powerful, and manly eloquence' as a sign of a healthy and sound mind and censures Maecenas who used to appear in extravagant and sloppy dress as an effeminate, even castrated orator:[24] outward appearance reflects inward character, a fundamental belief in antiquity and the justification for scientific physiognomy, as we have already seen. Both terms Quintilian uses, 'manly' (*virilis*) and what has been translated 'a man of position' (*honestus*), are therefore not merely descriptive but normative – being manly implies the qualities of strength, valour, willpower and self-control, qualities most prominent in the ideal nobleman; *honestus* is someone who deserves to be honoured by his fellow citizens because of his high qualities – the 'honours' incidentally, being not abstract feelings, but the higher offices, the positions of power in the state with their tangible advantages. Cicero makes the connection explicit. Beauty, he writes in his *De officiis* (1. 130), is twofold, with sexual attractiveness being becoming to women and dignity to men: 'therefore, one must remove from one's appearance all dress unworthy of a man, and one should beware of similar mistakes in gestures and movements'.

Besides dress, initial gesticulation helps to create this same impression. We saw that gesticulation in the *exordium* should be slow and restrained and that this corresponds to the general character of the *exordium*. But there is more. The orator is advised not to start to speak immediately; he should pause, even pat his head or wring his fingers, 'pretend to summon all his energies for the effort, confess to nervousness by a deep sigh'; then he should stand quietly in front of his audience, upright, 'the shoulders relaxed, the face stern, but not sad, expressionless, or languid . . . while the right hand should be slightly extended with the most modest of gestures' (159).

Part of this procedure – patting the head, wringing the fingers – certainly serves to attract the attention. To stand upright – what Cicero had called 'a manly bend of the body' – signals nobility and liberty; a stoop, Quintilian advises, could be read as a sign of low origin and servile personality (83, cf. 69). Incidentally, Seneca had compared the dishevelled way Maecenas used to present himself to the posture of a servile character on the stage.[25] To incline the head to one side, on the other hand, expresses languor, a quality closely associated with effeminacy and as such the opposite of manliness. Quintilian, of course, disapproves of it.[26]

However, it should not be overdone: to stand too erect and fierce is a sign of arrogance or even barbaric hardness which is heavily advised against (69). Here, two norms conflict. With a certain insistence, Quintilian uses the term 'modest' (*modestus*) as a sort of catchword for the initial impression. Cicero is even more explicit: as Crassus, his spokesman in *De oratore*, says 'even the best orators appear impudent and arrogant, if they do not begin their pleading with due shyness and seem nervous at the beginning' (1. 119) – a rather strange demand, according to our modern taste. The young Roman orator wins his audience by appearing not only as a proud and manly aristocrat, but at the same time as a person naturally given to respect and subordination in front of the magistrates of the Republic who preside over all occasions of formal speech.

There are other, even more surprising restrictions imposed upon gesticulation. Any frenetic movement, such as frequent nodding, intense shaking of the head (72) or the hands (103), jerking of the shoulders (130) or wild gesticulation which 'delivers such a rain of blows to the rear that it is scarcely safe to stand behind him' (118) is ill-suited. Gesticulation has only a limited amplitude: the hand should never be raised higher than the eyes or lower than the chest (112), and it should never move further to the left than the shoulders (113). Gesticulation, finally, is mainly a matter of the right hand, the left being only auxiliary (114).

It is certainly possible to explain one or other of these limitations without recurrence to a more general system. The left hand of a Roman orator is restrained by the fall of the toga: it is natural to use it less; besides, the dominance of the right hand may be fundamental to human action (and, thus, to symbolism) in general.[27] As to the upper limit for the lifted hand, in Imperial Rome it also has the function of distinguishing an ordinary orator from members of the Imperial house whose gestures of public address allow a higher lifting of the arm, as representations of emperors and magistrates show.[28] But individual explanations help only partially since they cannot explain all limitations. There is a more general reason behind the insistence upon restricted movements.

Moderation in movement is, in Roman opinion, characteristic of certain classes of men. In general, it is peculiar to a free man – only slaves run, a free man has leisure.[29] But being a free man is not only a social category, it is a way of living, thinking, and being; being a free man means also having a free soul, a specific personality. Gestures, according to a widespread ancient conviction, express character – Seneca's remarks on Maecenas make the point. Strictly moderated and limited gestures, then, are an indication of a moderate and self-controlled character – and this, of course, is another requirement of an exemplary Roman aristocrat and orator.[30]

All this – the restrictions and the selection of gestures – points in the same direction: rhetorical gestures are highly conventional, they are a selection and adjustment of gestures from daily conversation to the purpose of public speaking. Quintilian leaves no doubts: many common gestures, not only pictorial ones, are abhorred because they are too coarse and too vulgar; in one instance, he accepts a gesture though it is 'a common rather than professional gesture' (102).

One may reasonably suspect that approved gestures underwent modification and streamlining to improve precision and lessen ambiguity, but it is a difficult matter to substantiate this. One clue is the subtle distinction in meaning between similar gestures. 'Placing the middle finger against the thumb and extending the remaining three' has a variant where 'the middle and third fingers are also sometimes turned under the thumb'; the function of the two is different, the latter being more impressive and thus prohibited in *exordia*, as we have seen; to lightly grip the top joint of the index finger 'on either side, with the outer fingers slightly curved' is 'a gesture well suited for argument', while 'holding the middle joint of the finger and contracting the last two fingers still further' is a sign for more vehement argumentation (95). In both cases, the basic gesture is attested for daily conversation,[31] although one wonders whether these distinctions really were always observed there. In one case, at least, it seems possible to demonstrate the process: the nice gesture to touch one's lips with the fingertips to express wonder and admiration (103) is found both on Greek vase paintings and in the novel of Apuleius. But, typically enough, these attestations show some variation in form

without any discernible difference in meaning or chronological
distinction – sometimes only the index finger touches the lips, in
another case it is the thumb and index put together rather than all
the fingers of the hand.[32]


## GESTURES, STAGECRAFT, AND ELOQUENCE

This brings us to the strict demarcation between orator and actor,
pulpit and stage. Romans in general shared this feeling: the famous
orator Hortensius, the story went, used to perform rather
theatrically – which earned him the nickname Dionysia, the name
of a famous cabaret dancer of the time.[33] Appearing like an actor
could mean looking like a woman, that is, not appearing manly
enough. Dionysia was, moreover, of low social standing, her
profession certainly did not qualify for a *honestus*, and her name
contained an allusion to Dionysos-Bacchus the god of socially
disapproved ecstasy and total loss of self-control; Quintilian
explicitly forbids 'tossing or rolling the head till the hair flies free'
because it recalls an ecstatic.[34] Cicero once severely rebuked an
agent who had bought him two statues of maenads, the ecstatic
followers of Dionysos: 'where have I room for maenads?' In the
same letter, he disapproved of a statue of Mars because he, Cicero,
was a maker of peace, not war; this confirms that he disapproved
of the maenads too because he thought they did not fit his
character.[35] Thus, to give the impression of an actor did not fit the
image of a reliable aristocrat, the impression the orator had to give
to recommend himself to his audience.

Among the Greeks, by the way, the situation was no better.
Usually, to prove the contrary, modern scholars refer to the story
that Demosthenes had been instructed by an actor. A closer look at
the main account in Plutarch's *Life of Demosthenes*, however,
shows that the actor offered himself and had to persuade
Demosthenes to accept such a training – obviously instruction by
actors was unheard of in Athens also.[36] Thus, the case of
Demosthenes is the only exception to a more general rule – that
oratory and theatre were different things in Greece as well as in
Rome.

Since the Roman sources make us believe that gesticulation in acting and pleading were quite close, it would be interesting to at least catch a glimpse of the stage. The task is difficult. Roman acting – as with most technicalities of the Roman stage – is largely unattested,[37] and the tragedies (with the doubtful exception of Seneca) are lost. Still, there is some information on comic gesticulation to be gathered from the plays themselves, especially from Plautus.[38]

One preliminary remark is important: gesticulation varied according to character type – after all, Roman comedy employed stock characters. Exuberant gesticulation and movement were characteristic of slaves; a free man does not run, but the running slave was a stock type, presumably with a special stage technique for running. Other violent gestures belong either to slaves or to low class free-born: shaking the head with anger or being swollen with it; grinding one's teeth and slapping the thigh in anger.[39] This confirms our findings for the orator where frenetic movements were strictly forbidden – low origin and lack of self-control obviously going together.

More comes from a particular scene in the *Miles Gloriosus*, one of Plautus' best comedies (vv.200–215). The clever slave Palaestrio racks his brains to find a way to thwart the schemes of a fellow slave; in a splendid example of metatheatre, his neighbour, the old man Periplectomenus, comments on Palaestrio's gestures. First, with a stern face, he beats his chest with his fingers; turning to the side, he rests his left hand against his left thigh while he counts on the fingers of the right hand, slapping it against the right thigh in between. Then he snaps his fingers, shifts his posture several times, shakes his head ('he does not like what he thinks'); finally, he stands triumphantly erect having found the solution.

At the end, the onlooker Periplectomenus remarks that Palaestrio acts 'like the slave in comedy' (*dulice et comoedice*): his gesticulation is typical, conventional. Conventionality is what we would expect from the gestures of comic stock characters; as to gestures, the little evidence there is confirms it.[40] But it is obvious that the raw material for this conventionalization (so to speak) was gestures of daily life: thigh-slapping or counting on one's fingers was widespread among Greeks and Romans as well as with modern Europeans.[41] Conventionalization must have enforced certain characteristic elements in order to obtain better theatrical effects –

greater clarity, unequivocal significance and better adaptation to
the standard role; with slave roles, therefore, having better comical
effects.

Most of Palaestrio's gestures are also discussed in Quintilian: a
comparison is revealing. Slapping one's thigh is a strong gesture
which had been introduced into public speaking by the vulgar
Athenian politician and *rhetor* Cleon; nevertheless, both Cicero
(*Brutus* 278) and Quintilian (123) accept it – 'it is becoming as a
mark of indignation', which holds true for Palaestrio as well as for
the slave mentioned above; 'and', adds Quintilian, 'it excites the
audience', a strong argument in favour. Counting on the fingers –
or, rather, counting arguments on the fingers – is permitted, but
better with both hands, and certainly without slapping one's thighs
in between (115); forming the numerals with the fingers, however,
is very vulgar indeed (117).[42] Chest-beating the professor advises
against: it is a theatrical trick, *scaenicum* (115); on rare occasions
one may touch the chest with the fingertips to accompany words
of exhortation, reproach, or commiseration. Thus, Palaestrio's
gesticulation is stronger than Quintilian would allow for, it is
typical for a slave, *dulice*, as Periplectomenus has it;[43] but there is
at least a common stock of gestures.

We have seen how the gestures of *rhetors* are just as conventional
as those of the actor – this is one of the reasons for the difficult
demarcation between the two. Like theatrical gesture, rhetorical
gesture and gesticulation is a sort of self-sufficient sign system,
based upon gestures and gesticulation of daily life but selecting and
refining this raw material according to the principle of decency,
*decorum*. It differs from scenic gesture only in the principle of
selection, not in the fact of conventionality as such.

Rhetorical and theatrical gestures have not only their conventionality in common. Such a conventional system is teachable, in
fact has to be taught: there are teachers of stagecraft,[44] as there are
teachers of rhetoric. But gestures which are taught are not
spontaneous any more – therefore some people had misgivings: a
fundamental difference between stage and court was that the actor
dealt with fictional things, whereas the orator dealt with real life[45]
– would not an orator acting-out taught gestures incur the danger
of appearing a fake and lose all credit with his audience? Quintilian
himself answers this question in the affirmative: it would deprive

the orator of his credit, his *fides* and *auctoritas* – again two values central to the Roman *patronus* (184). Quintilian is also aware of the ultimate consequence, to renounce instruction in *gestus*. As a professional teacher, he has to reject it of course. In the introduction to his chapter on *actio* he attacks certain people 'who consider that delivery which owes nothing to art and everything to natural impulse is more forcible and the only form of delivery which is worthy of a man' (10).[46] This reference to the ideal of manliness shows that these people thought all teaching of delivery unmanly, presumably because it was considered too theatrical. To rely solely on 'nature' for the delivery would avoid the danger inherent in taught delivery: the presentation of the speech would then appear to come spontaneously from the heart. Quintilian agrees with his opponents that nature, of course, would have to play a part, but that it was much better to improve nature by art – without appearing unnatural; in fact, the aim of his teaching is to achieve the impression of natural spontaneity.[47]

## CULTURE AND GESTURES

Quintilian is well aware that the gestures he teaches have a special position: he distinguishes them not only from theatre and common use, but also from those of the past and those of other people and schools. Although many gestures seem to be common to both Greeks and Romans, there are those which only Greeks use or which 'foreign schools' – presumably again Greek teachers in Rome – recommend; typically enough, Quintilian advises against this gesture because it is too theatrical (103). What he prescribes, then, is (to use the term of the Neapolitan scholar) a specific Roman upper-class dialect of gestures.

This dialect has of course a historical dimension. Although in many instances Quintilian can refer back to Cicero as authority, once he confesses to a general development during the 150 years between Cicero's and his own teaching – namely, that modern gesticulation is generally somewhat livelier and more violent (184). He is not alone in making this observation, and more conservative observers connected the change with the decline of both rhetoric and morals.[48]

A millennium and a half later, in his *Elementa Rhetorices* of
1532, the German humanist Philip Melanchthon came to a similar
conclusion: 'delivery today is very different from that among the
ancients'.[49] Given the high conventionality of gestures and
especially gesticulation, it need not come as a surprise. Among
Quintilian's examples, few could be recognized today; mostly,
they are pictorial gestures, Quintilian's 'imitative' ones. Counting
on the fingers, for example, pictures a natural way of counting and
so is still understandable to us. We would understand too that
pressing the fist to the chest would have something to do with
emotion (to this extent, the gesture is pictorial); I doubt, however,
whether we would recognize it as expressing remorse – this
specialization is arbitrary, culturally defined. Slapping one's thigh
is even more arbitrary – we use it in our culture not to denote anger
as in Plautus and Quintilian, but together with loud laughter as a
somewhat vulgar expression of exhilaration.[50]

The distance is even greater with finger signs. Plain pointers are
still recognizable: pointing with the index seems to have a deep
natural basis; the vulgarity of pointing with the thumb – not quite
recommended by Quintilian (104) – is still recognizable by us
today. The highest degree of conventionalization seems to lie with
ideographs; though even today one may sometimes see the 'most
common' sign, thumb against middle finger, I doubt whether the
users know what they are doing. Other signs recommended by the
Roman have fallen out of use, others again changed into pictorial
signs and are heavily advised against – 'to put the tip of index and
thumb together to form a ring' was used by Greek dialecticians to
round off their conclusions; 'to stretch out the forefinger and the
little, the three others being closed' was to Quintilian a slightly more
forceful sign during narrating and arguing. Among contemporary
Swiss, the former gesture would be as abusive as the latter is to
modern Italians. A time-traveller would be well advised to learn,
amongst much else, the ancient art of gesticulation.

## NOTES

1  A. de Jorio, *La mimica degli antichi invesitgata nel gestire Napoletano* (Naples, 1832, repr. 1964), p. xx.
2  De Jorio, *La mimica*, p. xxii. The metaphor, as we know, has become current, see the early book by M. Critchley, *The Language of Gestures* (London, 1939).
3  *Actio quasi sermo corporis* ('delivery is, in a way, the language of the body'): Cicero, *De oratore* 3. 222; *actio quasi corporis quaedam eloquentia* ('delivery is a sort of eloquence of the body'): Cicero, *Orator* 55; compare also Quintilians *Institutio Oratoria* 11. 3. 1.
4  For a history of research see Adam Kendon, 'The study of gesture: some observations on its history', *Recherches Sémiotiques/ Semiotic Enquiry*, 2 (1982), pp. 45–62; for a bibliographical survey see the bibliography at the end of this volume.
5  See Cicero, *De oratore* 1. 128 'in an orator . . . there must be the shrewdness of a dialectician, the thoughts of a philosopher, the words nearly of a poet, the memory of a lawyer, the voice of a tragic actor and the delivery practically of the best stage-performer' (*in oratore . . . acumen dialecticorum, sententiae philosphorum, verba prope poetarum, memoria iuris consultorum, vox tragoedorum, gestus paene summorum actorum est requirendus*).
6  For a brief history from the classicist's point of view, see Ursula Maier-Eichhorn, *Die Gestikulation in Quintilians Rhetorik* (Frankfurt and Bern, 1989), pp. 35–47; to her references, add Robert P. Sonkowsky, 'An aspect of delivery in ancient rhetorical theory', *Transactions and Proceedings of the American Philological Association*, 90 (1959), pp. 256–74.
7  For Thrasymachos, see the fragments in Hermann Diels, *Die Fragmente der Vorsokratiker* (from the 5th edn, ed. with additions by Walther Kranz), 7th edn (Zurich and Berlin, 1954), no. 85 B 5 (Aristotle, *Rhetorica* 3. 1. 1404a13); for Aristotle, his *Rhetorica* (without a special chapter on delivery, but see bk 1 ch. 2; a very brief survey in Andrea G. Katsouri, *Rhetorike Hypokrise* (Ioannina, 1989), pp. 26–33; for Theophrastos, Diogenes Laertius 5.48 preserves only the title *Peri hupokriseôs* among definitely rhetorical treatises (see also Cicero, *De oratore* 3.221); for the few fragments of Demetrios' rhetorical writing see Fritz Wehrli, *Die Schule des Aristoteles. Heft 4: Demetrios von Phaleron*, 2nd edn (Basel and Stuttgart, 1968), frgs. 162–9.

8 Explicitly stated in Quintilian 11.2.1; Cicero presupposes this bipartition in many places, e.g. *De oratore* 1.128, cited in note 5.

9 The only commentary on the chapters on *gestus* is the recent doctoral dissertation of Maier-Eichhorn, *Die Gestikulation* – a useful booklet which, however, neglects the wider relationship of gestures to general cultural background; here, Burkhard Fehr, *Bewegungsweisen und Verhaltensideale: Physiognomische Deutungsmöglichkeiten der Bewegungsdarstellung an griechischen Statuen des 5. und 4. Jh.v.Chr.* (Bad Bramstedt, 1979) is still a pioneering work, though with no interest in Roman culture; see also the new edn with French translation and notes by Jean Cousin (ed.), *Quintilien. Institution Oratoire. Vol. 6: livres X et XI* (Paris, 1979). Appearing only after the colloquium on which this volume is based was Katsouri, *Rhetorike Hypokrise* (see note 7), a survey of the Greek and Roman material on gesticulation in rhetoric (13–140) and on the stage (141–99) from Homer onwards, with the main sources and ample illustrations. The chapter on Quintilian (124–40) contains few new insights, its main aim being to show that the famous illuminations in the manuscripts of Terence can illustrate Quintilian and that they derive from a tradition of gesticulation going back to the fifth century BC Athenian stage (133–40); for the former thesis, heard since Friedrich Leo (1883), see now Maier-Eichhorn, *Die Gestikulation*, pp. 145–53 (149: 'Für die Erklärung der Quintilianpassage gewinnen wir also aus den Bildern nichts, wenn sich auch mehrere, mindestens äussere Übereinstimmungen feststellen lassen'); the latter is highly speculative.

10 Here and in the following citations, passages from bk 11 ch. 3 of Quintilian's *Institutio Oratoria* are cited by their paragraph number only; the translations follow H.E. Butler's Loeb edition.

11 David Efron, *Gesture and Environment* (New York 1941), reprinted as *Gesture, Race and Culture* (The Hague, 1972); Paul Ekman and Wallace V. Friesen, 'Hand movements', *The Journal of Communication*, 22 (1972), pp. 353–74; a short discussion of this terminology in Adam Kendon, 'Introduction. Current issues in the study of "nonverbal communication"', in *Nonverbal Communication, Interaction and Gesture: Selections from 'Semiotica'*, ed. Adam Kendon (The Hague, Paris, and New York, 1981), pp. 31f.

12 Cicero, *Orator* 59: among the virtues of the perfect orator is 'a finger which does not beat rhythmically', *non ad numerum articulus cadens.*

13 The first preserved Roman rhetorical treatise, the anonymous *Rhetorica ad Herennium*, already warns 'not to change from an oratorical way into a tragic one' (*ne ab oratoria consuetudine ad tragicam transeamus* 3.24), and more generally 'in carriage and

gesticulation, there should be neither conspicuous beauty nor ugliness, lest we make the impression of an actor or a workman' (*convenit . . . in gestu nec venustatem conspiciendam nec turpitudinem esse, ne aut histriones aut operarii videamur esse* 3.26).

14 Macrobius, *Saturnalia* 3.14.11f. tells the story of Cicero and Roscius; the actor wrote, Macrobius adds, a treatise on the relationship between oratory and stagecraft. For Cicero's ideal orator see note 5.

15 See *Institutio Oratoria* 1.11.1–14.

16 The term in Plato, *Phaedrus* 261A. Still indispensable is Friedrich Solmsen, 'Aristotle and Cicero on the orator's playing upon the feeling', *Classical Philology*, 33 (1938), pp. 390–404, reprinted in his *Kleine Schriften* (Hildesheim, 1968), vol. I, pp. 216–30.

17 On the three 'duties of the orator' (*officia oratoria*) – *persuadere, movere, conciliare* in Cicero's terms, which Quintilian (154) repeats – see Rudolf Schottlaender, 'Der römische Redner und sein Publikum', *Wiener Studien*, 80 (1967), pp. 125–46.

18 See Cicero, *De officiis* 2.128–30 'the way to stand, walk, sit, lie down, the expression of the face and the eyes, the movement of the hands should preserve this befitting appearance' (*status, incessus, sessio, accubitio, vultus, oculi, manuum motus teneat illud decorum*). Especially important is the way one walks, as already in the late second century BC the epitaph of a noble Claudia shows, among whose virtues is 'modest walking', see *Carmina Latina Epigraphica*, ed. F. Bücheler, A. Riese, and E. Lommatzsch (3 vols, Leipzig 1895– 1926), vol. I, no. 52, 7 (*incessu commodo*); for the way of walking which indicates vice, see e.g. Seneca, *Epistulae Morales* 52.12, 114.3; Juvenal, *Satires* 2.17. Still important is Elizabeth C. Evans, 'Roman descriptions of personal appearance in history and biography', *Harvard Studies in Classical Philology*, 46 (1935), pp. 43–84; see also the commentary on Juvenal's *Satires* by Ludwig Friedländer (Leipzig, 1895), p. 166; Fehr, *Bewegungsweisen und Verhaltensideale*, pp. 7–12, and Bremmer, this volume, ch. 1, 'Walking'.

19 Cicero, *De oratore* 3.216 (*corpusque totum hominis et eius vultus omnesque voces, ut nervi in fidibus, ita sonant, ut a motu animi quoque sunt pulsae*).

20 Gregory Bateson, 'Redundancy and coding', in *Animal Communication. Techniques of Study and Result of Research*, ed. Thomas A. Sebeok (Bloomington and London, 1968), pp. 614–26, the citation p. 615; the modification in Kendon, 'Introduction. Current issues in the study of "nonverbal communication" ', p. 6f.

21 Quintilian 100: *est admirationi conveniens ille gestus, quo manus modice supinata ac per singulos a minimo collecta digitos redeunte*

*flexu simul explicatur atque convertitur*; 104: *compressam etiam manum in paenitentia vel ira pectori admovemus.*

22 Quintilian 92: *est autem gestus ille maxime communis, quo medius digitus in pollicem contrahitur explicitis tribus . . . cum leni in utramque partem motu modice prolatus, simul capite atque umeris sensim ad id, quo manus feratur, obsecundantibus.*

23 Cicero, *De oratore* 3.220: *non hic (sc. gestus) verba exprimens scaenicus, sed universam rem et sententiam non demonstratione sed significatione declarans.*

24 Seneca, *Epistulae Morales* 19.9.114, esp. paras 6 and 22; even more revealing are the metaphors in another description of Maecenas, *Epistulae Morales* 92.35: 'he had an abundant and manly nature, but success ungirded his dress' (*habuit enim ingenium et grande et virile nisi illud secunda discinxissent*).

25 See his *Epistulae Morales* 114.6.

26 Quintilian 69; see also Cicero, *Brutus* 220, on the *orationes languidiores* of Curio, not a favourite of Cicero, and *De oratore* 1.2 on Epicurus as a 'philosopher, so weak, so slothful, so spineless, so referring everything to bodily pleasure and pain' (*philosophus tam mollis, tam languidus, tam enervatus, tam omnia ad voluptatem corporis doloremque referens*). See also Bremmer, this volume, ch. 1, 'Walking'.

27 See for these explanations, Maier-Eichhorn, *Die Gestikulation*, pp. 114–16; for the biological and symbolic aspect, see R. Hertz, *Death and the Right Hand* (London, 1960); Adam Kendon, 'Gesticulation, speech and the gesture theory of language origins', *Sign Language Studies*, 9 (1975), p. 350

28 See Richard Brilliant, *Gesture and Rank in Roman Art. The Use of Gestures to Denote Status in Roman Sculpture and Coinage* (New Haven, 1963), pp. 9f.; Maier-Eichhorn, *Die Gestikulation*, p. 111 is muddled.

29 The earliest and most explicit testimony is Plautus, *Poenulus* 522s. *liberos homines per urbem modico magis par est gradu ire; servile esse duco festinantem currere* ('that free men walk through town at a temperate pace is more befitting; it is, I think, slavish to run in haste').

30 See for gesture control and self-control: Fehr, *Bewegungsweisen und Verhaltensideale*, pp. 16–23; for the wider context, Norbert Elias, *Über den Prozess der Zivilisation: Soziogenetische und psychogenetische Untersuchungen* (2 vols, Basel, 1939), esp. vol. II, pp. 312–41.

31 See the representations (mostly from Greek vases) in Gerhard Neumann, *Gesten und Gebärden in der griechischen Kunst* (Berlin, 1965), pp. 13–15.

32 The basic gesture: Karl Sittl, *Die Gebärden der Griechen und Römer*

(Leipzig, 1890). pp. 272f.; Maier-Eichhorn, *Die Gestikulation*, pp. 99f.; formed only with the index finger: Sittl, *Die Gebärden*, p. 272 7n.; Apuleius, *Metamorphoses* 1.8; thumb and index in Apuleius, *Metamorphoses* 4.28, perhaps with ritual significance.

33 The story in Gellius, *Noctes Atticae* 1.5.2.

34 Quintilian 71 (*fanaticum est*, 'it is typical for an ecstatic'); see for this typical movement Jan N. Bremmer, 'Greek maenadism reconsidered', *Zeitschrift für Papyrologie und Epigraphik*, 55 (1984), pp. 276–86, esp. pp. 278f., with earlier bibliography.

35 In a letter to M. Fadius Gallus, at the end of 62 BC, Cicero, *Epistulae ad familiares* 7.23.2; for the episode see D.R. Shackleton Bailey, *Cicero* (London, 1971), pp. 25f. (who prefers to call him Fabius); Manfred Fuhrmann, *Cicero und die römische Republik* (Munich and Zurich, 1989), pp. 165–6.

36 Besides Plutarch's *Life of Demosthenes* 7, where the actor has the name Satyros, see also Pseudo-Plutarch, *Vitae X oratorum* 845A (with the actor Andronikos), whereas in ibid 844F Demosthenes pays another actor, Neoptolemos, handsomely for his instruction; the story might go back to the late fourth century BC, see Demetrios of Phaleron, fr 164–66 in F. Wehrli, *Die Schule des Aristoteles*.

37 What the grammarian Aelius Donatus tells us in his commentary on Terence would be helpful – were it not information destined for rhetorical declamation rather than deriving from stage practice, see John Wiliam Basore, *The Scholia on Hypocrisis in the Commentary of Donatus* (Baltimore, 1908). And the illuminated manuscripts of Terence are no certain witness for theatrical practice, with due respect to Katsouri, *Rhetorike Hypokrise*, pp. 132–40.

38 Basic (but rather faute de mieux) is Barthelemy-A. Taladoire, *Commentaires sur la mimique et l'expression corporelle du comédien romain* (Montpellier, 1951), whom Katsouri in *Rhetorike Hypokrise*, pp. 182–5, follows closely; there is still some information to be gleaned from Boris Warnecke, 'Gebärdenspiel und Mimik der römischen Schauspieler', *Neue Jahrbücher für das Klassische Altertum* 13. Jahrgang, vol. 25 (1910), pp. 580–94, and even from Torkel Baden, 'Bemerkungen über das komische Geberdenspiel der Alten', *Neue Jahrbücher für Philologie*, Supplementband 1 (1831), pp. 447–56.

39 The running slave in Taladoire, *Commentaires*, pp. 41–3; for head-shaking, the best example is Saurea, the doorman slave, in Plautus, *Asinaria* 403; swollen with anger is e.g. the vulgar soldier in Plautus, *Bacchides* 603; the soldier Stratophanes in Plautus, *Truculentus* 601 'grinds his teeth and slaps his thigh' with rage.

40 For example, Seneca, *Epistulae Morales* 11.7 or Petronius, *Satyrica* 19 on theatrical laughter (*mimicus risus*).

41 Slapping one's thighs as an expression of anger and sorrow, Sittl, *Die Gebärden*, pp. 21–5 (rarely and late as an expression of merriment, ibid., p. 12); counting on the fingers: ibid., pp. 252–62.

42 The special system of finger counting, however, seems to have been in high esteem, at least in later antiquity, see Sittl, *Die Gebärden*, pp. 254–62 for the key text of Bede; see also Apuleius, *Apologia* 89 where finger counting perhaps is regarded as rather simplistic, as in Quintilian.

43 'He stands like the slave in comedy' (*astitit et dulice et comoedice*) comments Plautus, *Miles Gloriosus* 213. The theoreticians themselves point this out: Quintilian 1.11.3, and the *Rhetorica ad Herennium*.

44 The expression is Quintilian's, 11.3.71 (*doctores scaenici*), cf. 1.11.4.

45 Explicitly and with some weight in Quintilian's introduction to our subject, 11.3.4f.

46 One of these extremists was Dionysius of Halicarnassus, *Demosthenes* 54 – the position is understandable for an Atticist. One could, of course, refer to Aristotle, *Rhetorica* 3.1.1404a12 for a justification: Aristotle already put nature much higher than art in delivery.

47 Quintilian 1.11.3; anticipated in *Rhetorica ad Herennium* 3.27 'a good performance has the result that the discourse appears to come from the heart' (*pronuntiationem bonam id perficere, ut res ex animo agi videatur*).

48 See the elder Seneca's remark, with a typical moralistic twist, *Controversiae* 5.6 (*apud patres nostros, qui forensia stipendia auspicabantur, nefas*), and the general discussion of the decline of rhetoric in the Imperial Age: Gordon Williams, *Change and Decline: Roman Literature in the Early Empire* (Berkeley and Los Angeles, 1978), pp. 26–48; Konrad Heldmann, *Antike Theorien über Entwicklung und Verfall der Redekunst* (Munich, 1982).

49 *Elementorum Rhetorices Libri Duo* (1532): *actio vero longe alia nunc est quam qualis apud veteres fuit* (cited in Maier-Eichhorn, *Die Gestikulation*, p. 38).

50 In this signification, it is rarely attested and late; see Sittl, *Die Gebärden*, p. 12.

# 3

# The rationale of gestures
# in the West:
# third to thirteenth centuries

## JEAN-CLAUDE SCHMITT

The culture of the Middle Ages has sometimes been called a 'culture of gestures' or a 'gestural culture'. Such expressions have a double meaning: first the movements and attitudes of the human body played a crucial role in the social relationships of the past. Second, medieval culture itself thought about its own gestures, and indeed constructed a medieval theory of gestures.

## THE IMPORTANCE OF GESTURES

According to some historians, the weakness of literacy explains the importance of gestures in the Middle Ages. Marc Bloch, for example, pointed out the ritualization of feudal society, the formalism that was expressed by gestures and words more than by written records.[1] We would scarcely imagine today that a simple gesture could possess legal power or could commit people more efficiently than a written form drawn up by a notary and signed by both parties. At least until the thirteenth century, however, when cities and commercial activities began to develop rapidly and when growing state bureaucracies helped to spread literacy, gestures were much more powerful than such documents.

However, for two reasons I will not oppose 'gestural' culture and 'literate culture' schematically. First, the Middle Ages always knew both gestures and literacy (as we do today), although the balance between them changed from one century to the next and from one social group to the next. On the one hand, medieval culture gave writing and reading an even greater emphasis since they were rare and were used to spread God's Word, itself called 'Scripture'. For this reason literacy was for centuries monopolized by the Church, by the clerics who were accustomed to write in Latin. Second, we should not forget that writing too was a kind of gesture at a time when the only form of writing was writing by hand.[2]

Indeed, very few people could write and therefore commitment had to be made through ritual gestures, formal words, and symbolic objects (a reliquary, the host, a sword, etc.). Gestures transmitted political and religious power; they made such transmission public, known by all, and they gave legal actions a living image, as for example when a lord received in his hand the homage of his vassals or when a bishop laid his hand on the head of a newly consecrated priest. Gestures bound together human wills and human bodies.

In fact, the human body was of greatest importance in medieval society and culture. The human being was thought of as double consisting of a soul and a body, an invisible *inside* and a visible *outside* linked by a dynamic relationship. Such a relationship was a fundamental feature of all the medieval ideas about mankind, space, social order, and cosmos. Gestures figured, or better, *embodied* the dialectic between *intus* and *foris* since they were supposed to express without the 'secret movements' of the soul within.

However, the body was ambivalent. On the one hand, it was thought of as the 'prison of the soul', the servant of sin, an obstacle on the way to salvation. That negative judgement did not spare gestures, especially when they seemed to transgress the proper limits imposed by ethics and social custom: those 'bad' gestures were termed 'gesticulations'.[3]

On the other hand, salvation had to be reached through the

body and especially by means of ritual gestures of charity, penance, and piety. For Christians (unlike dualist heretics), the body was a sort of necessary evil that could be used positively. The Bible, from Adam to Christ, illustrated and taught all manner of gestures – both sinful ones that bore the label of the Fall as well as virtuous gestures that permitted the redemption of mankind.

Society itself was metaphorically thought of as a 'body' whose 'members' – the head, the arms, the sides, the belly, the legs, the feet – represented the different social groups with their distinctive functions and values, languages, signs, coats of arms, and also their individual gestures. Lay people, monks and canons, knights and merchants, scholars, made up different 'gestural communities'. In such a society, there was little room for individuals: everyone belonged to an *ordo*, a word with a non-coincidental reference to the ritual *ordines* of liturgy. Thus, society was strongly ritualized; gestures permitted everyone to confirm his belonging to one particular group. They also expressed hierarchies between the social groups and, within each one, between different ranks and dignities. Thus, all gestures had their importance: not just the most solemn rituals (royal coronations, marriage, the mass), but all the small gestures of everyday life such as making the sign of the cross when entering a church, beginning to eat, or facing danger.

A person was never alone while performing gestures. Even the hermit in the desert (that is, the medieval forest) or the monk in his cell acted at least under God's omniscient 'eyes'. More commonly, gestures were always performed towards someone else – to speak or to fight with, to greet or to challenge. Between individuals, and between individuals and God, in order to communicate or to pray, people continually made gestures that involved both their bodies and their souls. They gave their gestures all the values of their faith (in the double meaning of the medieval *fides*, secular homage and religious belief ), all the symbolic values of their social rank, and all the hopes of their life until and even after their death.

Therefore, we cannot doubt that the study of gestures, from the most solemn to the most ordinary and even unconscious, allows the historian to enter deeply into the functioning of medieval society, its symbolic values, its ways of life, and its modes of thought.

When historians today speak of medieval gestures, they cannot avoid comparing them to gestures of their own. Like ethnologists working within other cultures, historians face societies different from their own and realize that they have grown up and live in a different 'gestural society'. Although we usually think that we are using fewer or more moderate gestures than our ancestors or our neighbours (the Italians as viewed by the French, the French by the Americans), in our own culture gestures fulfil crucial ideological and practical functions. They serve obvious public and private rituals and they are means of non-verbal communication. We make more gestures than we realize.

However, gestures change from one place to another and from one time to another. Some gestures may even disappear through history and others may emerge. Some metaphorical expressions such as 'to throw down the gauntlet' or 'to take off one's hat' remind us of past gestures that would no longer actually be performed. For instance, we use the expression that the administration is 'making a gesture' toward another country or toward workers on strike, with the hope that a limited concession may have the same result as a more substantial (military or financial) action. The expression is quite ambiguous. It shows that real gestures no longer resolve social or diplomatic conflicts, but it also indicates that we identify 'gesture' with almost nothing that is material, just what we call a 'symbolic' act. Nevertheless, we notice that such a symbolic act does produce something, that it has real efficacy.

Thus, even when there is no real gesture we remember and underline the power of gestures, and not just the technical efficacy of gestures of work or 'body techniques' (the *techniques du corps* studied by Marcel Mauss in his pioneering study)[4] but the symbolic power of many gestures and rituals. And this is especially true for medieval culture.

## How to reconstruct medieval gestures?

Gestures, like words, belong to an ephemeral world. Usually they do not leave any traces for historians. There are only a few exceptions. For example, by studying the shape or *ductus* of a letter, paleographers can reconstruct the movement of the hand that drew it centuries earlier. Some sculptures or paintings also disclose the technical gestures of the artists, the movements and pressure of the hand. Bone deformations permit archaeologists to understand ancient modes of crouching. But usually historians do not grasp anything but textual or iconographic *representations* of gestures. These representations are of differing kinds.

Some texts simply mention isolated gestures but do not describe them. We might know that King Arthur and his knights met to eat, but we do not know how they ate, how they held their knives or moved their heads or their feet. Sometimes, we get better descriptions. We know for instance how Charlemagne expressed grief by pulling his heard and crying with an abundance of tears.[5] Occasionally we even find a moral or aesthetic judgement or an abstract thought about the meanings and social values of such gestures.

However, unlike the anthropologist who can observe them directly, in all such cases – from the merest mention to the most elaborate description – we can never reach the gestures themselves. This means that we have to take into account all of the biases, the weight of vocabulary, and the ideologies that intrude between the gestures, the texts, and ourselves.

This interference is equally present when we observe images. Medieval art was essentially anthropomorphic. The human figure was depicted everywhere, and invisible beings (God, the devil, the angels) were likewise given a human figure. So there are countless images of gestures. But such representations of gestures depend at least as much on the specific rules of figuration in medieval art as on direct observation of gestures by the artists. To begin with, the fixity of medieval images creates a huge problem. All the gestures that were mere movement (for example blessing while making the sign of the cross) had to be frozen by the artist. But at what point? The artist could choose to emphasize the hand held up rather than down, but he could not suggest the movement itself, its direction, or its speed.[6]

Dealing with literary or legal texts and with images, some historians have attempted to build up typologies of medieval gestures according to the parts of the body with which they were concerned (gestures of the head, of the arms, of the hands, etc.) or according to the possible meanings of gestures (gestures of grief or joy, of greeting, meeting, or leaving; gestures of respect, prayer, homage, blessing, etc.).[7] Many studies are more limited, referring to a single illuminated manuscript (for example, Eike von Repgow's *Sachsenspiegel*),[8] one kind of gesture (gestures of prayer, gestures of despair), or to the work of one single artist (Giotto).[9]

My own purpose is neither to trace the history of one particular gesture nor to limit myself to one particular piece of literary or iconographic evidence, nor even to construct a typology or dictionary of medieval gestures. I ask a more general question: what actually constituted 'making a gesture' in the Middle Ages? How and by whom were gestures not only performed but also thought about, classified, and figured? What cultural patterns, what attitudes towards persons and the body, what social relationships were expressed in all of these judgements? Was there a medieval theory of gestures?

## MEDIEVAL IDEAS ABOUT GESTURES

A large and diverse body of evidence including theological, legal, literary, pedagogical, and medical texts; monastic rules and customaries; liturgical *ordines*, vision narratives, treatises on prayer and preaching, liturgical dramas; and mirrors of princes, among others, may help answer such broad questions. As for images, particularly helpful are series of pictures showing different aspects of the same gesture which attempt to suggest movement, and, more generally speaking, express an attempt to think of gestures figuratively.

Altogether, it seems to me that medieval ideas about gestures, their functions, and their values may be summarized according to three notions. First, the notion of *expressivity*. Gestures were considered expressions of the inner movements of the soul, of feelings, of the moral values of individuals. In the West this notion belonged to a very old tradition. From one age to another it acquired different connotations: ethical ones in antiquity or in the Christian tradition, more psychological ones today when we enquire into the physical expression of feelings. In the Middle Ages, gestures seemed to be the outer expression of the 'movements of the soul', whereas the 'discipline' of gestures (drawn for instance from a monastic rule) was supposed to improve the soul.

A second axis consisted of what today we call *non-verbal communication*. It has slowly emerged from the old tradition of rhetoric inherited from pagan wisdom. But within Christianity, the symbolic values of the Word changed the balance between speech and gestures, whereas the social conditions of public communication were changing as well. Space and time shifted from the agora and the ancient theatre to the medieval pulpit. Also the principal actors gesturing on the social stage evolved from the rhetorician to the priest, the teacher, or even jugglers.

The third axis was concerned with *efficacy*, with its double meaning: the practical efficacy of technical gestures (sawing, moving, writing, etc.) and the symbolic efficacy of political or sacramental rituals.

Expression, communication, efficacy: such issues did not remain unchanged throughout the long Middle Ages. From late antiquity until the thirteenth and fourteenth centuries gestures and their medieval interpretations had a complex history. This history was hardly linear, but showed successive attempts to give gestures new interpretations, new kinds of figurations, as well as to impose on them a tighter control. Such attempts were part of the elaboration of new ideas about the body, the individual, the interactions between social actors, and attitudes toward nature and the supernatural. In short, since gestures involved both the individual and society, the soul and the body, the human and the divine, the observation of gestures became a laboratory for the new forms of rationality that developed during the Middle Ages. This was especially true at three different periods: late antiquity, the 'Carolingian Renaissance', and above all during the revival of an urban civilization in the West during the twelfth and thirteenth centuries.

Late antiquity was a period of reception and transformation of pagan representations of gestures and a time of important innovations. From antiquity,[10] the Middle Ages inherited many gestures (for instance rhetorical gestures of *declamatio*, legal gestures of *dextrarum iunctio*, the *orans* gesture of prayer) as well as intellectual tools with which to think and speak about gestures. The words and notions of *gestus*, *gesticulatio*, *motus*, came from antiquity along with their intellectual, moral, or scientific context: the ethics of social behaviour; the art of rhetoric (whose fifth and last part dealt with *actio* or *pronuntiatio*, the physical performance); the medical enquiry about the body and its movements; and the musical and mathematical notions of harmony that ought to rule all movements of the body as well as the entire universe. Christianity took up all of these notions, combining them with other patterns inherited from the Bible. Thus gestures had to fit new social and religious models. The *orator* was no longer a *rhetor* but a praying member of the faithful or a priest. After the Church was born, clerics sought to distinguish themselves from the laity. They wanted to benefit from gestures of allegiance partly borrowed from imperial ceremonial and they assumed that their new dignity reflected these marks of respect from their own persons onto God. Augustine played a key role for Christian understanding of gestures, while defining them as conventional signs making communication possible between all beings, human and supernatural, between man and God, the angels or the devil (tracing here a distinction between 'superstitious' gestures and legitimate gestures of prayer or sacramental gestures).

Typical of the Christian ethics of that time was the interiorization of the notions of sin and shame that led to a greater distrust of the body and, along with it, of gestures. Gestures were easily judged as expressions of the vices of pride (*superbia*) and lust (*luxuria*) that had to be contained and punished. Finally, monasticism developed as a completely new gestural institution with a large range of ascetic and penitential gestures and with new forms of collective prayer and liturgy.

The 'Carolingian Renaissance' partly revived these traditions from late antiquity. Within the framework of the liberal arts (rhetoric and music) Remigius of Auxerre was the first author to give gestures a definition. He opposed the gesture (*gestus*) of a single limb to the movement (*motus*) of the whole body. Simultaneously, liturgical gestures were codified in *ordines* and explained systematically by Amalarius of Metz. Iconography (such as that of the *Utrecht Psalter* or the *Stuttgart Psalter*) emphasized the central role of the hand of God as a pattern for human gestures and the main tool for ruling man and transforming the world.

Thus, in addition to the old pattern of a moderate *gestus*, as opposed to the demonic *gesticulatio* of those who were possessed by the devil, there was another kind of 'holy gesticulation' inspired by God. It was illustrated in the Bible by the sacred dance of David, jumping naked before the ark, and it was carried out by liturgical procession, collective psalmody of monks, or even dancing in churches. I would call such behaviour *gesta* or 'la geste' (as in 'la chanson de gestes') rather than *gestus*, 'le geste', a word that became much rarer during the same period. Actually, the idea prevailed that men could not control all of their gestures, that supernatural powers ruled their bodies and movements (as we can see in many images of the Psalmist or of the Evangelists). These powers were ruling their fate on earth as well: history too was termed *gesta*.

The twelfth and thirteenth centuries brought radical changes. First, we can see in the texts of this period how the question of gestures was reformulated while at the same time the word *gestus* once more became common. One of the main reasons for this revival was the diversification of society and the resulting necessity for everyone and for each group to distinguish themselves from the others by showing, among all kinds of signs, different gestures and attitudes (laity v. clerics, knights v. peasants, Cluniacs v. Cistercians, etc.).

In this context, the pedagogy of gestures became a necessity – above all in monasteries that became reluctant to accept children as oblates and took older novices instead.[11] The later they entered, the more secular gestures novices had to forget before they could become monks. Teaching novices the right behaviour gave birth to numerous prescriptions in the customaries and specific treatises of pedagogy. The best example was Hugh of Saint-Victor's *Institutio novitiorum*, which provided the most elaborate theory of gestures of the entire Middle Ages. Gestures (*gestus*) were defined as a movement (*motus*) of the whole body and a *figuratio*.[12] The external expression of the movements of the soul had to make up a 'figure', a symbolic image of the body in the eyes of God and man. Hugh also underlined the different modes (*modi*) or modalities of gestures and classified them in order to show how virtuous gestures held the middle ground between opposing bad gestures which neutralized each other. Finally, following the famous metaphor developed at the same time by John of Salisbury, Hugh compared the discipline of gestures to the government of the kingdom and the human body to the body politic. In fact, Hugh's theory of gestures was part of the broader ethical, political and aesthetic ideology that emerged in the Parisian schools of the twelfth century.

From that time on, the pressure of lay society made itself increasingly felt.[13] On the one hand, chivalric romances, books of *manières* and *contenances de table* were developing similar notions of moderate gestures, but with some other ideological goals: at stake were the self-identification of aristocracy and the definition of specific rules for young knights, for women (as for example in the *Roman de la rose*), for their children, and for the king (in the mirror of the prince).

Gestures of ordinary people also merited greater attention. Typical for them were gestures of work that were now described and depicted in a less symbolic manner. Manuscript miniatures pointed out the effective combination of physical energy, technical use of tools, and professional skills.

Other questions were now raised about the 'language of gestures', especially the ability of gestures to replace or match speech. The oldest lists of monastic sign language, the development of liturgical dramas, the rise of preaching, and finally the birth of an urban secular rhetoric aided such questioning.

Religious life, which was undergoing profound changes during this period, was one of the fields for these experiments. Kneeling and holding both hands together became the most typical gesture of Christian prayer. There was also a growing interest in distinguishing all the possible modes of prayer and their attitudes and gestures in terms of different occasions and intentions. The Parisian theologian Peter the Chanter first provided such a list of gestures at the end of the twelfth century. It consisted of seven modes of prayer, each of them depicted in a single miniature. Some years later the *Nine modes of prayer of Saint Dominic* consisted of a remarkable series of textual descriptions and images, teaching people how to behave and how to move while praying, from the most common mode of prayer to the most extraordinary mystical ecstasies.[14]

Eventually, the great question of symbolic efficacy also arose. Some gestures seemed able to transform living beings or material things. For example, making the sign of the cross was supposed to repel the devil or death. Gestures used for ecclesiastical sacraments (baptism, eucharist, and marriage) were especially discussed. Some theologians wondered whether sacramental words alone played a role in transubstantiation, although some precise gestures (crossing the host and elevating it) also had to be performed by the priest in order to complete the ritual.

## CONCLUSION

As we have seen all too briefly, there was no linear evolution reducing the role of gestures, submitting them to explicit rules and to the constraints of rationality. On the one side, the enforcement of ethics, the development of literacy, and the growing complexity of social encounters limited the scope of gestures in the context of other modes of communication and submitted them to more stringent control. On the other side, the development of figurative arts, the diversification of rituals, the forms of public speech, the scholastic explanations of religious gestures, and the new patterns of behaviour inspired by late medieval mysticism drew the question of gestures to the very centre of ideological debate.

Gestures and the human body have a long history. In suggesting its complexity and pointing out some of its main turning-points in the course of a thousand years, I have simply tried to unveil some of the historical problems with which we are still deeply concerned.

## NOTES

This article is a brief summary of my book, *La raison des gestes dans l'Occident médiéval* (Paris, 1990).

1 M. Bloch, *La société féodale* (Paris, 1939).
2 R. Marichal, 'L'écriture latine et la civilisation occidentale du Ier au XVIè siècle', in *L'Ecriture et la psychologie des peuples* (Paris, 1963), pp. 199–247.

3 J.-C. Schmitt, '*Gestus/Gesticulatio*. Contribution à l'étude du vocabulaire latin médiéval des gestes', in *La lexicographie du latin médiéval et ses rapports avec les recherches actuelles sur la civilisation du Moyen Age* (Paris, 1981), pp. 377–90.

4 M. Mauss, *Sociologie et Anthropologie* (Paris, 1950), pp. 363–86.

5 G. J. Brault, *The Song of Roland. An Analytical Edition* (2 vols, University-Park and London, 1978).

6 F. Garnier, *Le langage de l'image au Moyen Age. Signification et Symbolique* (2 vols, Paris, 1982–9).

7 E. Lommatzsch, *System der Gebärden, dargestellt auf Grund der mittelalterlichen Literatur Frankreichs* (Diss. Berlin, 1910); W. Habicht, *Die Gebärde in englischen Dichtungen des Mittelalters* (Munich, 1959); D. Peil, *Die Gebärde bei Chrétien, Hartmann und Wolfram: Erec – Iwein – Parzival* (Munich, 1975); R. G. Benson, *Medieval Body Language. A Study of the Use of Gesture in Chaucer's Poetry* (Copenhagen, 1980).

8 K. von Amira, *Die Handgebärden in den Bilderhandschriften des Sachsenspiegels* (Munich, 1905), pp. 161–263; R. Schmidt-Wiegand, 'Gebärdensprache im mittelalterlichen Recht', *Frühmittelalterliche Studien*, 16 (1982), pp. 363–79.

9 M. Barasch, *Gestures of Despair in Medieval and Early Renaissance Art* (New York, 1976) and *Giotto and the Language of Gestures* (Cambridge, Mass., 1987).

10 K. Sittl, *Die Gebärden der Griechen und Römer* (Leipzig, 1890); R. Brilliant, *Gesture and Rank in Roman Art: The Use of Gestures to Denote Status in Roman Sculpture and Coinage*, (New Haven, 1963).

11 M. de Jong, *In Samuel's Image: Child Oblation in the Early Middle Ages* (Leiden, 1991).

12 J.-C. Schmitt, 'Le geste, la cathédrale et le roi', *L'Arc*, 72 (1978), pp. 9–12.

13 J. Bumke, *Höfische Kultur* (2 vols, Munich, 1986).

14 J.-C. Schmitt, 'Between text and image: the prayer gestures of Saint Dominic', *History and Anthropology*, 1 (1984), pp. 127–62, repr. in R. C. Trexler (ed.), *Persons in Groups* (Binghamton, 1985), pp. 195–220 (in French).

# 4

# The language of gesture in early modern Italy

PETER BURKE

'Come all'historico sia necessaria la cognitione de' cenni'
Bonifacio, *L'arte de' cenni.*
'Evvi mai cosa più visibile, più comune e più semplice del
gestire dell'uomo?
E pure quanto poco si riconosce di esso!!'
De Jorio, *La mimica degli antichi.*

In the last few years the territory of the historian has expanded to include gesture, as well as the history of the body in general. For the practitioners of the so-called 'new history', or 'history of the everyday' (German: *Alltagsgeschichte*), everything has a past and nothing is too unimportant to receive historical attention. Even smells have a history which can be recovered and written.[1]

Opponents of the new history assert that historians of this school trivialize the past. Three responses to this charge seem appropriate. The first is to recognize the danger of trivialization wherever a 'new-historical' topic is pursued for its own sake, without any attempt to show connections with anything else. For an example of this approach one might cite Câmara Cascudo's historical dictionary of Brazilian gestures, a scholarly and fascinating book (and a good basis for future work) but a study which collects information without raising questions.[2]

A second response might be to argue that the notion of the 'trivial' needs to be problematized and relativized and more specifically that gestures were not taken lightly in early modern Europe. Italy may lack spectacular debates over gesture of the kind to be found in England (the Quaker refusal to observe 'hat-honour'), or in Russia (blessing with two fingers or three), but in the early seventeenth century a Genoese patrician, a crusader for the vanishing ideal of republican equality, claimed that he was imprisoned unjustly on account of his *gesti del corpo* (for example, his proud way of walking into the room and his failure to stand up straight before the Chancellor), gestures regarded by the government as a form of 'dumb insolence'.[3] This phrase, still current in the British Army, reminds us that in some quarters at least, the rules of gesture continue to be taken seriously.

The third response might be to follow Sherlock Holmes, Freud, and Morelli (not to mention Carlo Ginzburg), and to assert the importance of the trivial on the grounds that it provides clues to what is more significant.[4] We can study gesture as a sub-system within the larger system of communication which we call 'culture'.

This assumption is shared by many social historians. It may even seem obvious. So it may be useful to remind ourselves of the existence of a 'universalist' approach to gesture, recently reincarnated in the well-known books of Desmond Morris (despite the unresolved tension in his work between universalizing zoological explanations of the gestures of the naked ape and attempts to map their cultural geography).[5] As an example of more rigorous (indeed, 'scientific') analysis pointing in the opposite direction, we may cite Birdwhistell's famous demonstration that even unconscious gestures, such as modes of walking, are not natural but learned, and so vary from one culture to another.[6]

It is, however, the 'culturalist' approach which I shall attempt to pursue here, in the case of a society in which – according to its northern neighbours, at least – the language of gesture was and is particularly eloquent: Italy.

To follow this road to the end, it would first be necessary to reconstruct the complete repertoire of gestures available in a given culture, the 'langue' from which individuals choose their particular 'paroles' according to personality or social context. The way would then be clear for a general discussion of the relation between that repertoire and other aspects of the culture – such as the local contrasts between public and private, sacred and profane, decent and indecent, spontaneous and controlled, and so on.

The surviving sources are of course inadequate for these tasks, although they are as rich as an early modern historian has any right to hope. The literary sources range from formal treatises such as *L'arte de' cenni* (1616) by the lawyer Giovanni Bonifacio or Andrea De Jorio's *La mimica degli antichi* (1832) – both attempts to compile dictionaries of gestures – to the more casual observations of foreign travellers like John Evelyn, who recorded at least one insulting gesture (biting the finger) which the two lexicographers missed. In the second place, Italian judicial archives often note the gestures of insult leading to cases of assault and battery, and (among other things), confirm Evelyn's hermeneutics.[7] The Inquisition recorded another gesture absent from Bonifacio and De Jorio, the denial of Christianity by pointing the index finger of the right hand heavenwards.[8] In the third place, the art of the period can and must be utilized as a source, despite the difficulty of measuring the distance between painted gestures and gestures in daily life.

The task described above is clearly too ambitious for a short paper. So, instead of attempting to reconstruct the complete repertoire of Italian gestures of greeting, insulting, praying, and so on, or to comment on regional variation (from Venice to Naples), I shall simply offer a few observations on change over time, the time-span being three centuries or so, *c*.1500–*c*.1800. Following the available sources, I shall be forced to devote disproportionate attention to upper-class males.

The changes which will be emphasized here are not unique to Italy. They may be summed up in three hypotheses. The first is that of an increasing interest in gestures in the period. The second hypothesis is that a movement which might be called a 'reform' of gesture occurred in much of Europe in this period. The third and last hypothesis attempts to link this reform to the rise of the northern stereotype of the gesticulating Italian.

A NEW INTEREST IN GESTURES

Jean-Claude Schmitt has noted 'a new interest in gestures' in the twelfth century.[9] A similar argument might be sustained in the case of western Europe in the early modern period, more especially in the seventeenth century. In the case of England, for example, this interest can be seen in the work of Bacon; in Bulwer's guide to hand gestures, the *Chirologia* (1644); and in the observations of travellers abroad, including Thomas Coryate, John Evelyn, and Philip Skippon. In the case of France, one finds penetrating analyses of gesture in the work of Montaigne, Pascal, La Bruyère, and La Rochefoucauld, as well as a full discussion in Courtin's *Nouveau traité de la civilité* (1671). The history of gesture and posture attracted the attention of scholars and artists such as Poussin, whose *Last Supper* shows that he knew of the ancient Roman custom of reclining to eat.

In the case of Spain, it may be worth drawing attention to Carlos García's treatise of 1617, famous in its own day, on the 'antipathy' between the French and the Spaniards revealed in the different ways in which they walk, eat, or use their hands. For example: 'Quand le François a quelque fantaisie et se promeine, il met la main sur le pommeau de l'espée, et ne porte son manteau que sur l'une de ses épaules; l'Espagnol va jetant les jambes çà et là comme un cocq, se recoquillant et tirant les moustaches. Quand les François vont en troupe par les rues ils rient, sautent, causent et font un bruit si grand, que l'on les entend d'une lieue loing; les Espagnols au contraire, vont droits, gravement et froidement, sans parler ny faire aucune action qui ne soit modeste et retenue'.[10]

García's work is not without relevance to Italy. It went through thirteen Italian editions between 1636 and 1702. The influence of this book (or of the commonplaces it articulated with unusual vivacity and detail) can be seen in an anonymous account of the Venetian Republic, written in the late seventeenth century, which divided 100 leading politicians into those with a 'genio spagnuolo' (in other words a grave manner), and those with a livelier 'genio francese'.[11]

Linguistic evidence points in the same directions. In the first place, towards an increasing interest in gesture, revealed by the development of an increasingly elaborate and subtle language to describe it. In the second place, towards the Spanish model, for this language developed in Italian by borrowing from Spanish such terms as *etichetta, complimento, crianza* (good manners), *disinvoltura* (negligence), and *sussiego* (gravity).[12]

The multiplication of texts discussing gesture, confirms the impression of increasing interest. These texts include treatises devoted specifically to the subject, such as Bonifacio's *L'arte de' cenni*, which claimed to be addressed to princes because their dignity required them to gesture rather than to speak, as well as *La mimica degli antichi* of Bonifacio's severe critic de Jorio. The literature of morals and manners, most obviously Castiglione's *Cortegiano* (1528), Della Casa's *Galateo* (c.1555), and Guazzo's *Civile conversatione* (1574), also contains many relevant observations. So does the literature of the dance, including the treatise *Il ballarino* (1581) by Fabrizio Cornazano which discusses not only the various kinds of step but also how to deal with one's cloak and sword, how to make a proper bow, how to take a lady's hand, and so on. It is also worth looking at the literature of the theatre, including G. D. Ottonelli (1661), who discusses 'l'arte gesticolatoria', and A. Perrucci (1699), who is concerned with 'le regole del gestire'.[13] The relation between happenings on and off the stage is not a simple one, but to foreign visitors at least it may appear that actors stylize and perhaps exaggerate the gestures current in a given culture.

In their different ways, the books cited above reveal considerable interest not only in the psychology of gestures, as outward signs of hidden emotions, but also – and this is the innovation – in what we might call their 'sociology'; in other words a concern with the ways in which gestures vary (or ought to vary) according to what might be called the 'domain of gesture' (the family, the court, the church, and so on), and also to the actor (young or old, male or female, respectable or shameless, noble or common, lay or cleric, French or Spanish, and so on). In other words, there was at this time an increase in concern not only with the vocabulary of the language of gesture (exemplified by Bonifacio's attempt to compile a historical dictionary), but also with its 'grammar' (in the sense of the rules for correct expression) and with its various dialects (or sociolects). The connections between this interest in gesture, the contemporary concern with social variations in language and costume, and, more generally, with the study of men and animals in the so-called 'age of observation', deserves emphasis.[14]

## THE REFORM OF GESTURE

A reform of gesture formed part of the moral discipline of the Counter-Reformation. In the *Constitutions*, which he issued for his diocese of Verona around the year 1527, the model bishop Gianmatteo Giberti ordered the clergy to show gravity 'in their gestures, their walk and their bodily style' (*in gestu, incessu et habitu corporis*). The term *habitus* was of course widely known from the Latin translations of Aristotle before Pierre Bourdieu made it his own. San Carlo Borromeo, another model bishop, also recommended *gravitas* to the clergy of his diocese. San Carlo, however, concerned himself with the laity as well, recommending decorum, dignity and 'moderation' (*misura*) and warning them against laughing, shouting, dancing, and tumultuous behaviour.[15] A little later, the anonymous *Discorso contro il Carnevale* discussed the need for order, restraint, prudence, and sobriety (*ordine, continenza, prudenza, sobrietà*) and underlined the dangers of *pazzia*, a term which might in this context be translated not as 'madness' but as 'loss of self-control'.[16]

Similar recommendations to those just quoted were made on rather different grounds (secular rather than religious, prudential rather than moral) by the authors of a number of treatises intended for members of the nobility, lay or clerical. In the fifteenth century, the humanist Maffeo Vegio had already warned noble boys to concern themselves with the modesty of their movements and gestures (*de verecundia motuum gestuumque corporis*), while similar recommendations for girls may be found in the treatise *Decor puellarum*.[17] Another clerical humanist, Paolo Cortese, in his treatise *De Cardinalatu* (1510), warned against ugly movements of the lips, frequent hand movements, and walking quickly, and recommended what he called a senatorial gravity.[18] When Baldassare Castiglione, in a famous passage in *Il Cortegiano*, warned his readers against affected gestures, he was taking his place in a Renaissance tradition. It is also clear from these humanist texts that the authority of Cicero and Quintilian was taken as seriously in the domain of gestures as in that of speech.

The tradition continued to inspire writers after Castiglione. The physiognomist-dramatist Giovanni Battista della Porta recommended his readers not to make gestures with their hands while speaking (in Italy!). Stefano Guazzo discussed the dignity and the eloquence of the body and the need to find the golden mean, as he put it, between 'the immobility of statues' and the exaggerated movements of monkeys (*l'instabilità delle simie*). As for Caroso's treatise on dancing, it has been argued that it expresses a more restrained ideal than its predecessors, suggesting that the court dance was diverging more and more from the peasant dance in this period.[19] After reading this corpus of texts, many Renaissance portraits may well appear as translations of their recommendations into images. Whether the portraits express the ideals of the artist, the self-image of the sitter, or the artist's image of the sitter's self-image, the gestures portrayed – which to post-romantic eyes often seem intolerably artificial – may be read as evidence of attempts to create new habits, a second nature.

The most detailed as well as the best-known Italian recommendations for the reform of gesture are to be found in Giovanni della Casa's *Il Galateo*. The ideal of this Catholic prelate is actually as secular as Castiglione's; it is to be elegant and well-bred (*leggiadro, costumato*). To achieve elegance, it is necessary, according to Della Casa, to be conscious of one's gestures in order to control them. The hands and legs in particular need discipline. For example, noblemen are advised, in the author's version of the classical topos, not to walk too quickly (like a servant), or too slowly (like a woman), but rather to aim at the mean.[20]

Della Casa's points are mainly negative; one suspects that this inquisitor kept in mind, if not in his study, an index of forbidden gestures. Yet it would be a mistake to discuss the reform of gesture in purely negative terms, as part of the history of repression. It can be viewed more positively as an art, or as a contribution to the art of living. This is the way in which Castiglione sees it, not to mention the dancing-masters – and in the seventeenth century, if not earlier, dancing formed part of the curriculum in some Italian noble colleges. It was a festive mode of inculcating discipline.[21]

If the reformers of gesture had a positive ideal in mind, what was it? It might be (and sometimes was) described as a Spanish model, influential in Italy as in central Europe and including gesture as well as language and clothes. If it had to be summed up in a single word, that word might well be 'gravity'. The contrast made in Castiglione's *Il Cortegiano* between 'quella gravità riposata peculiare dei Spagnoli' and 'la pronta vivacità' of the French was, or was becoming, commonplace.[22] Indeed, Italians frequently perceived Spanish gesture as an absence of gesture. Thus Pedro de Toledo, Viceroy of Naples, surprised the local nobility by the fact that when he gave audience he remained immobile, like a 'marble statue'.[23] The phrase was, or became, a topos. One of Toledo's successors was described as so grave and motionless 'that I should never have known whether he was a man or a figure of wood'.[24] The Venetian ambassador to Turin in 1588 described the prince's wife, a Spanish Infanta, as 'allevata all'usanza spagnola . . . stà con gran sussiego, pare immobile'.[25] Guazzo's remark about the need to avoid the immobility of statues, quoted above, must have had a topical ring.

In employing the term 'model', I do not want to suggest that the Italians of the period always idealized the Spaniards. On the contrary, they were much hated and frequently mocked, the mockery extending on occasion to their gestures. Their gravity was sometimes interpreted as the stiffness of arrogance. Think, for example, of the figure of 'Capitano' on the Italian stage and of his stylized *bravure*: in other words aggressive, macho gestures intended to challenge or provoke his neighbours. Again, an eighteenth-century description, by the nobleman Paolo Matteo Doria, of Naples when it was under Spanish hegemony, gives a highly critical account of the mutual suspicion of the upper nobility, each observing the gestures of the others, and of the gestures themselves, an 'affected negligence' and 'determined, arrogant movements' failing to hide the desire to 'show superiority over others'.[26]

Nor do I want to assert that Spaniards always followed this particular ideal. It was probably restricted to the upper classes, and it may have been restricted to formal situations, especially to rituals (though curiously enough, the stiff rituals of the Spanish court seem to have been brought there from Burgundy only in the mid-sixteenth century).[27] Nor do I want to suggest any facile explanation of change in terms of 'influence'. The appeal of the Spanish model was surely that it met a pre-existing demand for the reform of gesture, in other words for stricter bodily control.[28]

The history of that demand has been written by Norbert Elias in his famous study of the 'process of civilisation' (by which he generally means self-control), concentrating on northern Europe but including a few observations on the Italians (who were, after all, pioneers in the use of the fork).[29] More recently, the late Michel Foucault has offered an alternative history of the body, examining the negative aspects in his *Discipline and Punish*, the more positive ones in his *History of Sexuality*, and emphasizing control over the bodies of others as well as over the self.[30] Elias and Foucault were of course concerned with the practice rather than the theory of gesture and the control of the body. It is time to ask whether or not the Italian reformers of gesture succeeded in their aims.

## THE GESTICULATING ITALIAN

The reform discussed in the previous section was not peculiarly Italian, but part of a general Western 'process of civilisation' (there are parallels in other parts of the world, such as China and Japan, but their history remains to be written). The hypothesis I want to present here is that the reform of gesture, if not more rigorous, was at least more successful in the northern Protestant parts of Europe such as Britain and the Netherlands than in the Catholic south; that the stereotype of the gesticulating Italian, still current in the north, came into existence in the early modern period; and that it reflects a contrast between two gestural cultures, associated with two styles of rhetoric (more or less copious) and other differences as well.[31]

The contrast is not between the presence and the absence of gesture, though it was sometimes perceived as such. What we observe in this period – at second hand – is rather the increasing distance between two body languages, which we might call the flamboyant and the disciplined. (I do not mean to imply that one body language is 'natural' and the other 'artificial' or 'civilized'; on the contrary, I assume that all body languages are artificial, in the sense of being learned.)

If the Italians perceived the Spaniards as gesturing too little, the northerners perceived the southerners as gesturing too much. The Dutchman Van Laar's view of the gesticulating Italian is discussed in Herman Roodenburg's contribution in Chapter 7 of this volume. In English, 'gesticulate' is a pejorative term (defined by the *Oxford English Dictionary* as the use of 'much' or 'foolish' gestures) and it is documented from 1613 onwards, a point which supports the hypothesis of a new interest in gesture at this time.[32] From about this time onwards, if not before, we find British writers commenting with surprise or disdain on what they regard as the excessive gestures of the Italians (or the French, or the Greeks). Thus Thomas Coryate, in Venice in 1608, noted what he called 'an extraordinary custom', 'that when two acquaintances meet . . . they give a mutual kiss when they depart from each other.' In the church of San Giorgio, he commented still more explicitly on 'one kind of gesture which seemeth to me both very unseemly and ridiculous', that of people who 'wagge their hands up and downe very often'.[33] Philip Skippon, in Rome in 1663, described a Jesuit preaching on Piazza Navona 'with much action and postures of his body'.[34] Frenchmen as well as Italians came in for this kind of criticism. In 1691 *The English Spy* mocked the French for 'so many Shruggs and Apish Gestures . . . Finger-Talk as if they were conversing with the Deaf'.[35] In Naples, the language of the body was even more apparent than it was elsewhere, at least to the British visitor; to John Moore in 1781, for example, describing the 'great gesticulation' of a story-teller, or to J. J. Blunt observing 'infinite gesticulation' during a reading of Ariosto.[36] In the early nineteenth century, an American, Washington Irving, was still more explicit in his diagnosis of the symptoms of the Italian national character, as he viewed from his café table on Piazza San Marco a conversation conducted 'with Italian vivacity and gesticulation'.[37]

These texts are of course insufficient to support any grand hypothesis, but at least they make an interesting problem more visible. The simple contrast between north and south, Catholic and Protestant will of course have to be refined. Where, for example, does one place Poland? In what ways did Spanish gravity differ from British self-control? To what extent were these stereotypes of national characters, expressing themselves through the language of the body, generalizations about a single social group, the noblemen? There is ample scope here for further discussion and also for comparative research.

## NOTES

1 A. Corbin, *Le miasme et la jonquille: l'odorat et l'imaginaire social, xviii–xixe siècles* (Paris, 1982).
2 L. de Câmara Cascudo, *Historia dos nossos gestos*, São Paulo n.d. (*c.*1974).
3 'Parve alle serenissime Signorie loro ch'io entrassi nella sala coraggiosamente, altri dissero con alterigia . . . stavo col corpo e col capo storto', A. Spinola, *Scritti scelti*, ed. C. Bitossi (Genoa, 1981), p. 126.
4 C. Ginzburg, 'Spie: Radici di un paradigma indiziario', in *Crisi della ragione: Nuovi modelli nel rapporto tra sapere e attività umane*, ed. A. Gargani (Turin, 1979), pp. 57–106. Cf. Ginzburg, *Myths, Emblems, Clues* (London, 1990), pp. 96–125, 200–14.
5 D. Morris, *Manwatching: A Field Guide to Human Behaviour* (London, 1977) and Morris et al., *Gestures: Their Origins and Distribution* (New York, London, 1979).
6 R. L. Birdwhistell, *Kinesics and Context: Essays on Body-Motion Communication* (Philadelphia, 1970); cf. M. Mauss, 'Les techniques du corps', *Journal de psychologie normale et pathologique*, 39 (1935), pp. 271–93.
7 *The Diary of John Evelyn*, ed. E. S. de Beer (Oxford, 1955), Vol. II, p. 173; cf. Rome, Archivio di Stato, Tribunale del Governatore, Processi Criminali, '600, busta 50, 'mittendosi la dita in bocca'.
8 B. Bennassar, 'Conversion ou reniement? Modalités d'une adhésion ambiguë des chrétiens à l'Islam (XVIe–XVIIe siècles), *Annales E. S. C.*, 43 (1988), pp. 1349–66, esp. p. 1351.
9 J.-C. Schmitt, 'Between text and image: the prayer gestures of Saint Dominic', *History and Anthropology*, 1 (1984), pp. 127–62, esp. p. 127.
10 C. García, *La oposición y conjunción de los dos grandes luminares de la tierra, o la antipatia de franceses y españoles*, ed. M. Bareau (Edmonton, 1979). Quotation from ch. 14. It is not clear whether this treatise, produced to justify Louis XIII's marriage to the Infanta, was originally written in Spanish or French. It went through at least twenty-eight editions by 1704 (in French, Spanish, Italian, English, and German).

11 Venice, Bibliotheca Marciana, Ms. Gradenigo 15, 'Esame istorico politico di cento soggetti della republica Veneta'.

12 G.-L. Beccaria, *Spagnolo e spagnoli in Italia: Riflessi Ispanici sulla lingua Italiana del Cinque e del Seicento* (Turin, 1968), pp. 161–207.

13 G. Bonifacio, *L'arte de' cenni* (Vicenza, 1616); G. D. Ottonelli, *Della cristiana moderatione del teatro* (Florence, 1652); A. Perrucci, 'Dell'arte rappresentativa', in E. Petraccone, *La Commedia dell'Arte* (Naples, 1927), pp. 70f.

14 The idea of 'dialects' of gesture goes back to A. De Jorio, *La mimica degli antichi investigata nel gestire Napoletano* (Naples, 1832, repr. 1964), p. xxii; see also Thomas, p. 3 and Graf, p. 36 in this volume.

15 F. Taviani, *La commedia dell'arte e la società barocca* (Rome, 1969), pp. 5–43; cf. *San Carlo e il suo tempo: Atti del convegno internazionale nel IV centenario della morte (Milano, 21–26 maggio 1984)* (Rome, 1986), pp. 911, 926–7.

16 'Discorso contro il carnevale', in Taviani, *La commedia*, pp. 67–81.

17 M. Vegio, *De liberorum educatione* (Paris, 1511), Bk 5, ch. 3.

18 P. Cortese, *De cardinalatu* (Rome, 1510), pp. xcvv–viii.

19 *Dizionario Biografico degli Italiani*, s.v. 'Caroso'.

20 Giovanni della Casa, *Il Galateo* (Florence, 1558), ch. 6.

21 F. Brizzi, *La formazione della classe dirigente nel Sei-Settecento: I seminaria nobilium nell'Italia centro-settentrionale* (Rome, 1976), pp. 254–5. On the relation between dancing and body language in general in this period, R. zur Lippe, *Naturbeherrschung am Menschen* (Frankfurt, 1974).

22 B. Castiglione, *Il Cortegiano* (Venice, 1528), Bk 2, ch. 37: Federico is speaking.

23 F. Caraffa, 'Memorie', *Archivio Storico per le Provincie Napoletane*, 5 (1880), pp. 25–7.

24 T. Boccalini, *La bilancia politica* (Châtelaine, 1678), vol. I, p. 215.

25 Quoted in Beccaria, *Spagnolo e spagnoli*, p. 174.

26 P. M. Doria, *Massime del governo spagnolo a Napoli*, ed. V. Conti (Naples, 1973), p. 59: 'il titolato di prima sfera pretende con la sua affettata disinvoltura, e con i suoi movimenti risoluti e disprezzanti . . . ostentare superiorità sopra gl'altri'.

27 Chr. Hofmann, *Das Spanische Hofzeremoniell von 1500–1700* (Frankfurt, 1985).

28 A point made for the domain of language by J. Brunet, 'L'influence de l'Espagne sur la troisième personne de politesse italienne', in *Présence et influence de l'Espagne dans la culture italienne de la Renaissance* (Paris, 1978), pp. 251–315.

29  N. Elias, *Über den Prozess der Zivilisation: Soziogenetische und psychogenetische Untersuchungen* (2 vols, Basel, 1939).
30  M. Foucault, *Surveiller et punir: naissance de la prison* (Paris, 1975); idem, *Histoire de la sexualité* (3 vols, Paris, 1976–1984).
31  The possible link between gestural discipline and Protestantism (especially Calvinism) deserves investigation. It is interesting to find a French Calvinist, Henri Estienne, criticizing the gestures of the Italians. See H. Estienne, *Deux dialogues de nouveau langage françois italianizé et autrement desguizé*, 1st edn 1578 (Paris, 1980 edn), p. 322.
32  Cf. and contrast J.-C. Schmitt, '*Gestus/Gesticulatio*: Contribution à l'étude du vocabulaire latin médiéval des gestes', in *La lexicographie du latin médiéval et ses rapports avec les recherches actuelles sur la civilisation du Moyen Age* (Paris, 1981), pp. 377–90.
33  T. Coryate, *Crudities* (London, 1611), pp. 399, 369.
34  P. Skippon, *An Account of a Journey made thro' part of the Low-countries, Germany, Italy and France*, in A. and J. Churchill, *A Collection of Voyages and Travels* (London, 1752 edn), vol. VI, p. 665.
35  *The English Spy* (London, 1691), p. 123.
36  J. Moore, *A View of Society and Manners in Italy* (Dublin, 1781), Letter 60; J. J. Blunt, *Vestiges of Ancient Manners* (London, 1823).
37  G. Crayon [pseud. of Washington Irving], *Tales of a Traveller* (2 vols, Paris, 1824), vol. I, p. 103.

# 5

# The Renaissance elbow

## JOANEATH SPICER

'Hand resting provocatively on his hip, Mick Jagger leads
the press conference like a pied piper teasing a pack of
rats.'
J. Hunter, 'Satisfaction', *Report on Business Magazine*

Renaissance Man may have been a creature of many parts, but it
has generally been his rational 'speaking hands' which have
attracted the attention of historians. I am, however, more
fascinated by Jagger's swaggering ancestors and will concern
myself with Renaissance Man's more emotive and increasingly
assertive (but hitherto neglected) elbow. Written references to
gestures associated with the elbow in the period under consideration
– the late fifteenth to seventeenth centuries – are largely limited to
admonitions to restrain them, and thus they fit more easily under
the controversial heading of 'natural' as opposed to 'taught'
(though whether they still might be said to be 'learned' remains to
be resolved). They are for that no less expressive of 'the motions of
the mind', nor no less rewarding to decode than those long
identified from the canon of ritual or rhetoric – as fingers resting
lightly on the chest – which, as Fritz Graf shows (see p. 50),
Quintilian had already suggested be used to indicate sincerity.

Portraits of any period are obviously not candid photographs; they are as composed as any narrative scene. The decorum of ritual and daily life provides the background code of comportment upon which portraitists drew: for example, the self-abasing body language of the devotional portrait versus the often prideful assertion or nonchalance of the secular. All this is hard to do well. As Leonardo succinctly put it, 'the intention of the mind' is difficult to paint because it 'has to be represented through gestures and movements of the limbs.'[1] This is echoed in the writings of others of the period, some like the later Dutch theorist and painter Karel van Mander further emphasizing the decorum or appropriateness of gesture and comportment: for example, that men act like men, and women like women.[2] The introduction of purposeful gestures will usually represent a distillation of generally accepted societal codes which rise out of collective experience – otherwise they wouldn't be recognized – and which convey an impression which the sitter is content to give off, seen through the prism of the individual artist's aesthetic sensibilities. In ordinary life we are usually not directly conscious of the way our body language colours our spoken word, adapts it for our relation with the audience at hand. However, an artist sensitive, perhaps unconsciously, to the nuances of non-verbal communication will be able to adapt this for a pictorial system that can be applied as well, to permit a sitter, whether himself or another, to give off a desired impression. Though this is certainly a manifestation of the 'presentation of the self' the analysis of which can benefit greatly from the insights of sociology,[3] we must be careful to remember the distinction between the distillation and that from which it has been distilled.

The following essay is a kind of work-in-progress report with as many holes and uncertainties as there are proposals. As a true follower of Bacon rather than Descartes I have devoted myself first to gathering primary material and have not got far enough in my research to pay Descartes his due. This essay will chronicle, in a fashion more skeletal and suggestive than truly descriptive, the presumed first appearance, rise and apogee of the male elbow in gestures indicative essentially of boldness or control – and therefore of the self-defined masculine role, at once protective and controlling, in contemporary society and in the microcosm of the family – in painting, primarily portraits, from about 1500 to 1650.

My examples begin in Germany and Italy but are soon concentrated in Holland, where for reasons that surely have to do with a collective perception of social ties and duties rather than pure artistic invention, the elbow in its most perfectly evolved form – the arms akimbo – will come close to achieving the status of a national attribute as an integral aspect of the imagery of the alert, on guard, proud regent class who managed so successfully to inform the values of seventeenth-century Holland. This connection of 'gesture and culture' may be seen in another way as an essay in defining the meaning of one or two related 'words' in a vocabulary and syntax that are as yet little understood.

Before proceeding we may reflect on some general observations. At the close of the fifteenth century in the major artistic centres of western Europe, natural movement observed from life was increasingly playing a role in lending vitality to artistic interpretation of traditional themes in a way that had been rejected since antiquity. In the wider context of narrative from which portraiture takes many of its cues, the arm akimbo is found widely, but not randomly: typically a male military figure registering self-possession and control, either the assertion of success or defiance. The most frequent appearance of the gesture in fifteenth-century Florence is probably in sculptural interpretations of David triumphing over the head of Goliath. Around 1500, especially in German art and more especially in the work of Albrecht Dürer, the real movements of daily life were increasingly absorbed into the expressive canon. The dominance of idealizing tendencies in Italian and Italianate art would limit developments in narrative interpretation of gesture before the shift to an acceptance of comportment of real life in the early seventeenth century especially in the work of Caravaggio and artists in the Dutch Republic, which experienced an explosion of male elbows.

The body language of self-possession, which in most pictorially treated narratives is associated with authority, will colour our perception of the figure: he is typically a leader (or one who comports himself as one) giving a command with the one arm outstretched sometimes holding a sceptre, baton or whip, the other arm akimbo, his weight on one leg in a hip-shot pose with the other leg casually extended. The effect may be heightened by the subordinate body language of others. The High Priest in scenes of

**Figure 5.1** Pieter Gartner (attr.), *Calvary*, 1537. (Walters Art Gallery, Baltimore.)

*Cavalry*, as in this example of 1537 attributed to Pieter Gartner[4] (see figure 5.1) commonly asserts himself so; another negative type of power is provided by the chief executioner in Albrecht Dürer's *Martyrdom of Ten Thousand*[5] of 1508. Positive imagery includes such scenes as Rembrandt's *Scene of Clemency from Ancient History*[6] of 1626 or the many renderings of the *Magnanimity of Scipio* in Dutch art.[7] If a leader's chosen posture is statesmanlike restraint, then one of his men representing the power of the 'state' takes up this aggressive, self-possessive display.[8] When striding – or rather swaggering – the effect is rather like a cock ruffling his feathers for greater effect which is in keeping with patterns of threat display throughout the animal kingdom. Samson with jaw bone in one triumphant fist may take this pose; likewise Hercules. He may be hero or brutal executioner; there is no moral distinction. Though often defiant, this gesture is incompatible with humiliation or humility and only by the greatest exception is it a gesture of Christ's.[9] In the same vein it is characteristic of Old Testament heroes but not of New Testament apostles or of philosophers and learned men whether ancient or contemporary. On the other hand in scenes of low life such as by Pieter Brueghel or Jan Steen, whether peasant or urban, this and other assertive gestures are more casually encountered, even among women.

## THE SINGLE PORTRAIT

With this brief indication of the narrative patterns in mind we may turn to our portrait theme. Around 1500 we encounter not only cool, admirably restrained, disembodied descendants of Roman busts and coins as Giovanni Bellini's *Doge Leonardo Loredano*[10] of about 1503, but the increasingly frequent encroachment of hands claiming pictorial space as their own, especially in Flemish and also German portraiture. As far as I am aware, however, it is first in self-portraits by Albrecht Dürer, most clearly developed in that of 1498 (see figure 5.2) and slightly later by Perugino *c*.1503,[11] that the lower arm and elbow are used aggressively, seemingly as space markers on the parapet separating the sitter from the viewer. The admonition found already in a fourteenth-century etiquette book[12] to keep one's elbows off the communal eating table is clear

**Figure 5.2** Albrecht Dürer, *Self-Portrait*, 1498.
(The Prado, Madrid.)

acknowledgement of the perceived possessive intrusiveness of this gesture. If Dürer's *Self-Portrait* is indeed the first experiment with this form, such an 'invention' would be consistent with the prideful posturing which comes through in his writings and artistic self-imaging and indeed with the larger trends in intellectual self-assertion of the Renaissance as a whole. The effectiveness of this self-possessive assertion of territoriality by such a boundary marker is strengthened by the direct eye contact Dürer establishes with us and the alignment of the lower arm parallel to the picture plane, thus a barrier over which we are challenged to leap in order to enter the space behind. A typically more subtle modification is found in Titian's *Portrait of a Man*[13] of *c*.1510, now thought possibly to be a self-portrait, where brashness is replaced by the hauteur of this elegantly attired man who without condescending to look at us subtly controls the barrier dividing our space from his. Later portraits of artists, including self-portraits, from Parmigianino and Lorenzo Lotto to Gabriel Metsu, Van Dyck, or Rembrandt will show a marked preference for an assertive body language which, as we will see, would normally be associated with military power or social position of a kind rarely enjoyed by painters.

Dürer's Paumgärtner brothers (see figure 5.3) of *c*.1498 from the *Paumgärtner Altarpiece*[14] provide an early example of the Renaissance elbow in a second form that will carry on throughout the period under discussion: the military posture with arm akimbo attributed to the portraits of the brothers in the guise of their name saints, the knights George and Eustace. As they each carry a banner, their appearance takes on the body language of the contemporary mercenary flag- or standard-bearer. Indeed it can now be seen that this gesture – whether with the hand on the hip or even more provocatively resting on the pommel of a dagger or sword as a rather obvious aspect of threat display – was an accepted gesture, even attribute, of the standard-bearer already in such German woodcuts and engravings from the end of the fifteenth century on as by Albrecht Dürer *c*.1502[15] or Hans Sebald Beham's dashing Landsknecht of 1526[16] (see figure 5.4). He was, as John Hale has succinctly described him,

the soldier responsible for displaying and guarding from capture the flag that was an essential focus in combat to troops who had become scattered, and to commanders who had to send orders to the captains of companies. As the standard was also the focus of regional or unit pride, its bearer provided not only the pictorial

**Figure 5.3** Albrecht Dürer, *Paumgärtner Altarpiece*, c.1498 and c.1502. (Bayerische Staatsgemaldesammlungen, Munich.)

**Figure 5.4** Hans Sebald Beham, *Standard-bearer*, *c.*1526, engraving.

advantage of his swirl of cloth, but also an emotional charge. Seldom shown wearing armour, he was expected to die with the standard wrapped around him so that it would not be borne away as a trophy by the enemy.[17]

While on the march one might imagine that the standard-bearer might well walk with one hand at his waist simply to brace himself, as may St Christopher when he carries the 'weight of the whole world' or Samson carrying the doors of the gate at Gaza or a peasant woman carrying a load on her head, but most representations of the standard-bearer show him at ease.

In the sixteenth century in the Netherlands, central Europe, Italy, and Spain there is a steady increase in the use of more expressive, frequently bolder, body language especially in male portraiture of the more powerful segments of society. Often this means vaguely or explicitly military associations – to convey the manly virtues – through both attributes and body language, such as the arm akimbo, most frequently showing one hand on the hip by a sword or rapier, or, if a commander, with a baton.[18]

Pontormo's *c.*1537 *Duke Cosimo I de Medici as a Halberdier*[19] (see figure 5.5) depicts Cosimo at age eighteen in the guise of a German or Swiss Landsknecht, in which the effrontery and virile coarseness of the mercenary whose elbow grazes the picture plane – a militarily tough but socially despised 'front' Cosimo is said to have enjoyed affecting apparently even after personally assuming command of his forces in 1537 – constitutes a slap at decorum and just the sort of association to which youths in regulated roles are often attracted. That this is balanced by a striking, ambiguous grace and refinement that suggests a noble in lowlife disguise contributes to its fascination. A duke or king, as in Holbein's famous portrait of *Henry VIII c.*1539/40,[20] may comport himself as expansively as a lowly mercenary, though for different reasons. In any case, this is not the humble, dignified, ideal courtier of Baldassare Castiglione's 1528 treatise on court life *Il Cortegiano*! With this reference I would like to turn briefly to the subject of books on etiquette or comportment in the sixteenth and seventeenth century. The majority, like *Il Cortegiano*, are largely aimed at those at court or on the fringes of court life and are concerned first with ingratiating comportment in the presence of one's betters,[21]

**Figure 5.5** Jacopo Carucci, called Pontormo, *Duke Cosimo I de'Medici as a Halberdier*, c.1537.
(J. Paul Getty Museum, Malibu.)

not exactly an issue for Cosimo or Henry. The importance of honesty (humility) and modesty underline most advice. After the earlier texts largely aimed at table manners, Erasmus in his influential 1532 treatise on comportment *De civilitate morum puerilium* appears to have the honour of being the first to comment on the arm akimbo, referring with disapprobation to those who (in an English edition of 1540) 'stand or sit and set [the] one hand on [the] side which maner to some semeth comly like a warrior but it is not forthwith honest'.[22] This is a confirmation of the military associations we have already proposed on the basis of the visual evidence. In like manner, Giovanni della Casa, in his widely influential book on gentlemanly comportment *Il Galateo* first published in 1558, condemns the pride and boldness of those who would 'set their hands to their sides and go up and down like a Pecock'. Other references in texts on comportment either repeat the admonition to keep the elbows off the table or just to restrain their movement.[23] Bonifacio's *L'arte de' cenni* of 1616, the one text from the period devoted to an analysis of gesture, devotes a fascinating section to the elbow and the arm akimbo, which he describes as giving the impression of strength, as those who use them to push their way through crowds. He goes on to cite passages from various authors which imply criticism of men always with their hands on their hips, as a quotation from Plautus deriding those who go around with hands on hips whom he calls 'handle men'.[24]

The mention rated by this gesture in John Bulwer's *Chironomia* of 1644, the first example I know of in a text on rhetoric, is again highly critical: 'to set the arms agambo or aprank, and to rest the turned-in back of the hand upon the side is an action of pride and ostentation, unbeseeming the hand of an orator'.[25]

In part because of the continuing pressure of the war with Spain, by 1600 military portraiture was an important aspect of public and also private art in the northern Netherlands as it was not in Italy. Of course if you subtracted the portraiture of the Dutch regent class and compared only the portraiture of the blood aristocracy, the only class outside the Church really commissioning portraits in Italy, the differences would be minimalized. A characteristic type is the individual portrait of the *Standard-bearer* of a militia company (see figure 5.6) by Evert van der Maes of 1617 of the

**Figure 5.6** Evert van der Maes, *Standard-bearer*, 1617.
(Collection Haags Gemeentemuseum, The Hague.)

Orange Company of the St. Sebastian Guild in The Hague,[26] typically richly dressed in yellow or red and posed in a calculatedly casual hip-shot stance with his hand on his hip – just oozing macho assertion. The standard-bearer in a Dutch militia company was the third ranking officer, was normally from the social elite, and was required to be single and affluent, contributing to his symbolic role proclaiming the potency of the company. Instead of facing the viewer, he insolently looks down his elbow at us, jabbing it at the viewer in a way that would be incredibly rude in actual life. Other depictions of standard-bearers, whether in inn-scenes or as portrait types as Rembrandt's 1636 *Standard-bearer as a Landsknecht*[27] carry on the use of this pose as an expressive attribute. The brash insolence of this gesture, now touching the picture plane, is widely followed in other military portraits as in the *Smiling Cavalier*[28] (see figure 5.7) of 1624 by Frans Hals or in civilian portraits such as Hals's *Jaspar Schade*,[29] of *c.*1645, by contemporary reports a man not only wealthy but very vain. In like manner a 1670 emblem by Cornelis de Bie of 'impudence and stupidity' is represented by an ass sauntering along with one hand on his hip and the other carrying a bag of money.[30]

To the extent that single portraits of men depicted with this gesture can be identified, the overwhelming percentage are socially powerful or associated with the military, or both. Such men when on horseback, if they don't have their hands full, may take this posture as Pauwels van Hillegaert's *Prince Frederik Hendrik on Horseback*. Individual proclivities of artists are blended with the self-consciousness of the sitter, his class. Indeed men depicted with the arm akimbo are more likely to be identifiable than those depicted without specific gestures (or in bust length), and there is a clear correlation with regent class. This gesture expressive of social assurance is often correlated with a view into the distance (of a house or battle), the use of an elegant curtain, pillars, or garden sculpture and of course with armour or a baton as in Jan Lievens, *Maerten Harpertsz. Tromp, Vice-Admiral*,[31] or a walking stick serving as a baton-surrogate for a non-military 'commander' as Samuel van Hoogstraten's *Mattheus van den Broucke, Governor of the East Indies*[32] (see figure 5.8). Among the artists who used it the most often would figure Hals and his follower C. Versponck in Haarlem. In Amsterdam the usage was more widespread, continuing

**Figure 5.7** Frans Hals, *Smiling Cavalier*, 1624.
(The Wallace Collection, London.)

into the eighteenth century with C. Troost; but no one could rival Bartholomeus van der Helst in his adaptation of the arm akimbo in conveying the sense of self of his prominent patrons from such patrician Amsterdam families as Bicker, Coymans, or De Geer – for example his 1642 portrait of *Andries Bicker*.[33] In Van der Helst's 1665 *Egbert Meeuwis Kortenaar, Admiral of Holland*[34] his

**Figure 5.8** Samuel van Hoogstraten, *Mattheus van den Broucke,*
*Governor of the East Indies.*
(© Rijksmuseum-Stichting, Amsterdam.)

subject stands in three-quarter view behind a parapet facing us, right arm akimbo, the left holding a baton braced against his abdomen. The strategically placed cannon just below the parapet aimed out into our space strengthens the assertive potency of the stance. Boys might be depicted in similar poses as well, as Ferdinand Bol's, *Otto van der Waeyen as a Polish Officer*[35] which features the left arm akimbo, the right grasping a ceremonial war hammer braced against the thigh, other weapons strewn behind. However, almost every single depiction of an Easterner was likely to display this mark of pride. Both hands on the hips – Plautus' 'handle man' – is potentially such a strong statement of self-possession, normally identified in art with anger or defiance,[36] that it almost never appears in portraits, exceptions being a full-length portrait of a pugnacious, very short *Unidentified Man* by Pieter Quast[37] in 1631 and Rembrandt's three-quarter-length *Self-Portrait* in Vienna of 1652. The artist is dressed in studio attire, thumbs in his belt, obviously looking intently at himself in a mirror; his brow is furrowed in thought. In the recent literature the 'aggressive informality' of this 'proud, confrontational worker's stance'[38] has been astutely noted, but in the context of this present study the unique choice of this posture in Rembrandt's paintings of himself takes on more significance. As a self-portrait, this takes on the character of profound, personal stocktaking.

As for the weaker, perforce humbler sex, the arm akimbo might characterize a woman of princely status such as Queen Elizabeth I of England,[39] or a female warrior such as Juno or Athena, but it was not an appropriate gesture for middle-class women of good standing, though there were some exceptions for women from powerful or noble families. Standards of female comportment called for restraint on the part of the 'morally weaker' sex, containment, the avoidance of anything suggestive of personal pride or self-possession. It would lack propriety to be so bold; and the gesture is otherwise rarely encountered except in allegories of Pride or Vanity such as cautionary images of Lady World[40] or depictions of light company.[41]

## GROUP PORTRAITS: CORPORATE

The function of the brandished male elbow takes on further connotations in Dutch group portraiture, a kind of societal self-imaging hardly found outside the Republic with the exception of marriage portraits.[42] The issue of body language as an aspect of the group dynamics of 'men in groups' has not been really addressed in the recent literature on Dutch corporate imagery[43] and I can make only an exploratory foray into the material here. For example, in Rembrandt's 1642 *Nightwatch* or *Militia Company of Captain Frans Banning Cocq*[44] (see figure 5.9) which has been eloquently termed 'a living allegory of the soldier's calling', a 'role portrait of the militant citizen' framed around the narrative motif of the company preparing to move out. As E. Haverkamp Begemann has put it, 'Banning Cocq's company, strong and ready to act, was a visual metaphor for the might of Amsterdam and its willingness to protect its rights.'[45] There are two proud figures each with arm akimbo, the vividly dressed lieutenant Willem van Ruytenburgh and, once again, the standard-bearer or ensign Jan Cornilsz. Visscher, the second and third ranking officers within the company. In a surprising percentage of Dutch militia company pieces, especially of Amsterdam companies by the whole gamut of painters, this proud, assertive gesture characterizes the standard-bearer, as in Pieter Isaacsz., *Officers of the Amsterdam Company of Captain Jacob Gerritsz. Hoing*,[46] 1596 (see figure 5.10) and frequently the lieutenant or the captain (as in Rembrandt's only militia company piece or Joachim von Sandrart's *Company of Captain Cornelis Bicker c.*1642),[47] sometimes joined by another officer on the outer edge of the group, protective of the group in the face of outsiders (viewers). Most often the captain comports himself as the statesman who gives the orders while the next ranking officers suggest the aggressive potential. That the higher ranking officers were usually of a higher social class may contribute to their easy posturing. The centrality of the standard-bearer, whose individual characterization we have already treated, is obvious in the Dutch and German vocabulary, as it is not in English: the words for 'company', 'flag', and 'flag-bearer' all have the same root, thus more encompassing than the English 'ensign'

**Figure 5.9** Rembrandt van Rijn, *Nightwatch or Militia Company of
Captain Frans Banning Cocq.*
(© Rijksmuseum-Stichting, Amsterdam.)

signifying the flag, the flag-bearer (formerly) but not the company
itself. In Dutch, each militia company (*vendel*) had its own flag
(*vaan, vaandel*) which was carried by the flag or standard-bearer
(*vaandrager, vaandrig*). The macho imagery of these militia
companies, to which we will return, is especially interesting given
the decline in their military significance in consequence of the rise
in the effectiveness of the standing army.

Though images of the Amsterdam civic guard from the middle
of the sixteenth century with their insistently speaking hands,
direct gazes and straight backs exude stalwart firmness,[48] the
earliest possible example I have found of this more pugnacious
comportment centred on a standard-bearer with 'elbow drawn' is a
sketch attributed to Cornelius Ketel, presumably for a lost
*Company of Captain Herman Rodenburgh* dated 1581,[49] though
other more certainly dated works follow in quick succession.[50]

**Figure 5.10** Pieter Isaacsz, *Officers of the Amsterdam Company of Captain Jacob Gerritsz Hoing*, 1596. (Amsterdam Historisch Museum on loan from City of Amsterdam.)

This was in fact a pivotal time in the military history of Holland. In 1579 the provinces rebelling against Spain had signed the Union of Utrecht. In 1580 the Prince of Orange, as leader of the rebellion, came to Amsterdam to garner suppport; apparently as a consequence of this in September of that year a reorganization of the Amsterdam militia was initiated with the aim of producing a more efficient force.[51] It is thus very likely that there is a causal relationship between these events, capped by the declaration of the Republic in 1581, and the appearance of what seems to be a new mentality expressed in the new pride, self-assertion and more aggressive posturing in the imagery of the militia companies. The paintings themselves also became much larger and frequently full-length.[52] That there is a relationship between mentality and the impression these men were comfortable in giving off is further suggested by depictions of Amsterdam milita companies celebrating the Peace of Munster in 1648 by Flinck and Van der Helst which are far more relaxed and open in their body language; besides such overt signs as figures shaking hands, they are both almost entirely 'de-elbowed'.[53]

If we now return briefly to Rembrandt's *Nightwatch*, it should be clear that the arm akimbo of the highlighted standard-bearer and lieutenant play an integral role, subtly blending symbolism and narrative in expressing 'the might of Amsterdam and its willingness to protect its rights'.

The pattern appears to be far less consistent for group portraits of Haarlem militia companies. Though Hals's 1616 *Officers of the St George Company* (see figure 5.11) fairly bristles with elbows and self-satisfied but good natured bravado – all fascinating examples of upper middle class masculine posturing – the bold flag bearer at the right edge is more the exception than the rule and he is not at the centre.[54] The pattern of response envisioned by Hals is consistent with the impression given off by tightly bonded groups of men (or men with women) today when facing an outsider (viewer), as in the similar pattern of posturing of the male rock group the Sha Na Na (figure 5.12): again it is the figures on the front line of contact with the outsider-spectator who raise their weapons.

Depictions of the regent class sitting as the board of a charity or civic body normally involve less aggressive posturing,[55] as one

**Figure 5.11** Frans Hals, *Officers of the St George Company, Haarlem*, 1616. (Haarlem, Frans Halsmuseum.)

would expect. However, by the middle of the seventeenth century
– the high point of such corporate imagery – of the members
shown seated around their meeting table, there will commonly be
one man (not the chairman) who is seated next to the space at the
table visually left open for the approach of the intruder-viewer
(and thus either at the right or left edge or in front) and who turns in
his chair to look either at us or at an intruder within the scene (as an
orphan) and assumes this 'on guard' or 'ready' posture, for example
in Ferdinand Bol's *Regents of the Nieuwezijds Huiszittenhuis,
Amsterdam* 1657 (see figure 5.13).[56] The assistant in Rembrandt's
*Anatomy Lesson of Dr Deyman*[57] plays a similar part. This role
offers parallels to that played by the second- and third-ranking
officers in the military groups.[58] As might now be anticipated, in
portraits of all female boards the body language of the group as a
whole and certainly of the mediating figures tends to be either
neutral or more open and welcoming.[59]

**Figure 5.12** Press photograph of the Sha Na Na.
(Source unknown.)

**Figure 5.13** Ferdinand Bol, *Regents of the Nieuwezijds Huiszittenhuis, Amsterdam,* 1657.

(© Rijksmuseum-Stichting, Amsterdam.)

GROUP PORTRAITS: MARRIAGE AND FAMILY

The evolution of certain strands of marriage and family portraits runs parallel though the dynamics are different. A variety of pictorial conventions were called upon by Renaissance artists to evoke a sense of marital bonds;[60] some clearly evince a sense of territoriality, turf to be defended.

Raphael's splendid companion portraits of *Angelo and Magdalena Doni*[61] (see figure 5.14) of *c.*1505 convey the message of a marital unit with Angelo at the head, an early example of complementary assertive–passive body language. Where he is all angles pressing up to the picture plane, she is all curves flowing back, the potentially strong line of her left arm delicately broken by the overlapping counterpoint of her other hand as it is in portraits of women by other artists, such as Leonardo's *Mona Lisa*. While she looks away, he confronts the viewer with a direct gaze. He sits forward with his right arm nudging the picture plane, the highlighted elbow slightly forward, accentuating the structural L of this position which is further strengthened by the rectangle of the 'window frame' itself and anchoring the composition for the left to right visual scan characteristic of so much sixteenth- and seventeenth-century art. His gesture serves to mark the boundary signalling his territory. It is not so different from the modern male party-goer who possessively rests his arm on the back of his wife's or girlfriend's seat. Such male posturing is normally aimed at other males. Analogous uses of body language (though not the elbow) to express dominance are found in fifteenth- and early sixteenth-century Flemish and German painting, as in Jan van Eyck's *Arnolfini Wedding*[62] of 1434 and Jan Gossaert's *Double Portrait of a Couple*[63] from roughly a century later.

A more overtly assertive expression of the husband's prerogatives and duties, focusing on the man with (right) hand on his hip or pommel of a sword in a boldly casual hip-shot pose, was used by Dürer for the *Betrothal of Archduke Maximilian and Mary of Burgundy*, one of the vignettes designed by him for the woodcut *Triumphal Arch of Maximilian* of 1512–18. Whether or not this is the first use in portraiture,[64] the gesture seems to have already become a commonplace in depictions of couples in German

**Figure 5.14** Raphael Sanzio, *Angelo and Magdalena Doni*, c.1505. (Palazzo Pitti, Florence.)

allegories or scenes of domestic life, as in the work of Israel van Meeckenem and the Master ES.[65]

The issues are more clearly drawn in a *Family Group*[66] by an anonymous artist of the northern Netherlands dated 1559 (see figure 5.15). The militant gesture of the husband will reappear in Netherlandish and German marriage portraiture (but most especially in Netherlandish) and this piece exemplifies the allegorical origins of many conventions that eventually become commonplaces – so well understood that the apparatus of interpretation could be jettisoned. The painting is discussed by E. de Jongh in his stimulating study of marriage and family portraiture in seventeenth-century Holland.[67] He comments on the emblematic toys of the two children and the scene visible through the window to the rear – of Eve offering the apple to Adam – as underlining the harmony of marriage, based on the necessary hierarchy of the sexes resulting from female weakness. Though elsewhere De Jongh briefly refers to the 'generally greater freedom of movement' on the part of husbands in marriage and family portraits, he does not take the issue further. However, I would suggest that the husband's bold 'on guard' gesture of right arm akimbo coupled with his left hand resting possessively on his wife's shoulder while she looks down, and he at her, make the hierarchy and their respective roles in it palpably clear. His virtues reside in steadfast leadership. Hers lie in passive obedience. The codes that De Jongh has been so important in uncovering in terms of the emblematic sources for many objects are more obviously susceptible to decipherment with the aid of contemporary emblem books, but the kind of gestural vocabulary analysed here offers further important clues to interpretation without which our understanding is unnecessarily limited.

From this point we will concentrate on the Dutch husband and father whose sterner image and projected sense of duty more easily express themselves in such insistent gestures of prerogative and protection. While there are relatively few marriage portraits in Italian sixteenth-century painting, it is interesting to note how often they are infused with a degree of tenderness and absence of assertion.

While there are many ways through gesture and objects such as harmonizing musical instruments to illustrate the complementary roles of husband and wife, this one will evolve into one of the most

Figure 5.15 Northern Netherlands painter, *Family Group*, 1559.
(Koninklijk Museum voor Schone Kunsten, Antwerp.)

common formulas for seventeenth-century Dutch companion portraits of married couples. The man will normally be on our left (on the right before marriage, as De Jongh has shown) with hand resolutely on hip, often thrusting his elbow boldly in our direction, as in Frans Hals's companion portraits of an unidentified couple in Cincinnati[68] (see figure 5.16) or, less frequently but more discreetly, angled away as in the portraits of an unidentified couple of c.1650 in Washington[69].

Variations on this particularly resonant expression of male and female relations are found in the work of nearly every Dutch portraitist and many of the Flemish. In Anthony van Dyck's companion portraits of the small son and daughter of the Marchesa Cattaneo of 1623[70] four and half year old Filippo is shown in the same protective pose as the adult males with their wives or families. As De Jongh has pointed out, the marriage portraiture of royalty was often overtly concerned with conveying political messages; within that context body language often expressed a similar gloss on the relationship as found in those of lesser mortals: for example *The Archduke Albert and Archduchess Isabella Visiting a Collector's Cabinet*[71] (see figure 5.17) presently attributed to Jan Breughel and Frans Francken II. On the wall to the rear can be seen a typical pair of marriage portraits from c.1570/80 featuring the husband as a guardian figure. A variation on this relation between the sexes may be found in genre scenes such as Johannes Vermeer's *Soldier and Laughing Girls*[72] where this outwardly protective gesture has been turned around to the more erotic overtones of sexual threat display.

Images of women exhibiting this gesture of self-possession become more plentiful around 1650 for women of powerful familes in the Netherlands as in Van der Helst's companion portraits of *Samuel de Marez and Margaretha Trip*.[73]

A reflection of subconscious associations contemporaries made with such marital images must be behind intriguing alterations made in the depiction of paired, full-length portraits of Willem Prince of Orange and his son Maurits seen hanging together in the Leiden University library in an engraving by Willem Swanenburgh after Jan C. Woudanus in 1610 (see figure 5.18) for a series of views of the university.[74] In the first, unfinished state, Maurits, the brilliant military leader and stadhouder in 1610, stands at the left in

**Figure 5.16** Frans Hals, *Unidentified Husband and Wife*, c. 1650.
(The Taft Museum, Cincinnati, Ohio; bequest of Mr and Mrs Charles Phelps Taft.)

**Figure 5.17** Jan Brueghel and Frans Francken II (?) *The Archduke Albert and Archduchess Isabella Visiting a Collector's Cabinet*, c.1620. (The Walters Art Gallery, Baltimore.)

a classic military posture with right hand on his hip, the left bracing a baton against that hip, his weight on the right leg with left extended, next to a table upon which rests a helmet. To the right his father Willem, the founder of the university in 1575, here more in the guise of a statesman in a long robe, stands partially turned towards his son, his arms stretched out with palms up (a gesture traditionally recognized by rhetoricians as indicating 'openness' or appeal) – thus, in the context of this pairing and contemporary portrait modes, visually playing an inappropriately subordinant 'wifely' role. That this must have struck the printmaker, or the sponsor of the series, is suggested by the changes in the final state. Now Willem has been moved to the place of honour and dominance on the left, his right hand on his hip while his left hand rests on a table balancing off that in Maurits's portrait which has now been moved, in reverse, to the right. In the actual portraits[75] presented to the university by Maurits in 1598 upon which these were presumably based, Maurits lightly rests one hand on the pommel of his sword and the other on a table while Willem stands next to a table with his hands stuffed into the pockets of his robe! Both portraits were adapted in differing degrees to a more heroic, assertive mode as joint protectors of the university and, particularly since the more 'manly' figure is at the right, neither is left to play the wife.[76]

While portraits of whole families are found from the middle of the sixteenth century, I have not been successful in finding examples exhibiting this same kind of threat display until well into the seventeenth century, at which point they abound. As in Gabriel Metsu's *Family of Burgomaster Dr Gillis Valkenier*[77] of about 1657 (see figure 5.19) they will often centre on a proud paterfamilias shown seated or standing, sometimes in exaggerated ease, with his hand on hip casually conveying seigneurial territoriality and warning off encroachment on his preserve – a 'pictogram' of middle-class virtue.[78] In Peter de Hooch's contemporary *Family in a Courtyard*[79] with three adult males and two females, the two eldest males respectively sit and stand with arm akimbo at the right and left edges, 'bracketing' the group while their spouses offer them fruit – a common reference to fruitfulness in marriage imagery. A further variation on this theme focuses on a son or sons who instead take this watching, protective masculine

**Figure 5.18** Jan C. Woudanus (after), *Leiden University Library*, 1610, engraved by W. Swanenburgh (details of the first and second states showing the portraits of Prince Willem of Orange and his son Maurits).

stance *vis-à-vis* the outside world as in works by Frans Hals, Cuyp,[80] or in a stern *Family Group* by an anonymous northern Holland artist[81] where all the sons 'have their elbows out' while the girls, except for the baby, all wear pearls and carry flowers or fruit, symbols of chastity and hoped-for fruitfulness. This convention finds a parallel expression at the English court in Anthony van Dyck's *Portrait of Philip 4th Earl of Pembroke and his Family*[82] where the richly dressed two eldest sons and son-in-law play out this role while the soberly dressed father wearing the Order of the Garter takes the role of statesman. This role is again curiously comparable to that of the standard-bearer or lieutenant in militia

**Figure 5.19** Gabriel Metsu, *Family of Burgomaster Dr Gillis Valkenier*, c.1657.
(Gemaldegalerie. Staatliche Museen Pressischer Kulturbesitz, Berlin.)

pieces. In a double portrait of two brothers, it may be the elder whose arm akimbo expresses the message of his protective feeling toward his sibling.[83]

Beyond basic distinctions in societal roles, individual artists made greater or lesser use of different patterns of body language: for example Rembrandt's use of body language in portraiture is subtle but more frequently turned to the conveyance of contemplative values and less to aggressive posturing than in the portraits of Hals, Van der Helst, or Van Dyck. Surely this reflects a blending of his own sensitivities with the social sense of his Amsterdam patrons,[84] who indeed were generally not from the same very powerful regent circles as those of Van der Helst.

Did men of the regent, mercantile, portrait-commissioning class in the Netherlands posture more assertively than the more aristocratic or clerical patrons in Italy? How reflective are these portraits of actual mores? While much was made in contemporary travellers' tales of the almost proverbial gesticulating Italian observed in the marketplace, these gesticulators were, by and large, not from the class that commissioned portraiture. The ambience of the courts, so important elsewhere in Europe as the focal points for standards of comportment, with an emphasis always on restraint and the elimination of large movements away from the body, was not such a socially formative factor in the northern Netherlands, and indeed there is a dearth of new etiquette books after Erasmus's until adaptations of Antoine de Courtin's French manual at the end of the seventeenth century.[85] It is possible that the greater social and gender equality of Netherlandish society might have bred the urge in those holding power to accentuate the symbols of their hegemony and the respect due to their guardianship? How does one correlate this with the similar self-possessive body language lent(?) by Van Dyck to his noble English and Italian sitters?

Finally, were seventeenth-century Dutch burghers more aggressive in their manners than Netherlanders 100 years previously? While it may well be so for the specific case of military imagery, I can hardly think that it was so for Dutch husbands. Here the changes in the artistic prism may be the operative factor.

In this connection we cannot conlude without momentarily considering the limits of our pictorial evidence, a significant aspect of which is the historical shifts in the aesthetic predispositions

**Figure 5.20** Michelangelo Mierisi da Caravaggio, *Supper at Emmaus*, c.1600. (Reproduced by courtesy of the *Trustees of the National Gallery, London*.)

which inform visual imagery at any given period, and how these influence our perception of the mores we take to be reflected in the seeming naturalism of these paintings, more exactly what would appear to be the increasing level of aggression in male gestures. Important here are the shifts in the perception of pictorial illusion, of the function of the picture plane in contributing to the sense of a spatial continuum between the viewer and the man or narrative portrayed. In a simple representative contrast of the *Nativity* from the *Paumgärtner Altarpiece* by Dürer (figure 5.3) of about 1503 and Caravaggio's *Supper at Emmaus*[86] (see figure 5.20) of roughly 100 years later we are aware of dramatic differences in the perception of space. In the earlier composition the viewer is involved by being drawn into the rational illusionistic space back beyond the 'window' (in contemporary parlance) of the picture plane. While by the time of Pontormo's *Cosimo* the taste for more complicated rhythms would accommodate the effrontery of the ducal elbow, it is only in early seventeenth-century painting, so often characterized by thrusting rhythms challenging the picture plane, that the male elbow could reach its provocative apogee. Typically in Caravaggio's melodramatic, even alarming compositions the spatial continuum extends, even bursts out, into our space involving us in the emotive experience whether we want to be or not. The coarse figures shock with their gaggle of elbows rudely thrust upon us as Caravaggio surely intended. Whether conceived by Dürer, Pontormo, or Hals, the evolving interpretation of body language remains wedded to the evolution of contemporary aesthetic tastes.

A part of the fascination of expressive elbows is that such natural gestures, as opposed to more ritualistic ones, remain just as integrally a part of our own repertory – though not of our conscious conventions – and therefore are intriguing to decipher. While we today are not critical of men or 'even' women who habitually put their hands to their hips and make no associations with the military, the urge to make the gesture and to react intuitively to it goes unabated.

## NOTES

An initial interpretation of some of this material was first given at the Toronto Renaissance and Reformation Colloquium, *The Language of Gesture in the Renaissance* in 1983 but was not published with the proceedings. Bibliographic references have been kept to a minimum. Myriad sources including the photographic archives of the Rijksbureau voor Kunsthistoriche Documentatie in the Hague have been important in establishing a repertory of examples of the various gestural types. However, to make it easier for readers who are not art historians, as many as possible of the works cited in the notes below are illustrated in Bob Haak, *The Golden Age of Dutch Painting* (New York, 1984; hereafter 'Haak'. So many paintings cited belong to the Rijksmuseum or the Historisch Museum in Amsterdam that such locations are given as ARM and AHM, respectively.

1 *Trattato* I, 60v; M. Kemp (ed.), *Leonardo on Painting* (New Haven, 1989), p. 144.

2 Karel van Mander, *Den grondt der edel vry schilder-const* (Haarlem, 1604; ed. H. Miedema, Utrecht, 1973), chs 4, 'Attitude' and 6, 'Affecten'.

3 Erving Goffman's *The Presentation of Self in Everyday Life* (New York, 1959) remains a useful prompt, though the caveats are important. Beginning with his *Masks of Wedlock: Seventeenth Century Dutch Marriage Portraiture* (Ann Arbor, 1982), David Smith has frequently introduced the approaches of sociologists such as Goffman into his interpretations of portraiture. While his interpretations are not always persuasive, his initial premise, that such an approach can offer salient insights, is.

4 Baltimore, The Walters Art Gallery.

5 Vienna, Kunsthistorisches Museum.

6 Leiden, Museum De Lakenhal; Haak 577.

7 As those by G van den Eeckhout of 1669 (Lille, Musée des Beaux-Arts; Werner Sumowski, *Gemälde der Rembrandt – Schüler* (5 vols, Landau, 1983), vol. II, 474 (hereafter 'Sumowski')) or an earlier one (The Hague, Dienst voor Verspreide Rijkscollecties; Sumowski 411) or that by F. Bol (The Hague, Gebouw van de Eerste Kamer; Sumowski 93). Cf. Jan Lievens, *Brinio Promoted to General*, 1661 (Former Amsterdam Town Hall, now Royal Palace; Haak 46); F. Bol, *Aeneas Distributing Prizes c.*1662 (Rijksuniversiteit Utrecht, on loan from the Dienst voor Verspreide Rijkscollecties; Haak 50); F. Bol, *Three Marys at the Tomb*, 1644 (Copenhagen, Statens Museum; Haak 609).

8  For example the soldiers standing by in Albrecht Dürer's woodcut of *Christ Presented to the People* 1498/9; Claes van der Heck's *The Judgment of Count Willem III of Holland*, 1618 (Alkmaar, Stedelijk Museum; Haak 109); or Adrian van de Venne's *Adoration of the Magi*, 1644 (Stockholm, Nationalmuseum; Haak 705).

9  Occasionally seen in the *Raising of Lazarus*, as that by Carel Fabritius, *c.*1643 (Warsaw, Muzeum Narodowe; Haak 635) when Christ commands Lazarus to come forth from the grave.

10  London, National Gallery.

11  Florence, the Uffizi.

12  *Bouc van seden* in *Denkmäler altniederländischer Sprache und Literatur*, ed. E. Kausler (Tübingen, 1844), lines 660–2.

13  London, National Gallery.

14  Munich, Bayerische Staatsgemäldesammlungen. For other military saints similarly characterized in German art: Stefan Lochner, *Altarpiece of the Patron Saints of Cologne*, *c.*1440 (Cologne, Cathedral); Grünewald, *The Meeting of Sts Erasmus and Maurice*, *c.*1520 (Munich, Bayerische Staatsgemäldesammlungen).

15  Adam Bartsch, *Le peintre graveur* (Vienna, 1803–21), 87.

16  Bartsch, *Le peintre graveur*, 200. Others for example by Master MZ, *Four Soldiers*, 1490 (Max Lehrs, *Geschichte und Kritischer Katalog der deutschen, niderländischen und französischen Kupferstichs im XV. Jahrhunderts* (New York, 1973), VIII.263.13, hereafter 'Lehrs'. Master ES., *The Arrest of Christ*, *c.*1460 (L.38); Heinrich Aldegrever, *Standard-bearer* (Hollstein 177), Erhard Schön in *A Column of Mercenaries* (illustration in Keith Moxey, *Peasants, Warriors and Wives* (Chicago, 1989), 4.10).

17  John R. Hale 'The soldier in Germanic graphic art of the Renaissance', in *Art and History: Images and their Meaning*, eds R.I. Rotberg and Th.K. Rabb (Cambridge, 1986), p. 87. Though Hale notes the standard-bearer's typical 'strutting' and notes his importance as one whose role signalled him out for artistic attention in military imagery of the first decades of the sixteenth century, he does not further comment on the possible attributive function of gestures. More recently Keith Moxey, in his *Peasants, Warriors and Wives*, pp. 69–72, comments instructively on ways in which the standard-bearer in sixteenth-century German prints of military mercenary life, as Erhard Schön's *A Column of Mercenaries*, may serve as the symbol of the virility of the company and therefore of the cause it serves. Moxey's concerns do not encompass such sign systems of body language as are here discussed.

18  As Christopher Amberger, *Christoph Baumgärtner*, 1543 (Vienna,

Kunsthistorisches Museum) or various portraits of the Duke of Alva, e.g. by an unidentified artist in the AHM.

19  Malibu, the J. Paul Getty Museum. See most recently the discussion of the pose as a 'Landsknecht' in the separate catalogue of its sale by Christie's, New York, 31 May 1989.

20  Rome, Galleria Nazionale.

21  The most specifically applicable secondary text consulted on manners was Pieter Spierenburg, *Elites and Etiquette: Mentality and Social Structure in the Early Modern Northern Netherlands* (Rotterdam, 1981) which takes as its point of departure Norbert Elias's influential work *Über den Prozess der Zivilisation: Soziogenetische und psychogenetische Untersuchungen* (2 vols, Basel, 1939).

22  From the 1540 English translation *A Lytell Booke of Good Maners for Chyldren* by Robert Whitinton. The majority of uses from c.1400 on of the term 'arm akimbo' (source obscure) cited by the *Oxford English Dictionary* imply dominance or defiance; as English seems to be unique in having such a specific word, tracing the occasions of the gesture in other literature has thus far proved unfruitful.

23  S. Blankaart, *De Borgerlyke Tafel* (Amsterdam, 1683), p. 106; and Dirck Adriaensz. Valcooch, *Regel der Duytsche Schoolmeesters* (Amsterdam, 1597), p. 14.

24  Some of the quotations are taken out of context and do not, in the original text, appear to imply criticism.

25  John Bulwer, *Chirologia: or the Naturall Language of the Hand . . . Whereunto is added Chironomia: or the Art of Manuall Rhetoricke* (2 vols, London 1644), chapter on 'Certain prevarications against the rule of rhetorical decorum . . . ', section 9.

26  The Hague, Gemeentemuseum; Haak 459.

27  Paris, private collection; Rembrandt Research Project (hereafter 'RRP'), *A Corpus of Paintings by Rembrandt*, vol. III (Dordrecht, 1989), cat. A120, with references to early seventeenth century portraits of standard-bearers. However it should be noted that the man is wearing a gorget, which a 'Landsknecht' standard-bearer would not have worn. Rembrandt may not have known this; alternatively, he knew exactly what he was doing and delighted in the historical mixing of past and present. More generic imagery: G. van den Eeckhout, *Two Soldiers in an Inn*, 1673 (Amsterdam, private collection; Sumowski 518) or G. Dou, *Officer with a Flag and Weapons* (Budapest, Szepmüveszeti Muzeum; Sumowski 268). The flag-bearer is hardly the only officer to sport this gesture in scenes of military life.

28 London, Wallace Collection; Haak 477.

29 Prague, Narodni Galerie; Seymour Slive, *Frans Hals* (Washington, 1989) (hereafter, '*Hals*'), 62.

30 *Faems Waer-gaim, Werelts Soet-cap* (1670), ill. in M. F. Durantini, *The Child in Seventeenth-Century Dutch Painting* (Ann Arbor, 1983), fig. 73.

31 ARM. Cf. his *Cornelis Pompe van Meerdevoort* (The Netherlands, Private collection; Sumowski 872).

32 ARM; Haak 914.

33 ARM; Haak 475.

34 ARM. Compare Van der Helst's *Michiel Adriaensz. de Ruyter, Vice Admiral of Zeeland, Holland and West-Friesland* from 1667 commemorating his defeat of the English (ARM; Haak 48); F. Bol's portrait of de Ruyter, 1668 (Copenhagen, Statens Museum for Kunst; Sumowski 177).

35 Rotterdam, the Boymans van Beuningen Museum: Sumowski 146.

36 For example the depiction of the General Pyrrhus in F. Bol's *Intrepidity of Gaius Fabricius Lucinus in Pyrrhus' Camp* (Amsterdam, Former Town Hall and now Royal Palace; Haak 760).

37 Amsterdam, private collection.

38 H. Perry Chapman, *Rembrandt's Self-Portraits: A Study in Seventeenth Century Identity* (Princeton, 1990), p. 87.

39 Anonymous artist (Hatfield House).

40 H. Pot, *Lady World* (Frans Halsmuseum, hereafter 'FHM'; Haak 153).

41 E. van de Velde, *Garden Party* 1615 (ARM; Haak 380); Pieter Quast, *Merry Company* (Hamburg, Kunsthalle; Haak 707).

42 A review of the theories on why this should be so would carry me far beyond the purposes of this essay.

43 Most recently: M. Carasso-Kok and J. Levy-van Halm (eds), *Schutters in Holland, kracht en zenuwen van de stad* (cat. Frans Halsmuseum, Haarlem, 1988; hereafter *Schutters*) with bibliography, and *Hals*.

44 ARM; RRP III, cat. A146 with an elegant discussion of the interpretation, major points of which build on E. Haverkamp Begemann, *Rembrandt: The Nightwatch* (Princeton, 1982).

45 RRP III, p. 466; Begemann, *Rembrandt: The Nightwatch*, pp. 50, 73ff.

46 AHM. Representative sampling of Amsterdam militia pieces focusing similarly on the flag-bearer: Nicolaes Eliasz., *Company of Capt. Jan van Vlooswijck*, 1642 (ARM; Haak 625); F. Hals, *Company of Capt. Reynier Reael*, completed by Pieter Codde (ARM; Haak 482); A. van Nieulandt and Claes Lastman, *Capt. Abraham Boom with a*

*detachment sent in 1622 to defend Zwolle*, 1623 (AHM; Haak 62); P. Moorelse, *Officers of the Amsterdam Company of Capt. Jacob Hoynck*, 1616 (ARM); G. Flinck, *Company of Capt. Albert Bas*, 1645 (ARM; Haak 623).

47 ARM; Haak 621.
48 For example: C. Anthonisz., *Banquet of Amsterdam Civic Guard*, 1533 (AHM; Haak 185); Dirck Jacobsz, *17 Members of the Amsterdam Civic Guard*, 1529 (ARM; Haak 183). See also *Schutters*.
49 ARM, Printroom; K. G. Boon, *Catalogue of the Netherlandish Drawings of the Fifteenth and Sixteenth Centuries* (The Hague, 1978), cat. 329; Haak 359.
50 D. Barendsz, *Officers of the Company of Capt. Reynst Pietersz.*, 1585 (17th century drawn copy, London, British Museum); *Schutters* 61C; C. Ketel, *Company of Capt. Dirck Jacobsz Rosecrans*, 1588 (ARM; Haak 186).
51 *Schutters*, pp. 39–40.
52 Christian Tümpel, 'De Amsterdamse schuttersstukken' in *Schutters*, especially pp. 87–101, on the evolution of the companies from 1575 and also of the compositional format of the portraits. Tümpel's fine observations on the visual language of these pieces do not extend to the questions raised here.
53 Flinck (AHM; Sumowski II, 717), Van der Helst (ARM; Haak 190).
54 H. Pot, *Officers of the St. Adrian Company, Haarlem*, c.1630 (FHM; Haak 376).
55 Thomas de Keyser's *The Four Burgermasters of Amsterdam* (AHM) is interesting because of the gestural jockeying for dominance between four men equal in power.
56 ARM. Other examples: Pieter van Anradt's *Regents of the Oude Zijds Huiszittenhuis*, 1675 (ARM Haak 864); Jan de Bray *Regents of the Children's Charity Home*, 1663 (FHM; Haak 801). Other examples: Van der Helst, *Regents of the Walloon Orphanage*, 1637 (Amsterdam, Maison Descartes; Haak 617); Hals, *Regents of the Old Men's Almshouse, Haarlem*, 1664, (FHM; Haak 798, *Hals* 85); Jan de Baen, *Directors of the United East India Company, Hoorn*, (Hoorn, Westfries Museum; Haak 1001); F. Bol, *Regents of the Leper Asylum, Amsterdam*, 1649 (AHM; Haak 197); J. Backer, *Regents of the Nieuwe Zijds Huiszittenhuis, Amsterdam*, c.1650 (ARM; Haak 607). One of the most self-assertive of these is Van der Helst's *Governors of the Archers' Guild*, 1657 (ARM; Haak 198).
57 ARM; Haak 206. A much later example: Cornelius Troost's *Inspectors of the Collegium Medicum* 1724 (ARM).
58 The subjects of G. ter Borch's *Magistracy of Deventer*, 1667 (Town

126       *Joaneath Spicer*

Hall, Deventer; Haak 47) are, on the other hand, very restrained, as their office would lead one to hope.

59 For example Jacob Backer, *Regentesses of the Burgher Orphanage, Amsterdam*, c.1633 (AHM; Haak 196) or Adriaen Backer's 1683 portrait of the same body (AHM).

60 See Berthold Hinz, 'Studien zur Geschichte des Ehepaarbildnisses', *Marburger Jahrbuch für Kunstwissenschaft*, 19 (1974), pp. 139–218 (with interesting comments on marriage portraits as manifestations of the family tree and 'masculine self-consciousness' though without breaking much new ground on gesture), and E. De Jongh, *Portretten van echt en trouw: huwelijk en gezin in der Nederlandse kunst van de zeventiende eeuw* (Zwolle and Haarlem, 1986).

61 Florence, *Palazzo Pitti*.

62 London, The National Gallery.

63 London, The National Gallery.

64 See Lucas Cranach's companion portraits of *Duke Henry the Pious and Duchess Catherine of Saxony*, 1514 (Dresden, Gemäldegalerie, Staatlich Kunstmuseum).

65 For example: Meeckenem's engraved series *Couples in Scenes of Daily Life*, c.1495–1503 (Lehrs IX.389.499 and 398.508); Master of the Lake Constance Region, *Allegory of Life and Death*, c.1480 (Nuremberg, Germanisches Nationalmuseum); Master ES's engravings: *The Small Garden of Love* (Lehrs 207), *The Garden of Love with Chess Players*, c.1460–5 (Lehrs 214), for which see *Meister E.S.* (Munich, Staatliche Graphische Sammlung, 1987; catalogue by Holm Bevers) including in comparison as text ill. 40 a page from a North Italian *Tacuinum sanitatis* (Handbook of health) showing a maiden playing a lyre and a young man seated listening with arm akimbo and hand on upper thigh. There is no comment on the gestures. The configuration of these couples is curiously similar to Master ES's *Arms of the Passion* (Lehrs 188) in which the shield is supported by Christ at the left with his right hand to his side holding open his wound and the Virgin at the right (Lehrs 188).

66 Antwerp, Koninklijk Museum voor Schone Kunsten.

67 De Jongh, *Portretten van echten trouw*, p. 46.

68 Cincinnatti, The Taft Museum; *Hals*, cat. 63, 64.

69 Washington, National Gallery; *Hals*, cat. 71, 72.

70 Washington, National Gallery.

71 Baltimore, The Walters Art Gallery, for which Joaneath Spicer, 'Jaunty soldiers and good husbands', *Bulletin of the Walters Art Gallery*, summer 1990. See also Gerard van Honthorst, *Prince Frederik Hendrick and Princess Amalia van Solms*, c.1637 (The

Hague, Mauritshuis; De Jongh, *Portretten van echt en trouw*, fig. 27a; Haak 681). In his portrait of *Princess Maria Steward and Prince Willem II*, 1647 (ARM; De Jongh, *Portretten van echt en trouw*, fig. 27b), the royal status of the husband is lower and he is at the right but in spite, or perhaps because of this he is particularly militantly presented with half-armour, left arm akimbo (away from his bride) and with his right, gloved hand smartly bracing his commander's baton against his upper right thigh.

72 New York, Frick collection, *c.*1658.
73 Private collection; Haak 785, 786.
74 Hollstein (W.S. 29–32). See ARM, *Leidse universiteit 400, Stichting en eerste bloei* (1975).
75 Leidse Universiteit, C5, and C6.
76 This perspective offers intriguing insights into the aggressive–passive body language of Hans Holbein's double portrait of Jean de Dinteville and Georges de Selve, 1533 (London, The National Gallery).
77 Berlin, (Staatliche Museen Preussischer Kulturbesitz), Gemäldegalerie.
78 Selected examples: P. Soutman (attr.) *Berestyn Family*, *c.*1630–1 (Paris, Louvre; Haak 175); A. van Ostade, *Family Group*, 1654 (Paris, Louvre; Haak 179); Caspar Netscher, *Family Group*, 1667 (Rotterdam, Museum Boymans-Van Beuningen; De Jongh, *Portretten van echt en trouw*, cat. 59); Henrick ten Oever, *Family Group*, 1669 (Zwolle, Overijssels Museum; De Jongh, *Portretten van echt en trouw*, cat. 60; Haak 866); Jan Miense Molenaer, *Music-making Family* (Haarlem, Frans Halsmuseum; De Jongh, *Portretten van echt en trouw*, cat. 69); Abraham van den Tempel, *Family Group* (Leiden, prentenkabinet der Rijksuniversiteit; De Jongh, *Portretten van echt en trouw*, fig. 11). The formula is frequently encountered in the following centuries in American and English painting influenced by Netherlandish types, for example John Singleton Copley's *Sir William Pepperrell and his Family*, 1778 (Raleigh, North Carolina Museum of Art).
79 Vienna, Akademie der bildenden Künste (De Jongh, *Portretten van echt en trouw*, fig. 37f). On fruit, see De Jongh *Portretten van echt en trouw*, under cat. 37.
80 Jacob Cuyp, *Family Portrait*, 1631 (Lille, Musée des Beaux Arts; Haak 727); Frans Hals, *Family Group in a Landscape*, *c.*1648 (Castagnola-Lugano, Thyssen-Bornemisza; *Hals* cat. 67); Jan Mijtens, *Mr. Willem van den Kerckhoven en zijn gezin*, 1652 (The Hague, Gemeentemuseum; De Jongh, *Portretten van echt en trouw*, cat. 52); Herman Doncker, *Family in a Dune Landscape* (location unknown; De Jongh, *Portretten van echt en trouw*, fig. 30a); Wybrand de Geest,

*The Verspreeck Family of Leeuwarden* 1621 (Stuttgart, Staatsgalerie; Haak 465).

81 Baltimore, The Walters Art Gallery; discussed in Spicer, 'Jaunty soldiers and good husbands'.

82 Wilton House, Wiltshire, collection of the Earl of Pembroke.

83 Herman Doncker, *Two Brothers in a Landscape* (Baltimore, The Walters Art Gallery; Spicer, 'Jaunty soldiers and good husbands'); Rubens, *Albert and Niclaas Rubens* (Vaduz, Prince of Liechtenstein) in which Albert has his right hand on his hip, and his left arm around his brother.

84 On Rembrandt's patrons see G. Schwartz, *Rembrandt His Life, His Paintings* (New York, 1985) and S. Alpers, *Rembrandt's Enterprise* (Chicago 1988); for Haarlem see Pieter Biesboer, 'The burghers of Haarlem and their portrait painters' in *Hals*.

85 *Traité de la Civilité* (Paris, 1677). See Spierenburg, *Elites and Etiquette*, pp. 16ff; Roodenburg, pp. 154–157 of this volume.

86 London, The National Gallery.

# 6

# The order of gestures: a social history of sensibilities under the Ancien Régime in France

## ROBERT MUCHEMBLED

When Jean-Claude Carrière and Daniel Vigne decided to make a film based on a sixteenth-century legal case, *The Return of Martin Guerre*,[1] they encountered the fundamental problem of how to transfer gestures and attitudes of the characters onto the screen. The work was a great success.

The work or the works? It existed in at least four different forms: (1) the preparatory historical study which was entrusted to the American historian Natalie Zemon Davis; (2) 'a story, a tale', drawn from her work by Carrière and Vigne; (3) the scenario (a very 'technical' job according to these authors); (4) finally, the film. One only has to compare these four versions to note that the descriptions – and often mere suggestions – of gesture were not made in an identical way.

This is an exciting problem which demonstrates the necessity for historical reflection that pays attention to the daily realities of life in the past. For how is it possible to understand bygone ages if we do not try to mentally reconstruct the framework of daily life and the bodily movements of those people of the past, as every good film-director has to do?

Since the pioneering work of Norbert Elias such a perspective has become perfectly respectable: the body is now an important object of historical reflection.[2] Consequently, even the most fleeting gestures must command our attention, as they define manners of behaviour inscribed in collective sensibilities, i.e. in the general cultural codes and rites which transmit values through norms. Indeed, that is also the lesson of non-European anthropology: for example, by observing the gestures and attitudes of spectators of cock-fights, Clifford Geertz was able to disentangle the web of Balinese culture and arrive at its founding principles.[3]

If we want to apply this technique to the Ancien Régime in France, we are of course confronted by an area of reseach too vast to be covered by this contribution. For that reason I will limit myself to a few essential notions by which I hope to open up avenues for future study. In my opinion, no human society is purely 'natural'; in this sense, gestures equally partake of culture. So it is important first to define such an anthropological theory as it is the basis of what follows. Relying on some of my earlier studies which I will not repeat in detail here,[4] I would like to stress the effects of a growing cultural bipolarization expressed through the body and gestures. This process is in no sense specific to France but can be observed, with various nuances, throughout Europe. It is well demonstrated by Flemish and Dutch genre-painting (pictures that were also popular in France) and deeply revealing of a new 'art of gesture'.

THE HISTORY OF GESTURE:
A CULTURAL ANTHROPOLOGY

How do we write a history of gesture? In my opinion, a workable method has to introduce anthropological curiosity into a solidly historical framework. The studies by Erving Goffman and those of ethologists, in particular Edward T. Hall, may serve as guides in this field, though they cannot be transferred directly to situations in the past because they rest on observations and sociological experiences of the present.[5] But at least, they will provide us with some fundamental notions which the historian has to combine with his own thoughts – the thoughts of a 'man of paper', who mentally tries to reconstruct worlds which he can no longer experience physically.

In my own investigation I will be guided by two operational concepts. The first, borrowed from Goffman, defines the world as a theatre where the social relations are the object of a continuous staging. The second, derived from ethology, notes the importance in all animal and human societies of a 'territory of my own' which every individual uses in order to come into contact with others or to avoid them. We issue signals (especially gestures) codified to indicate an expression of respect, a demand for consideration, or even a desire for a confrontation.[6] Taken together, these two principles define systems of comportment based on a ritual segmentation of the body – or, more simply, on a usage of the latter – which differs according to civilizations.

By being attentive to social and chronological dimensions, the historian can make his own contribution to such an anthropological theory. Studying gesture presupposes before everything a precise statement of the typological role of every actor and his frame of reference. For it is important to know whether one is speaking of Europe, France, a region, or just a small village, in as much the Ancien Régime is not a uniform world. Even more important is the social situation of those whose gestures one analyses. Is it not evident that attitudes, comportments, and sensibilities change in meaning depending on criteria of wealth or poverty? Equally they differ according to sex, age-group, or even type of situation as, for instance, the normality of working days or the inversive character of festivals.[7]

Since the historian cannot walk the streets of the past in order to observe ordinary situations, he usually has to work with incomplete documentation which is more often biased towards the exceptional than to the normal events of everyday life. Regarding the study of gestures, this situation is not necessarily a handicap as departures from normality allow us to pass from observable attitudes to underlying sensibilities much easier than ordinary occasions do. For example, legal sources furnish precise information about gestural codes used in insults, thus allowing us to deduce the conception of personal and collective honour of the social groups in question: the point of honour amongst nobles, the protection of virgins' and women's purity by their fathers, husbands and brothers; the macho ethic of young men on the brink of marriage who proudly carried the symbols of their power: the feather in their hat and sword at their side.[8] In this way I have been able to study the signs of conflict in the countryside of Artois: mimicry, hissing, the habit of 'beating the street' or a tree with one's sword, of moving close to someone else and brushing against him – these are often the start of fatal fights between bachelors.[9]

In this way common structures of conflict emerge behind such brutal gestural codes, illuminating the relations between ages and sexes, permitting us to define the conditions of the normal social equilibrium. In a similar way war, plague, situations of great fear, strong demographic growth – in short everything that disturbs norms and traditions – bring about conflicts and attempts at restoring the equilibrium. The gestures employed in these cases, for example during a charivari, supply us then with the keys to interpret the culture in which they are expressed.

One of the difficulties in such a study arises from the fact that every historical document can give indications about gestures but no well-defined series of sources, except legal ones, is specifically oriented to this area of research. For this reason it is important to concentrate our research on what I will call 'fields of coherence' (*champs de cohérence*). To start with, nothing is as important in my opinion as familiarity with criminal archives, not because a sociology of delinquency might be found there (which would be another project) but because one can draw from it countless elements of familiarity with the ordinary structures of life in the past. The depositions of witnesses or the letters of remission not only illuminate the actual crime, but numerous seemingly insignificant or accidental details relate the realities of the age.[10] In fact, the most interesting social situations for a history of gestures are those of 'social friction', i.e. the circumstances where people meet: the church, the tavern, festivals, crowds, and public places. In other words, we must concentrate our attention on normal cultural codes, on the expressions of sociability which cannot fail to appear when the supplicant conjures up the circumstances of his crime. This concern for veracity is particularly marked in the letters of remission as a pardon was only granted if the guilty person could argue strong extenuating circumstances and had related in minute detail how he had acted, thus enabling the legal officers to verify his account.

Admittedly, some historians may have reservations about looking for norms in documents principally oriented towards deviancy. In order to reassure them and to complete my approach it is important to support the connections discovered in this way with those that emerge from other evidence, such as literature or theatre, etiquette books, and even better – at least in my opinion – in painting.[11]

## SOCIAL CODES AND CULTURAL BIPOLARIZATION FROM THE SIXTEENTH TO THE EIGHTEENTH CENTURY

All gestures can appear natural but all are equally cultural because as we have learned from the ethnologists, no human society is 'primitive'. Everywhere we can observe codes of behaviour which are based on a specific world-view. Perhaps those communities which we used to call 'uncivilized' distinguished themselves from ours by a certain homogeneity despite differences in social status, age, or gender. But Europe, at least since the Middle Ages, has shown important differences between popular culture (admittedly, a simplifying term) and that of the dominant groups in society. Already half a century ago Norbert Elias demonstrated in a remarkable way the changes in comportment of these elites since the fourteenth century, a result of a process of 'civilization of manners'.[12] Picking up his dossier in the case of France and the Netherlands I have described in my *L'invention de l'homme moderne* (1988) the results of this growing cultural bipolarization.[13] Within this brief study, I would simply like to stress the close tie between gestures and culture in the lower and the dominant classes of society, as well as the slow transition from the notion of a magic body to that of a sacred one.

Gestures are in fact mediations which permit the passage from nature to culture, i.e. from the body (gender, sensation) to comportment, the latter being the transmitter of collective mentalities. Considered in this way, gestures of peasants, as described in legal, religious or literary texts, have a profound meaning, often unrecognized by the outside observers who have left us the testimonies in question.

In his *Contes et discours d'Eutrapel*, published in 1585, the Breton Noël du Fail describes the *veillée* (the gathering of women from surrounding farms or villages in someone's barn to spin or sew) on winter evenings. He brilliantly evokes the postures of the youth of both sexes, for whom this is a good occasion 'to make love through marriage', i.e. to practise a form of courtship consisting of minor liberties, of diversions, and of laughs. The gestures made at these evenings can be analysed at two levels. Some only transmit conventional sentiments, specifically those supported by a group's ethics. The boys, for example, try to touch the girls to steal a kiss from them, or to amuse them. But if in the heat of action they indecently show the 'upper part of their trousers open' the girls 'start to laugh loudly with their hand half-hiding their eyes'. In this way our source defines a boundary of female modesty and a small transgression which is possible in the context of the *veillée*, while implying that such comportment is not admissible in general. In the same text, a second level of gestures permits us to recover the proper codes: the boys, who would have liked 'to make eyes, to put back in place the breasts which had slipped down to the armpits through the continuous movement of the spindle, and secretly to steal a kiss by tapping the shoulder from behind, were controlled by a group of old women whose hollow eyes pierced right into the cow-shed, or by the master of the house who was lying on his side in his bed near-by . . . and in such full view that nothing could be hidden from him.'[14]

This *veillée* constitutes a kind of peasant micro-society, bringing into contact within a limited space age-groups and sexes. Numerous other descriptions demonstrate that this occasion was fundamental to the transmission of culture, as the courting described here was strictly codified. Like everywhere else, sexuality is not something free in the rural world. The normal gestural latitude allowed to adolescents of both sexes is precisely defined by the supervision of the old women and the heads of the families. But Noël du Fail does not only describe anecdotal events. He allows us to understand the functioning of a structure of relationship which imposes upon everybody obligatory codes regarding marriage since that is the fundamental element for the succession of generations and the stability of society. Under the watchful eye of the master of the house, who represents the authority of the established adults, the female world mimes the eternal game of supervision (the old women) and fascination (the girls) in front of the third element, the male youths. Each of the members of this triad has its own role to play and to express it by gesture, even though sometimes things get out of hand.[15]

Two centuries later these roles and gestures remain essentially the same in the country despite the impact of the 'civilization of manners'. Some twenty years before the French revolution, Nicholas Restif de la Bretonne (1734–1806) described at length the manners of the peasants of his birthplace, Sacy (Yonne). The separation of the sexes was obligatory: the girls distrusted the big youths who lusted for their virtue and the fathers or brothers continued to supervise this symbolic good on which the honour of the family depended. This is shown by the codes employed at the *veillée* and elsewhere. For example, in courting a girl it was advisable first to hang around

the house for some months before it is possible to speak to her. People talk about it in the countryside and the girl learns that a Pierrot or a Jacquot hangs around the house because of her. One evening, out of pure curiosity, she finds an excuse to go out . . . but the parents are not fooled. If the boy suits them they don't say a word and the girl can go out of the house. If, however, they don't like him, the mother or father stands up, pushes the girl back into her chair or seat, and says: 'Stay there, I'll go myself' . . . But if the girl is left to go out, then the boy approaches her and caresses her . . . Subsequently, she goes out every evening . . . On Sundays they talk without doing anything, and that is the day that the boy will take a chance and kiss her, but it is rare that the girls are not sensible.

Restif adds that the companionship normally lasts two or three years and that marriage in the first winter is usually out of the question. The parents of the girl rarely ask the boy about his intentions before the second year of the companionship and then with the question: 'What are you coming here to do, Jacquot?'[16]

In fact, words are rare and chaste in evoking marriage or other questions of prime importance such as sex. In general, gestures suffice as they carry precise messages that everybody in the rural world can interpret without difficulty. Folklorists have noted the endurance of these practices until modern times, such as conveying one's refusal to grant the hand of one's daughter by seemingly insignificant and irrelevant gestures: only giving eggs to a guest, stirring the fire, not giving a chair to a suitor who enters the house, and so on.[17]

Such a codification is not at all arbitrary. It is normally expressed in interrelationships between persons who know each other's position (wealth, power, age, gender) exactly and in the purpose of the request. Admittedly, when analysing gestures it is often difficult to recover the entire chain of meaning in question. Gestures are only the visible parts of types of behaviour proper to adult males, women, male youths, children, or marginal groups. Despite regional differences and developments between the sixteenth and eighteenth centuries, all these categories are inserted in a conception of the world typical of inhabitants of the country. About 1700, the prior of Sennely-en-Sologne described it well, despite his prejudices as a man of the church faced with 'superstitions':

The Solognots all have the looks and manners of simpletons, they seem to be stupid, practically numb, and yet there are few people who are more spirited. They are shrewd and such masters in dissimulation that they can cheat even the most prudent people . . . Even the children are reserved in their conversations and cautious in not saying anything that can trap them. They keep a gloomy silence which surprises those who do not know their natures and they are imagined to be as spirited as statues. They never deviate from their maxim, which is to speak little but well.[18]

For Solognots of 1700 as for the Bretons of the sixteenth century as depicted by Noël du Fail, the gestural codes form a language parallel to that of the word. The body is profoundly expressive and it is magical. After all, is the eye of the sorcerer not capable of casting a spell? With grumbling forbearance the prior of Sennely translates this idea by claiming that his parishioners are 'baptized idolaters'. He illustrates his view by relating some examples of gestures, particularly at the hour of death:

Letting the yoke of a plough catch fire they regard as an error punishable by death, and the poor sick are often seen in their agony hiding themselves under the pillow of their bed from fear that they inadvertently had let one catch fire. They are also scrupulous in doing the washing at a time when a sick person has received extreme unction. They doubt the salvation of a person who dies turned towards the wall, claiming that the devil is watching to seize the souls of those who die at that side.[19]

Story-tellers, authors, observers like the prior of Sennely, or keepers of legal records of rural areas allow us to recover the gestures of peasants and interpret them. Unfortunately, the objects of our interest were often illiterate at that time and therefore left little direct evidence. So in general we will have to analyse the comportments and mentalities through documents deriving from the higher cultural strata. We must be careful, of course, to distinguish descriptions of realities from the usually more or less prejudicial judgements with which they are interspersed but if we do so, two quite distinct fields of coherence emerge: popular and elite culture. The second allows us to test the progress of the cultural bipolarization during modern times, as each witness defines, at least subconsciously, the distance he perceives between the strange comportments of which he speaks and those which he himself has assimilated.

There is no need here to repeat the analyses by Norbert Elias of the 'evolution of manners' in French court circles and urban elites.[20] It will be enough to note, in the wake of numerous scholars, that the standards of taste or lack of taste, and those of shame, changed slowly within the upper social minorities.[21] The 'modernization' of gestures manifests itself in a repudiation of everything that is too animal in man. As in Molière's *Tartuffe* (1664), it involves a minimum of hiding, not only 'that breast I would not know how to look upon' but also the exercise of one's natural functions, nudity, sexuality, and those postures which make one resemble the animals. The development was, admittedly, neither linear nor rapid and we have to take heed of numerous subtle distinctions so as not to distort the phenomenon. It is a fact that both France and the Catholic southern Netherlands witnessed the triumph of the morality of the Counter-Reformation, sustained by the absolutist state from about the seventeenth century onwards. It is a minor but none the less enlightening detail, that the tendency of religious authorities to combat all indecency finally led to the painting over of Renaissance nudes, now deemed too provocative; the nudes of Michelangelo in the Sistine Chapel are a case in point.

All this points to a rejection more of the magical or animal body than of sexuality alone. The new morality is a philosophy of life which aims at focusing the efforts of Christians on their salvation at the expense of gratifications sought in the material world and sensual pleasures. Reaching for holiness by mortifying the flesh and ignoring one's needs was obviously not within the grasp of ordinary people but everybody had to try and control his passions so as not to become their slave. The combined efforts of the religious and civil authorities joined with the moralizing or educational tendencies of the day in an effort to push the magical body back into the demonic realm of darkness and to encourage the well-to-do to see their physical body as a sacred envelope linking them directly to God and to his lieutenant on earth, the absolute king.

Confronted with the resistance of the popular classes, especially the peasants, the authorities and the members of the upper classes expressed in derogatory terms the gestures, customs, and 'mentalité' of that other cultural pole which they no longer understood. From then on police regulations are teeming with symptomatic prohibitions.[22] The seignorial law of Cerny-les-Bucy, in the bailiwick of Vermandois, for example, prohibits dancing in the street or in public places on Sundays and holidays. It threatens with a fine of twenty *livres* 'all young men and others' who insisted on a 'bien venue' or presented 'bouquets on the occasion of weddings, betrothals, baptisms'. The law even instructed mothers 'to keep their children close to them in the churches, not allowing them to run about, wander, or make a noise, and not give them toys', and prohibited any person from taking a dog into the said churches, on pain of a fine of forty sous. The police regulations of the bailiwick of l'Isle-Adam (Val d'Oise), dated 1 September 1780, contain similar orders, notably prohibiting everyone 'of all ages and all sexes from defecating in cemeteries around churches on pain of a fine of three pounds fifteen sous', as well as from letting animals graze in the cemeteries, even if one had bought the grass for the church's profit, and finally, prohibiting all 'merchants, traders and others from displaying goods and foodstuffs for sale in the cemeteries and church porches on pain of a fine of ten pounds'.[23]

The constant repetition of such orders suggests the resistance of the peasants. The gestures evoked in these documents mix the sacred with the profane and are sometimes indecent, dirty, or disorderly. None the less, they do belong to the cultural traditions of the countryside, as is demonstrated by the use of the cemetery or the church, or by the evocation of the customary rights of bachelors organized into 'abbayes de jeunesse' to impose on new members a 'welcome' and to demand gifts in kind or cash on the occasion of a marriage or a baptism. The logic of the police rests on a conception of the body which is, yes, policed, but it comes into collision with the tenacity of the codes behind the gestures in question. We find an indifference to demands for hygiene soon to be imposed in the cities as the eighteenth century approached, combined with the maintenance of an intense sociability, even in the places reserved for the dead. And the same tenacity could be found in the still intact power of social roles, as represented by the bachelors and by the world of women who still raised their children in a way that did not please the authorities.

Thus the underlying logic that appears in these documents stems from the norms mainly practised by the upper classes, as much at court as in the cities. The ecclesiastical leaders were obviously well-placed to formulate this growing cultural bipolarization. Just as the prior of Sennely did, so Jean-Baptiste Thiers, the curate of Champrond-en-Gâtine in the diocese of Chartres, deplored the fact that the people abandoned themselves to countless 'superstitions', which he enumerated in his *Traité des superstitions* (1679). Numerous gestures, which appeared strange or were disapproved by the curate (*his* morality and not that of the peasants, of course) relate to the magical body I defined earlier. Thus, newly-weds dreaded particularly the spell of 'cording', the symbolic act of tying a cord which prevents a husband from fulfilling his conjugal duties as a result of the malevolence of a magician. Amongst the formulas to get rid of the spell, Thiers mentions the following: 'the newly-weds to be completely nude and the husband to kiss the wife's big toe on the left foot and the wife the husband's big toe on the left foot', or 'urinate in the keyhole of the church where they were married'.[24] A twentieth-century psychologist would undoubtedly see many sexual symbols here and, in the first 'remedy', an amusing way to arouse a dormant libido. In this first example however, we find a concrete and precise gesture of untying, applying a magical corporal symmetry; during the wedding ceremony the magician had made knots in a piece of cord, binding in this way the sexual capacities of the husband which therefore had to be disentangled, in the literal sense of the word, by the proposed gymnastics. The symbolism of the keyhole and the urine in the second case is obvious enough not to need stressing: the magical body returns to the locations of the double rite, religious and maleficent, in order to destroy the latter by reinforcing the former.

I cannot analyse Thiers' entire book here. Having waged war against the peasants' errors, the author provides us with a very important harvest of ethnological data, though the facts are insufficiently dated and insufficiently localized. When used with other descriptions of this kind and with the notes in legal sources (which are more limited but better embedded in their historical context) this book may enable us to draw up repertories of gestures and reach back to the codes of behaviour from which they derive. The field of marriage offers numerous gestures to be studied. For example, 'when there is a widow or some girl to be wed in a house and their hand is sought in marriage one must be very careful of removing logs from the fire, because that drives away those in love.'[25] Was this a proverb? Or an allusion to some obscure magical act? Neither, for this was a simple social ritual which was poorly understood by Thiers. We have already seen that courting proceeded slowly, without verbally expressing what one hoped for. In this case, taking away the logs was simply part of a well-established code of a father's refusing the suitor of his daughter. No wonder this gesture drove away those in love!

In a peasant world that is inclined to signs and gestures, many actions derive a solid meaning from a silent language. Other gestures reveal a magical view of the human body: as Thiers observed, 'Some take a dead man's bone from a newly-dug grave, soak it in water for one day and one night and make their intended wife drink this water.' Elsewhere, he condemns the practice of baptizing 'a particular membrane called "le nombril de l'enfant" [the caul], when it is seen coming from the mother's womb and it still encloses the baby's body.'[26] This rite improves the luck that is supposed to accompany the child being born with the caul. And if it wears the remains of this amniotic membrane around its neck, it will become totally invulnerable to any weapon whatsoever.

Working for the good of the Church, Thiers cannot admit such beliefs, or, more generally, any attitude which departs from official orthodoxy. Like so many of his contemporaries within the civilized or upper strata, he indiscriminately condemns phenomena of a mental order, especially magical beliefs, and social practices such as dances, ways of courting, or customs attached to the rituals of private or public life (marriage, charivari, youth festivals etc.). In other words, official culture sets itself up as unique and refuses to admit a general logic other than its own, labelling everything deviating from the norm as 'superstitions'. We have seen, however, that the historian can still recover the internal logic of popular culture, as expressed in the gestures painted from life by observers such as Thiers. The peasant world displays an extraordinary capacity for passive resistance, thus preserving the substance of its world view as is demonstrated by the rich harvest of practices and beliefs collected by the folklorists of the nineteenth and twentieth centuries.[27] As for the other cultural pole, that of the 'modernization' of gestures, it frequently expresses itself in the form of a new art of experiencing one's body.

## THE ART OF GESTURE

The body certainly reflects cultural practices. The body of the sixteenth-century courtier, the seventeenth-century 'honnête homme', and the eighteenth-century 'homme éclairé' distinguishes itself both from animals and from the rude or gross manners of the lower classes. In fact, the peasant often constitutes a kind of counter-example because both eye-witnesses and painters like to emphasize those traits which bring him close to the animal world. The standards of shame and of the whole theatre of gesture among the upper classes underwent far-reaching changes in the early modern period. From the publication in 1530 of Erasmus's *De civilitate morum puerilium* onwards, the children of the most prominent families (later also the pupils at the *collèges*) acquire the new rules of courtesy which spread gradually among the upper classes and even among some prominent peasants.[28] The structuring of body and gesture is profoundly altered within these sections of the population and that distinguishes them more and more from the majority of the rural population and from the lowest classes in the towns.

It is impossible to sketch here in detail this major process of the *invention de l'homme moderne*, one which runs along different lines according to the social groups involved.[29] I will confine myself to an attempt to determine the exact place of genre painting within such a mechanism. Produced in the Low Countries and much valued in France (at least, apparently, amongst the well-to-do classes in the towns), this style develops a moralist viewpoint, disparaging the imperfections of the lower classes and imparting to those who enjoy this painting a feeling of superiority that highlights the cultural bipolarization mentioned earlier. So it plays a part which compares with that of Thiers's *Traité des superstitions* or similar texts. Exposing such errors, either through humour or the severe admonitions of the Church, probably served more to educate the elite who bought these books and paintings than to genuinely change the attitudes of the peasants or the poorer townsfolk. This line of development, which for lack of a better term we may call 'bourgeois', is different from a rigid imitation of superior models which we find more often among the courtiers or the aristocracy. Besides following the manuals on civility, these latter groups also had to master such 'techniques de corps' as the art of fencing or horse riding, thus establishing a major distance between themselves and the 'bourgeois gentilhomme' who in Molière's famous play attempts to mimic them (1670). The upper classes preferred portraits and allegorical compositions to genre painting, because 'la figure de l'homme est le plus parfait ouvrage de Dieu sur la terre', as Félibien put it in 1667.[30] Those who admired the picture of Richelieu by Philippe de Champigne[31] or those who had themselves portrayed by Pierre Subleyras in eighteenth-century Toulouse tried to come as close as possible to the sources of distinction and power by adhering to the artistic standards of classicism.

Genre painting, then, does not express the taste of the elite in its entirety. Research in notarial archives, for example in inventories of the deceased, may enable us to refine this sociological sketch. In the meantime, we can only define the theoretical message by what the great French masters considered a minor form of pictorial representation.

Paul Vandenbroeck has convincingly demonstrated that Hieronymus Bosch gave visual expression to the social ethic of the prosperous citizens of towns in the Netherlands and southern Germany by labelling the excesses of Carnival and, more generally, all sexual or bodily expressions as madness.[32] One can detect here the starting point for the moralization and modernization of gesture within these urban upper classes. Subsequently, Pieter Brueghel the Elder resumes this theme of rustic rudeness but with more sympathy for the lower classes. Can it be that the drunkard, or the figure urinating or defecating in the sight of everyone in a corner of the painting, makes the buyers of these paintings laugh and enables them to distance themselves from those represented? Anyway, the metaphorical sense is often emphasized by the artist or his imitators. The *Ass at School*, engraved after Brueghel in 1557, has a Latin legend which explains that a stupid animal, even though sent to Paris for study, will remain what he is (see figure 6.1). I would like to interpret this scene as a highly ironic denunciation of the attempt at educating children, in particular those of the common people, as is suggested by the background and the mention of Paris – a cultural centre that is supposed to transform the donkey into a horse. The piling up of bodies, grimaces, the showing of bare bottoms or genitals close to the teacher, various postures that are never upright or well-controlled (with the exception of that of the teacher): everything is the exact reverse of the gestures recommended in Erasmus's manual on civility. For a literate person, the undisciplined and obscene children represent a (wrong) state of nature which contrasts with the education recommended for the well-to-do, and which reminds us also of the fact that the peasants who do not even go to school are as incapable as the donkey of changing their comportment.

*The Pedlar Pillaged by the Apes*, engraved in 1562, expresses the disturbances of the natural state in a similar fashion (see figure 6.2). At a time in which an ethic was established that disapproved of

144        *Robert Muchembled*

**Figure 6.1** Pieter Brueghel (after), *The Ass at School*, 1557, engraving.
(© Rijksmuseum-Stichting, Amsterdam.)

looseness and indecency, it was wiser to use a group of monkeys
rather than humans to portray natural activities. Two of the ape-
like creatures imitate children by jumping around on hobby-horses
(for the monkey can be represented with much greater liberty in
this area). The cottage in the background alludes to the countryside
at the edge of which a hawker has fallen asleep. The undisciplined
animals are pillaging his stock-in-trade, dispersing the objects that
symbolize urban progress: gloves, mirror, spectacles. In other
words, the innovations are the object of facetious behaviour or of
appropriation by these little people symbolizing the peasants, as
some gestures clearly demonstrate. Four apes are dancing in a
circle to the sound of instruments which have come from the
pedlar's basket as young peasants used to do during a feast. In the
foreground, a monkey defecates into the pedlar's hat. In the tavern
numerous quarrels arose from behaviour of this type. Perched on
the back of the merchant, another monkey searches for lice on his

**Figure 6.2** Pieter Brueghel (after), *The Pedlar Pillaged by the Apes*, 1562, engraving. (© Rijksmuseum-Stichting, Amsterdam.)

head while another one holds his nose near the behind of the
sleeper. The scatological dimension, so well presented by Rabelais,
aims at making us laugh at the natural odour and lice which
accompany man during his whole life. The peasants did not at all
doubt the usefulness of delousing and in fact it was known as a
gesture of affection among those close to another. Without trying
to force the interpretation, it seems evident that Brueghel plays
with the opposition between nature and culture. By being amused
the urban upper classes that owned such prints were able to see a
difference between the 'animal world' of the countryside and their
own. Surely this is the first stage on the path to a moralization
which would lead to an aversion to the lower part of the body and
vulgar gestures.

But this process was not complete. Painting, like the theatre,
purges the passions, teaching the eye and mind of the citizen to
distinguish himself from the unruly and licentious realm of people
depicted by the artist. Brueghel, however, belonged to a particular
moment in history, when the morals of the upper classes
sometimes still incorporated such behaviour. As a consequence,
their judgements remained indulgent; some buyers probably did
not even notice the cultural distance that Brueghel rendered in
metaphor. But in the second half of the sixteenth century the
situation gradually became more clearly defined, leading in the end
to a very sharp cultural differentiation in the seventeenth century.
In France the aversion at that time taken to the 'dirty' works of
Rabelais went hand in hand with the dismissal of nudity and all
verbal obscenity, to be noticed, for example, among the works of
the *précieuses*.

At that moment a second phase had been reached; genre painting
now increasingly relied upon the image of otherness, i.e. of
difference, to structure a representation of self common to the
artists and the buyers of their work. A recent exhibition held at
Antwerp testifies to this: the phenomenon unfolds across the
whole of Europe between the fourteenth and the eighteenth
centuries, assuming various forms successively. Amongst its
constants we find the definition of civilized life, city-life in
particular: the artists love to suggest it by painting its contrary, the
uncivilized existence of the peasants.[33]

One ought to examine genre painting systematically in order to

**Figure 6.3** Jacob Jordaens, *Feast of the Epiphany*, 1640.
(Koninklijk Museum voor Schone Kunsten, Antwerp.)

determine its precise role in the gestural and bodily education of
the upper classes. Some paintings clearly demonstrate what was
not deemed proper, reinforcing in this way the lesson of the
manuals on civility, though perhaps offering as well the gratification
of a little transgression, given the gratifications contrary to the
teachings of the Church and civility. The *Feast of the Epiphany*
(before 1656) by Jacob Jordaens takes place in a sumptuous
interior (see figure 6.3). There reigns an atmosphere of disorder,
drunkenness, and luxury as underlined by the gestures, grimaces
and postures of the majority of the diners. Only the queen chosen
by the old pot-bellied king (himself appointed by lot) stands out
by her distinguished and elegant comportment, the mark of a good
education. On the right, a drunkard is vomiting, almost hitting the
feet of the spectator. Above the group is the moral of the story, in
the form of a Latin device: 'Nothing resembles a fool more than
the drunkard'.

It is worth noting that the process of civilization of manners

**Figure 6.4** Jan Steen, *Beware of Luxury*, 1663?, Oil on canvas. (Kunsthistorisches Museum, Vienna.)

described by Norbert Elias did not only apply to court. Written for the education of a Burgundian prince, Erasmus's *De civilitate* was quickly adopted and imitated by the urban elites of the Netherlands because it fitted so well with the civility they had been striving for since the time of Hieronymus Bosch. Jordaens, and many other painters, are the heirs of this double tradition. Their success with prosperous city-dwellers all over Europe spread the messages involved, producing a 'bourgeois' state of mind, the traces of which can equally be found in the United Provinces. The denunciation of excess and the insistence on a real sense of bodily economy are expressed, for example, in a painting by Jan Steen, *Beware of Luxury* (1663?). Here, intemperance and licentiousness dominate as everyone pursues vain pleasures. Their gestures suggest insouciance, and the bodies of the characters deny the order which the manuals on civility instilled. But the proverb written on a slate at the lower right cautions to be careful at the very moment when one is having a good time. Above the joyous scene a basket containing sticks and swords makes clear that punishment is not far away (see figure 6.4).

It is difficult to conclude, as I have sketched a path of research rather than given a complete history of gestures in the modern period. Perhaps the best I can do at the moment is simply to stress the fact that there is a profusion of material: legal sources, manuals on civility, literature, religious tracts and genre painting, all of which offer a wealth of information. As for the period chosen here, it provides us with a good observation point, as it is a time of a slow but all-pervasive cultural bipolarization. Though devalued, gestures attached to a magical conception of the body do not always disappear completely but they do fall into an inevitable decline. In France, as in other countries, court circles and the bourgeoisie defined themselves more and more by a philosophy of the sacred, producing an 'economy' of gesture which was quite different from that of the peasants and the poor city-dwellers. The history of gesture, then, provides us with keys to interpret such phenomena which continue in our day.

## NOTES

1 Natalie Zemon Davis, Jean-Claude Carrière, Daniel Vigne, *Le Retour de Martin Guerre* (Paris, 1982), esp. p. 9.

2 Norbert Elias, *Über den Prozess der Zivilisation: Soziogenetische und psychogenetische Untersuchungen* (2 vols, Basel, 1939); see also the bibliography at the end of this volume.

3 C. G. Geertz, *The Interpretation of Cultures* (New York, 1973), pp. 412–53 ('Deep play. Notes on Balinese cockfight').

4 R. Muchembled, 'Pour une histoire des gestes (XVe–XVIIIe siècle)', *Revue d'histoire moderne et contemporaine*, 34 (1987), pp. 81–101; idem, *La violence au village: Sociabilité et comportements populaires en Artois du XVe au XVIIe siècle* (Turnhout, 1989), esp. pp. 143–60, 167–83, 247–68.

5 E. Goffman, *The Presentation of Self in Everyday Life* (New York, 1959) and *Interaction Ritual* (New York, 1967); E. T. Hall, *The Silent Language* (New York, 1959) and *The Hidden Dimension* (New York, 1969).

6 For examples see my works cited in note 4.

7 For a new initiative within the history of *mentalité*, see *Mentalités: Histoire des cultures et des sociétés*, edited by Robert Muchembled. No. 1: *Affaires de sang* (Paris, 1988); no. 2: *Injures et blasphèmes* (Paris, 1989); no. 3: *Violences sexuelles* (Paris,1989); no. 4: *Les marginaux* (Paris, 1990).

8 Muchembled, *La violence*, pp. 143–268.

9 Muchembled, *La violence*, pp. 253–60.

10 Muchembled, *La violence*, pp. 15–23; N. Z. Davis, *Fiction in the Archives* (Stanford, 1987).

11 For these various types of documentation see Muchembled, *L'invention de l'homme moderne* (Paris, 1988), p. 12.

12 See Elias, *Über den Prozess der Zivilisation*.

13 Muchembled, *L'invention*, esp. pp. 203–89.

14 This text is quoted by J.-L. Flandrin, *Les Amours paysannes (XVIe–XIXe siècle)* (Paris, 1975), pp. 121–2.

15 On this subject see Muchembled, 'Les "jeunes" et les groupes de jeunesse dans la société villageoise française (XVe–XVIe siècle)' in *Les Pouvoirs informels dans l'Eglise et la société du bas Moyen Age*, forthcoming.

16 Quoted by Flandrin, *Les Amours paysannes*, pp. 145–6.

17 A. van Gennep, *Manuel de folklore français contemporain* (Paris, 1943), vol. I, pp. 271–5.
18 'Le manuscrit du prieur de Sennely, 1700', *Mémoires de la société archéologique et historique de l'Orléanais*, 32 (1980), p. XI.
19 'Le manuscrit du prieur de Sennely, 1700'.
20 Elias, *Über den Prozess der Zivilisation* and *Die höfische Gesellschaft* (Neuwied, 1969).
21 Muchembled, *L'invention*, esp. pp. 230–89.
22 A. Combier, *Les Justices seigneuriales du baillage de Vermandois sous l'Ancien Régime* (Paris, n.d. [1897], p. 151.
23 J.-H. Bataillon, *Les Justices seigneuriales du baillage de Pontoise sous l'Ancien Régime* (Paris, 1942), p. 179.
24 Quoted by F. Lebrun, 'Le *Traité des superstitions* de Jean-Baptiste Thiers, contribution à l'ethnographie de la France du XVIIe siècle', *Annales de Bretagne et des pays de l'Ouest*, 83 (1976), esp. p. 454.
25 Jean-Baptiste Thiers, *Traité des superstitions: Croyances populaires et rationalité à l'Age classique*, ed. J.-M. Goulemot (Paris, 1984), p. 237.
26 Thiers, *Traité des superstitions*, pp. 239 and 180.
27 See the impressive study of Van Gennep, *Manuel de folklore*.
28 I quote from the French edition: Didier Erasme, *La Civilité puérile*, presenté par Philippe Ariès (Paris, 1977).
29 For more details see Muchembled, *L'invention*, pp. 239–89.
30 Quoted by G. Vincent, 'Normes et marges. De Poussin à David: une histoire cyclique?', *Mentalités*, 4 (1990), pp. 105–118, esp. p. 108.
31 On this portrait see Muchembled, *L'invention*, pp. 434–42.
32 Paul Vandenbroeck, *Jheronimus Bosch: tussen volksleven en stadscultuur* (Berchem-Antwerp, 1987).
33 Paul Vandenbroeck (ed.), *Over wilden en narren. Beeld van de andere, vertoog over het zelf* (Antwerp, 1987), pp. 149–51.

# 7

# The 'hand of friendship': shaking hands and other gestures in the Dutch Republic

## HERMAN ROODENBURG

'I think I can see the precise and distinguishing marks of national characters more in those nonsensical *minutiae* than in the most important matters of state'.
Laurence Sterne, *A Sentimental Journey*.

Among the many gestures we make each day, shaking hands is certainly the one taken most for granted. Because this popular greeting has been observed in numerous countries for many generations – at least in the Western world – we are easily apt to think that the handshake is among our most 'traditional' gestures.[1] But just how old is this greeting? In antiquity the handshake was widely known, though it was not the everyday gesture of greeting and leave-taking as we now know it.[2] Indeed, the same would seem to apply to early modern Europe. Foreign travellers in the Dutch Republic, for example, only recorded such salutations as bowing or taking off the hat; the handshake was not mentioned at all.[3] A remarkable event, which took place in 1612, confirms this picture. In that year a flaming row arose in one of Amsterdam's churches between Simon Episcopius, the future Remonstrant leader, and a couple of orthodox ministers. When Episcopius finally left the Church, he discovered to his anger that none of these ministers took the trouble of properly greeting him: 'there was no-one who raised his hat or hand.' Again, no mention of shaking hands.[4]

It is quite possible that, having collected these and other first-hand reports, we will not find a positive history but a negative one, a history of the anomalous, of refraining from particular salutations, and the affronts suffered by its victims. The Quakers, a Puritan sect that had most of its followers in England, Holland, and Pennsylvania, were even notorious for such behaviour. They deliberately violated the existing conventions of politeness, refusing to call someone 'your grace', when he was not in a state of grace, or to say 'your humble servant', when he was not their master at all. They even rejected the use of 'you' to a single individual, insisting instead on the more familiar or – in the presence of one's superiors – even insulting 'thou' and 'thee'. They also refrained from all the worldly gestures that accompany these modes of address, such as bowing, curtsying or taking off one's hat. Scorning all 'idle talk' and 'empty ritual', they took such conventions quite literally, thereby denying those phatic and ceremonial aspects of language and gesturing that have been stressed by sociologists, anthropologists, and sociolinguists alike. Of course, as historians we can only be grateful to the Quakers. Thanks to their 'rudeness', a fair number of first-hand reports on the daily gestures of greeting and leave-taking and the feelings and notions attached to them have been preserved. But it is once again remarkable that none of the gestures that were rejected by these men and women included our modern-day gesture of shaking hands.[5]

Are we to conclude from these few pointers that the handshake as a salutation was not even known in early modern Europe, that its history has been much shorter than we think? Before drawing such a conclusion it will be necessary to consider another source that, even if it says little about the handshake, will at least help us to establish the precise connotations of such gestures as bowing, doffing, or curtsying. I am referring to those many manuals on civility that, especially from the sixteenth century on, became so popular among the European elite. The wider connotations of these gestures are interesting because they were not isolated. They were directly related to notions of proper posture and usage. For centuries bowing, lifting the hat, and other gestures have been part of a whole 'science of conversing agreeably' – the actual subject of these manuals – by which the upper strata could distinguish themselves from the rest of the population. In other words, although the handshake may be absent from these treatises, we can at least deduce from these wider views on the body and its social meanings why it was not part of that 'science', and why it was not considered 'polite'. Being most at home with the history of the Dutch Republic, I have confined myself to the manuals published there.[6]

In addition to other material, I have made sparing use of pictorial evidence to support my argument. Using contemporary genre paintings can easily get a historian into trouble. Gerard Terborch's *The Suitor's Visit*, now in Washington, is a case in point (see figure 7.1). At first sight this wonderful painting seems to present a scene from polite society. We see a well-dressed man entering a room and making a bow to a young lady standing in front of him. A closer look at the painting, however, shows us that the woman makes a second gesture with her hands. We seem to recognize the 'fica', the obscene gesture in which the thumb is slipped between the index and the middle finger.[7] So, instead of an elegant scene we are apparently confronted with a very ambiguous scene in which all the details, including the elegant visitor, are put in another, rather mysterious light.[8]

## THE IMPACT OF THE MANUALS ON CIVILITY IN THE DUTCH REPUBLIC

Like other countries, the Dutch had their own traditions of *courtoisie* and *civilité*, especially in the seventeenth century as French manners became ever more popular among the Dutch elite. Unfortunately, the exact pace of this process is still a matter of debate. The famous manuals on civility, those of Castiglione, Erasmus, Della Casa, and De Courtin, were all translated into Dutch; the first edition of De Courtin's *Nouveau traité de la civilité* was even published in Amsterdam. But most of these translations were published after 1650. Before that time it was

**Figure 7.1** Gerard Terborch, *The Suitor's Visit, c.*1658.
(National Gallery of Art, Washington, Andrew W. Mellon Collection.)

mainly Erasmus's *De civilitate morum puerilium* that dominated
the market, though its actual reputation is difficult to assess.[9]
Other works, with the exception of Stefano Guazzo's *De civili
Conversatione* which found a translator in 1603, were not available
in Dutch during this period.[10] Even Castiglione's *Libro del
Cortegiano* was not translated until 1662.[11] Ten years later, in 1672
(a year after the original French edition), the first translation of De
Courtin's *Traité* was published in Amsterdam. Both the original
text and its translation were quite popular in the Republic. In 1675

and 1733 two other Dutch editions appeared, the latter undergoing three additional printings.[12] In 1715, Giovanni della Casa's *Galateo* was translated.[13] Finally, in 1735, a completely Dutch manual by C. van Laar was published, the first since Erasmus's little treatise. It was called the *Groot ceremonie-boek der beschaafde zeeden*. Remarkably enough, this book has gone unnoticed by Dutch historians, despite the fact that it has over 500 pages and was heavily influenced by De Courtin.[14]

It seems then that from the middle of the seventeenth century onwards Dutch, French, and Italian manuals on civility were fairly popular in the Dutch Republic. But what about the last decades of the sixteenth and the first half of the seventeenth centuries? It is difficult to believe that the Dutch at that time were hardly interested in any *courtoisie* or *civilité*, let alone that their manners were still as 'plain' and 'unfeigned' as Erasmus described them jokingly in his *Praise of Folly* of 1509.[15] Still, in 1651, Jean de Parival, the professor of French at Leiden University, concluded that the Dutch had long been notorious for their rude manners, but lately had become known for their refinement.[16] De Parival's comment seems to coincide nicely with the increased interest in the manuals on civility around the middle of the seventeenth century. However, already in the 1590s an English traveller, Fynes Moryson, had observed almost the same thing among the inhabitants of the province of Holland: 'In manners they were of old rude and are so to this day in some measure, and the Hollanders have of old beene vulgary called plumpe, that is blunt or rude. Yet since their last long warr they are much refyned in manners by their conversation . . . '[17] It is certainly risky to adopt such verdicts. Most travellers had at best an incomplete knowledge of the Dutch language and customs. Indeed, some of them just repeated the impressions of other travellers. Besides, the English often made the same comments about the French, the French about the English, and the Spanish about the French. Before using sources like these, we should always look at the wider context of such pronouncements.[18]

Actually, the Dutch upper classes had already adopted many of the foreign fashions and manners long before the manuals found a larger audience. In the late sixteenth and early seventeenth centuries they were clearly impressed by the more ostentatious lifestyle of the Flemish and Brabantine refugees who after the Fall of Antwerp in 1585 had fled in such large numbers to the north. Among them were the wealthiest families from Antwerp. Poets and playwrights, such as Roemer Visscher or Gerbrand Adriaensz. Bredero, scoffed heartily at the *courtoisie* of all these immigrants with their showy clothes and polished speech peppered with French words. But they also poked fun at many men and women who tried to imitate the refugees; evidently, the new lifestyle had caught on. Indeed, in 1615 one of Amsterdam's Calvinist ministers admonished his parishioners for blaming their worldliness on the Flemish, as they themselves had been all too eager to adopt these latest fashions.[19] In 1625 two ministers even reported that they had spotted the first mannequins in town.[20] By that time it was probably no longer the *courtoisie* of the wealthy Flemish families but more and more the fashions followed at the courts in the Hague or even Paris that worried them. It seems likely that after 1620 the wealth and manners of the refugees had been more or less accepted. For example, Rosette, a light-hearted character in Jacob Cats's extremely popular treatise on marriage, modelled herself on the manners and clothes then fashionable at the court in The Hague.[21] Apparently, in trying to secure itself a place among the other European courts, the stadholder's court had already developed sufficient standing to be alluring to young, worldly women such as Rosette.

Thus many of the new rules on civility must have reached the Dutch upper strata, not through the manners books but through other, largely oral channels – for example by making the Grand Tour,[22] by instruction at the fashionable 'French schools',[23] or by instruction by tutors and dancing-masters (dancing was held to be highly beneficial to a proper posture[24]) and, of course, one's parents. Direct influences from the court at The Hague were probably limited, though in its diplomacy (in which many of the city oligarchies were represented), it covered a wider range than merely court life itself.

## POSTURE, GESTURE AND CIVILITY

As Samuel Johnson once observed, 'all works which describe manners, require notes in sixty or seventy years, or less'.[25] If it was already difficult for contemporaries to grasp the precise meaning of the rules that were pertinent a few generations ago, then such problems certainly apply to us. Some fifty years ago, on the basis of these works, Norbert Elias reconstructed a centuries-old European 'process of civilization'. From the thirteenth century onwards the rules of etiquette changed continually. After originating among the highest nobility the new codes would diffuse themselves: first, among the middle classes from the sixteenth century onwards; then among the lower classes from the nineteenth century onwards. In the course of this process the essential activities of life became more and more stylized or were even pushed back from the 'stage' (public life) 'into the wings'.[26]

The manuals certainly provide us with a mine of information concerning such activities. Besides rules about urinating, defecating, or hiding one's nudity, they established other rules about blowing the nose, sneezing, coughing or spitting, in short, all those activities which 'we share with the animals' as De Courtin explained. It seems to me, however, that the bodily control propounded by the manuals went much further and that Elias discussed only one aspect of these treatises. Generally speaking, they established codes of behaviour, if only among the elite, for all sorts of 'relations in public'.[27] In fact, the insights and explanations set forth in these books constitute an early, though already highly accomplished, example of the study of 'non-verbal communication'. Thus many of the treatises deal at length with phenomena such as gestures, facial expression, or even 'paralingual phenomena' (the pitch or intensity of the voice, etc.). Attention to such details, so readers were told, was a prerequisite for the 'science of conversing agreeably' – one 'faux pas', one 'gaffe', was enough to break a man's career. The manuals are indeed teeming with all the larger and smaller social mistakes that were analysed so carefully by Erving Goffman.[28]

Control of one's every movement, even of the eye, was obviously the first thing one had to learn. The rules given were surprisingly consistent. Erasmus, for example, urged his readers always to keep their bodies erect; they should not lean backwards (a sign of conceit), nor let their head hang to one side or the other, or gesticulate too wildly. When standing, they should keep their feet firmly together; when walking, they should not stagger, nor go too slowly or too quickly; and as for sitting, it was improper to sit with arms akimbo (a very military thing to do), and unseemly to hold the knees apart, to keep the legs crossed, or to play with one's feet.[29] Such advice about proper posture would hardly change at all. In a way De Courtin's treatise was very different, as the 'science of conversing agreeably' had been greatly developed by his time. His manual now dealt with a host of awkward situations and was thus much larger and far more detailed than Erasmus's little treatise had been.[30] But that does not alter the fact that the author propounded a similar control of one's body. When standing, walking, or sitting a well-mannered person had to observe a certain 'measure and consonance', as De Courtin explained. Composure, a calm and erect posture, were strongly recommended. All in all, the rules remind us of Balzac's aphorism 'Le mouvement lent est essentiellement majestueux' or Nietzsche's observations on 'Was ist vornehm?': 'die langsame Gebärde, auch der langsame Blick'.[31] Of course, some people swayed their heads, rolled their eyes or waved their hands as if swatting flies, but all such behaviour was 'against civility'. Again, when walking in the street one should not go too quickly so as to gasp for breath, nor too slowly, or walk 'as a woman or a bride' (meaning, perhaps, with downcast eyes). One also had to distinguish oneself from those bad-mannered people who swung their arms or legs 'as if they would like to sow' or raised their feet 'as if continually lifting them out of a tub'. Finally, when sitting, one should not be agitated, fumble with one's clothes, or cross the legs.[32] It is indeed striking how all these rules resemble those in ancient Greece and Rome. To give just one example, Erasmus's and especially De Courtin's exhortations not to walk too slowly or too quickly are almost identical to those given by Cicero in his *De officiis*.[33]

The new conventions, especially those on proper posture, were probably widespread among the Dutch elite. We only have to think of the way peasants, beggars, and other 'simple folk' were portrayed in the paintings of Adriaen Brouwer, Adriaen van Ostade, and their many predecessors and contemporaries. We find no erect postures there. On the contrary, most of the figures are stocky and hunchbacked, their heads twisted to one side or the other. Of course, all these paintings, just like the seventeenth-century *kluchten*, offer a caricature of lower-class life. They depict the exact opposite of life among the upper urban classes, in which one's *courtoisie* or *civilité* was manifested first and foremost in one's comportment and gestures.[34] A proper posture was very important. In 1632 the famous poet and statesman, Constantijn Huygens, noticed much to his alarm that the head of his eldest son, Constantijn Jun. (for whom he had ambitious plans) inclined a bit to the left. Unfortunately, remedies such as a stiff collar, ribbons attached to his bonnet, or a treatment of steaming his neck were to no avail. Having seriously thought of taking his son to a certain peasant, probably a notorious bonesetter, the father finally decided for a university-trained physician from the city of Utrecht. This doctor made a gash of two inches long in the poor boy's neck, separating (according to his own report) the many entangled sinews there and greasing the whole machinery with some oil. To the parents's relief the operation was a great success. Indeed, being rid of this ailment, Constantijn went on to have a brilliant career as the personal secretary to Prince William III, the future king of England.[35]

What was actually developed in all the manuals was a growing discipline over one's own body, a growing self-control that would finally distinguish Dutch and other northern manners from Mediterranean, and especially Italian, codes of conduct. To the seventeenth- and eighteenth-century Dutch the difference was already clear. In the *Groot ceremonie-boeck*, the Italians 'who speak with their head, arms, feet and the whole body' were simply depicted as the antithesis of all civility. As the author explains, using a devoted 'instructor' as his mouthpiece, the French, the English, and the Dutch now rejected such strong movements. When speaking, the Dutch merely used the eye and 'a moderate movement of the hand to support [their] words'. Because of their lively gesticulation the Italians were put on a par with peasants or, even worse, the 'moffen' or Westphalians, the immigrants the Dutch loved to ridicule.[36]

We also find another distinction. In general, as the *Groot ceremonie-boeck* argued, the comportment of the body should be 'without affectation . . . erect, without stiffness or constraint, free and easy in its natural gestures'. Indeed, when walking, one should place one's feet 'in such a way that the edifice of the body will rest well on them', as the gait should be 'well-ordered, without

swaying the body to and fro' or, as the writer continued, 'keeping
it fixed in the Spanish way, as if not daring to turn one's head'.[37]
This last remark, an obvious reference to the Spanish 'gravity' in
manners, is interesting. In the 1650s some comparable observations
were made by a Dutch traveller, François Aerssen van Sommelsdijck,
on his travels through Italy and Spain. In the latter country he
observed the 'gravité naturelle ou affectée' that was especially
cherished at court, though he had found the same behaviour ('fort
rogue et fort fière') among all Spaniards. It was a solemnity that he
had not seen among the gesticulating Italians, except for the
Spanish-oriented aristocracy in Genoa.[38] Before, in his *Spanish
Brabanter* of 1617, Bredero had already ridiculed the 'pride' and
'gravity' of Jerolimo, the hero of his play.[39] Moreover, in the
streets of Amsterdam and other Dutch cities, the wealthy
Sephardim, who had fled the Iberian peninsula, must have
displayed their 'gravidade'.[40] In other words, like their English
contemporaries mentioned in Peter Burke's contribution to this
volume, the Dutch were probably quite aware of the gestural
cultures of other countries, making a sharp distinction between the
proud and haughty style of the Spaniards and the more exuberant
Italian style, the latter developing after the pioneering works of
Castiglione and Della Casa had already made their mark on
France, England, and the Dutch Republic.[41]

Elaborating a bit further on our critique of Elias and borrowing
a few basic distinctions made within the study of non-verbal communication, we could even say that the rules of civility, this whole
science of making oneself 'agreeable', had two important applica-
tions: first, how to avoid 'non-verbal leakage' and thereby betray
oneself, and second, how to avoid intruding upon another's
'personal' or 'social space'. Of course, one's verbal assertions and
the gestures that support them were the most important means of
making oneself 'agreeable'. As they could be easily controlled, the
manuals provided a host of instructions about how to accomplish
this. Much more difficult, however, was a person's unintentional
communication: one's posture or gait, or one's unintentional
gestures during a conversation. As Erasmus, De Courtin, and Van
Laar argued, this was precisely the part of a person's appearance
others would search for even the tiniest clue if they did not wholly
trust what he or she was conveying with words and with intended

gestures. In fact, they urged their readers not only to take heed of the 'expression they gave' but also of the 'expression they gave off', to borrow this phrase from Erving Goffman.[42] Erasmus, for example, cautioned that coughing while speaking was 'a gesture of those who lie' (*is gestus est mentientium*).[43] De Courtin pointed to such 'giveaways' as scratching the body or fumbling with one's hat, buttons, or gloves.[44] More mysterious is the admonition not to cross the legs while sitting and conversing.[45] Probably such asymmetry in the positioning of the limbs was seen as a sign of relaxation and thus of a certain carelessness, if not indifference, towards the other person.[46] We can find such carelessness, mixed with plenty of bravado, in the portrait of Willem van Heijthuysen, attributed to Frans Hals and now in Brussels. We see the man rocking on a chair, his legs crossed, holding a whip in his hands. Of course, our attention is also drawn to his prominent elbow (see figure 7.2). All these details were essential to portraiture. In his influential treatise on the art of painting Giovanni Paolo Lomazzo mentioned many of them, including the advice not to paint a high-born person with his legs crossed. For more information he referred the reader to Della Casa's *Galateo*.[47]

A second application of the 'science of conversing agreeably' was to avoid intruding into another's 'personal space'. Doing such, the treatises explained, will make the other person feel encroached upon. In fact, it was mostly here that the feelings of embarrassment and shame, analysed by Norbert Elias, came in.[48] Of course, a certain physical distance had to be observed. Touching a person, especially one who was of a higher rank than oneself, could be very embarrassing indeed. To grab an elevated person's buttons, sleeves, or coat while talking to him was considered a very serious slip. Another intrusion was kissing a woman of higher rank without her permission to do so. And even when she did offer her cheek, one should only fake the gesture without really touching her face.[49] Staring was deemed unseemly as well. Gazing at someone with one eye closed, as Erasmus explained, was quite discourteous; later, in the works of De Courtin and Van Laar, the rules were more subtle. The difficulties of being seated in a formal situation were another problem that might arise. When urged to be seated by someone of higher rank, one had to take a seat right opposite this person, but to look this man or woman straight in the eye after having done so

**Figure 7.2** Frans Hals, *Willem van Heijthuysen*, *c*.1637–9.
(Koninklijk Museum voor Schone Kunsten, Brussels.)

was seen as a serious lack of respect. It was better to sit sideways, with the head slightly tilted; one's gaze had to be modest and demure.[50] Speaking loudly, demanding as it were more space for oneself and speaking up to prominent persons, was understood as a similar violation of personal space.[51] The strongest feelings of embarrassment and shame, however, were evoked by bodily excreta. The manuals dealt at length with contemporary feelings on coughing, spitting, eating, urinating, and defecating, but they also noted minor annoyances such as bad breath or a disagreeable body odour.[52]

## THE ART OF GREETING

Respecting the personal space of one's superiors was very important. In fact, the manuals devote a great deal of attention to the delicate actions of doffing one's hat, kissing a person's hand, curtsying or giving the right of way. Behaving courteously, showing *heusheidt* or *wellevendheidt*, had become quite complicated since the times of Erasmus, based as it was on a host of hidden codes and implicit expectations which demanded from every 'civilized' man or woman a thorough knowledge of the rules and, moreover, a subtle and continuous appeal to their intuition. Readers of *Madame Bovary* will remember how Emma's father, the old Rouault, urged his future son-in-law to keep his hat on while in his house. By doing so he showed his respect for Charles Bovary as Charles himself, by taking off his hat each time he entered the house, expressed his esteem for the father of his future bride. Such intricate ritual was long-standing. We find it explained as early as the seventeenth century in De Courtin and, having become even more intricate, in the *Groot ceremonie-boeck*.

When entering the house of someone of higher rank one should always doff the hat, De Courtin explained. On being received by this person one had to make a deep bow, while taking the hat in the left hand and staying left of the other person so that he could keep his right hand free. Of course, this man (or woman) could always urge his visitor to cover his head again, but doing so without his special request would be quite discourteous. And even then, when this person had to sneeze, one had to bare one's head immediately. Moreover, to make things even more complex both De Courtin and Van Laar deemed it proper to doff the hat a second time even if one was invited to keep it on. If this was followed by another request then one simply had to obey.[53] Of course, asking one's superiors to do so was completely wrong.[54]

**Figure 7.3** Rembrandt van Rijn, *The Syndics of the Amsterdam Drapers' Guild*, 1661. (© Rijksmuseum-Stichting, Amsterdam.)

In his *Meaning in the Visual Arts*, the art historian Erwin Panofsky has drawn our attention to the problems of interpretation evoked by such a simple gesture as lifting the hat.[55] Surprisingly, in discussing this he did not use any pictorial evidence just as other art historians seem to have neglected such gestures in Dutch seventeenth-century painting.[56] Yet, the conventions behind such conduct, with its emphasis on deference to rank, can surely enlarge our understanding of these paintings. Rembrandt's *The Syndics of the Amsterdam Drapers' Guild* (see figure 7.3) is a case in point, as each of the men portrayed wears a hat except the servant Frans Hendricksz. Bel.[57] Likewise, in Rembrandt's *The Anatomy Lesson of Dr Nicolaes Tulp* (see figure 7.4), the famous physician and future burgomaster is the only person whose head is covered; all the surgeons have removed their headgear as an obvious token of respect.

Women had their own special ways of showing deference. They curtsyed and made other gestures, but they were also supposed to bare their heads in the company of their superiors. On entering the house of a high-born man or woman they had to take off their caps, unless these were merely adornments for their hair such as the fine-meshed caps then fashionable. Women also had their masks; we can still see them in the skating scenes painted by Hendrick Avercamp (see figure 7.5). In fact, it would have been strange if masks had not been there as they were intended above all to protect a lady's skin against a burning sun or a bitter wind. The manuals stipulated that a well-mannered woman should take her mask off in front of someone of higher rank. Nor was she allowed to put it on in this person's company unless expressly asked to do so.[58]

These complicated rules were made even more complex, because persons of higher rank needed more 'personal space' than others. At court, one was advised to doff one's hat even when a servant went by carrying the monarch's food. The same gesture was required in front of a royal portrait, or even when reading a letter coming from his majesty. In other, more concrete situations, the monarch, like every person of higher rank, had the right of 'precedence': the 'right hand' or *hogerhand* as it was termed in Dutch. In other words, one had to keep left of this man or woman, walking one step behind them. But spaces also had their 'right' and

**Figure 7.4** Rembrandt van Rijn, *The Anatomy Lesson of Dr Nicolaes Tulp*, 1632. (Maurishuis, The Hague.)

**Figure 7.5** Hendrick Avercamp, *Skating Scene near a Town Resembling Kampen and Utrecht* (detail), *c.*1610. (Amsterdam, Private Collection.)

'left hand', their *hogerhand* and *lagerhand*. Locating these spaces was relatively simple indoors: the left hand was usually where one had entered the room. But where was it in the streets? Normally, when walking one had to pass a prominent person on his left. But if the street had a gutter, then the left hand was always there, regardless of the other's position. However, if a wall ran along the street, then the left hand was not there, but on the other side. In other words, one had to give this person 'the wall'.[59]

It is striking that these last details were only mentioned in De Courtin's original text and not in the Dutch translation that was published only one year afterwards. In general, the Dutch rules were probably less strict than those in France. Rank and station were certainly valued in the Republic but modern historians agree that the differences between, for example, elite and popular culture were significantly smaller than elsewhere in early modern Europe. Simon Schama even dismissed the whole distinction and replaced it with a *brede middenstand*, a broad middle class 'which could include anyone from skilled artisans, members of a guild and earning more than ten stuivers a day . . . all the way up to the magnates of commerce, industry and finance, who would have disdained being classified as aristocrats.'[60] The author may have stretched his point, but the difference from other countries was certainly there. Foreigners often observed that the Dutch loved equality (a label they hardly applied to other European people), and the Dutch themselves agreed. In 1603, Gomes van Trier, the Flemish native who translated Guazzo's *De civili conversatione*, concluded that the Dutch were not interested in civility, one of the obstacles being 'that very great misunderstanding of some, who (under the appearance of humble people) want to promote equality here in this world'.[61] More than a hundred years later, in the 1730s, the author Justus van Effen likewise hinted at the Dutch love for equality, judging that all this consciousness of rank and station that went along with the rules of civility was more natural with strongly hierarchic states than with a 'common-wealth' (meaning his own country), 'where in a certain way all the inhabitants might be seen as each other's equals'.[62] Both observations are interesting because they make us aware of a crucial aspect of the manuals: their strengthening and crystallizing of social hierarchy, engraving its codes even on the body, on its comportment and gestures.

But even if the rules of *courtoisie* and *civilité* were toned down in the Republic, the major rules were certainly known. Of course, among the lower classes showing deference, lifting one's hat to superiors etc., was only natural.[63] Unfortunately, it is far more difficult to find out to what extent the minor rules were known. In Dutch diplomacy they were often observed. Indeed, the resemblance between the 'pointilles' cherished in these circles and the rules that were later expounded by De Courtin and Van Laar is really remarkable. Hat-honour, giving the right of way, and all the other codes were vital within international relations because the rank and honour rendered to an envoy were rendered first and foremost to his monarch and his country. Even modest gestures, such as lifting the hat, reflected a delicate and far from static order in which the French and English kings held the higher and the German electors the lower positions. Within this balance of power the Dutch would soon claim a position immediately after the Venetian Republic. That was certainly a position of distinction, as Venice itself held the last position in the line of European kingdoms.[64]

However, only in 1650 would the Estates-General finally capture the position they had been striving for. In that year Louis XIV rendered the new Dutch ambassador, Willem Boreel, the same honour that he had rendered thus far only to the Venetian Republic. Of course, in entering the hall where he was received in audience, Boreel had to doff his hat and bow three times in approaching the king; that was standard procedure. But at the third bow Louis had taken his headgear off and had asked Boreel, who had covered himself again, to follow his example. All this had happened even before Boreel had presented his credentials and started to deliver his solemn speech on behalf of the Estates-General. The whole event was a victory for Dutch diplomacy.[65] Still, in the years before the Estates-General had been less successful. Clearly afraid of receiving too little honour, they had repeatedly instructed their envoys to cover their heads even if the monarch did not request it. Yet in order to avoid an awkward situation they had to doff their hats again at the first possible opportunity.[66] It is this uncertainty and compromising within the bounds of possibility that remind us immediately of the complicated ritual expounded in the manuals. We find the same similarities in giving the right of way, in offering and taking seats, bearing in mind the 'right' and 'left hand', etc. Indeed, such considerations were crucial to the Munster negotiations in 1648 as they were to each international contact, whether audiences, visits, banquets, or other diplomatic meetings.[67]

Clearly, De Courtin, Van Laar and all the other authors of seventeenth- and eighteenth-century manners books took much of their knowledge from diplomatic circles. It also seems likely that even the Dutch upper classes adopted many of these minor rules.[68] There certainly was a relaxing of the rules, as is revealed by the cuts made by De Courtin's translator. But it is striking that contemporary jokes and anecdotes were only aimed at too much 'punctilio', at those men and women who always stood on their authority.[69] We also know that young men such as François van Aerssen, who made their Grand Tour through Europe, knew exactly how to value the honours rendered to them when received at court.[70] And we saw how rich patricians such as Nicolaes Tulp ordered paintings in which the codes of 'hat-honour' were strictly followed.[71] Even in circles where an outsider would have expected a different, more egalitarian style, the rules had made their mark. John Locke was clearly surprised that even the Labadists, a Protestant sect, bowed to each other or took their hats off when meeting a fellow member.[72] Was it perhaps another gesture, for example the handshake, that Locke had expected in these circles? It is certainly remarkable that among all the gestures and postures laid down in the manuals this one gesture was never mentioned. It is missing from the texts and from the illustrated title page of De Courtin's *Nouveau traité*. There we see a couple of figures bowing, doffing the hat or kissing a lady's hand, but no one is shaking anyone else's hand.

SHAKING HANDS

If the handshake was omitted from the early modern 'manners books', if this gesture did not fit in with the strengthening of rank and station that went along with the new rules of *courtoisie* and *civilité*, then we have to look elsewhere, in other situations – for example in the neighbourhoods of seventeenth-century towns where the gesture was definitely known, though in a very different sense.

Surprisingly, though community studies have proliferated in recent years only a few have been undertaken on neighbourhoods in the early modern town. In fact, Richard Cobb, writing on the neighbourhoods in eighteenth-century Paris (which he characterizes as 'urban villages'), has been one of the exceptions. It is probably the widespread theory that urbanization can only lead to a corrosion of social bonds and all traditional values of the countryside that has been responsible for this neglect. But it seems quite likely that this process has been less destructive, or at least less cogent, than historians have so far assumed. An interesting book by David Garrioch on the same Paris quarters studied by Cobb suggests a more opaque development. And the same seems to hold true for such neighbourhoods in the seventeenth-century Republic.[73]

Obviously, life in these neighbourhoods was quite intense. Rites of passage such as baptism, marriage, and funerals were the outstanding occasions where all the neighbours were invited for a communal meal, a custom in every town. In some of them we also find the so-called *jonkmalen*, occasions where the local youth would gather, or the *buurmalen*, organized once a year or every two or three years by the *buurt-* or *wijkmeester*, where all the inhabitants of a particular neighbourhood would gather. Neighbourhoods probably comprised no more than a couple of streets, side-streets, and alleys. In 1795, for example, The Hague had 71 neighbourhoods and Leiden 135. Most striking in the regulations issued by such quarters is the desire to promote the 'good peace and civil unity' (the *goede vrede ende burgerlijcke eenigheyt*) or the 'continuation of good neighbourliness and extension of friendship' (the *continuatie van goede buurschap ende vermeerderinge van vrientschap*) among the inhabitants.[74]

The *buurtmeesters* or neighbourhood officials were a familiar sight and were described by, among others, Jean de Parival. In his book, he mentions 'une certaine coustume' in Dutch towns, 'qui a pour but, la paix, amitié, et concorde'. He explains how the towns were divided into 'plusieurs voisinages', and how each of these quarters had its own 'maitre', supported by several 'conseillers'. He continues, 's'il arrive quelque different, les parties comparoissent devant ledit maitre qui tasche de les mettre d'accord'. Apparently, Dutch neighbourhood officials could act as arbitrators in disputes. What De Parival stumbled upon was, in fact, one of those 'extrajudicial' institutions described by Bruce Lenman and Geoffrey Parker: semi-official institutions where people could settle their conflicts without having to appeal to an official court of justice.[75] De Parival then goes on to say that if the 'maitre' had failed to reconcile both parties they could appeal to the twice-weekly sittings of the 'commissaires . . . constituez pour entendre les plaintes et pacifier les parties'. It was only after these commissioners were likewise unsuccessful that the parties were allowed to take the official course of justice. What interests us most, however, is the way in which these disputes were settled before the neighbourhood officials: that is, the precise way in which amends were made for the affronts and injurious words that had been suffered by one of the parties. According to De Parival such reconciliations were reached by a recantation and confession by the person who had been in the wrong, 'par celuy qui a blessé la reputation de l'autre, en disant qu'il le tient pour honneste homme et que la parolle a esté laschée par colere.' He then concludes: 'alors ils se donnent la main'.[76] An English traveller who copied De Parival's text word for word put it even more strongly: 'then they shake hands, and are made friends'.[77]

De Parival was probably writing about such reconciliatory rituals in Leiden where he was professor, or possibly those in The Hague and Haarlem where the neighbourhood officials fulfilled a similar function. Amsterdam also had its *buurtmeesters*, but there they seem to have had other responsibilities such as overseeing the poor. Leafing through the records of the Calvinist church, however, we come across numerous cases in which the handshake equally served as a confirmation, a seal of reconciliation. In cases where someone had been involved in a lengthy dispute or had scolded another church member or had slapped him in the face, the Amsterdam Calvinist consistory always tried to reconcile both parties. Problems such as marital discord and even separations of bed and board, seen by both Church and State as only a temporary parting, were dealt with in the same way. In all these cases the parties were summoned before the ministers and elders and, in the imposing ambience of the consistory, pressured to settle their dispute. The procedure was very similar to that employed by the neighbourhood officials. The party that had been most in the wrong would confess his fault and declare that he knew the other to be an 'honest' person. Finally he would ask the other party for forgiveness. Many of these reconciliations did not go smoothly as both parties often muttered all sorts of accusations. Still, most cases were finally concluded with formal reconciliation in which both parties gave each other the *hand van vriendschap* ('the hand of friendship'), the *hand van broederschap* ('the hand of brotherhood'), or sometimes even the *vredekus* ('the kiss of peace'), a simple but telling ritual that was accompanied by a firm exhortation to burn all discord in the fire of love.[78] Year after year the Amsterdam consistory dealt with numerous cases in which such *hantgevinghe* or *hanttastinghe* finally sealed the peace between both parties. Probably such reconciliations were standard routine for all consistories, whether Calvinist, Lutheran, or Mennonite.

It seems, then, that in the sixteenth and seventeenth centuries and probably for a good deal of the eighteenth century, shaking hands had a very different meaning from the ritual act we know today. It looks as if the gesture was not part of any greeting or parting behaviour at all but that it had quite different connotations which centred around such concepts as friendship, brotherhood, peace, reconciliation, accord, or mutual agreement. Seen from this perspective other situations in which the handshake was widely used easily spring to mind, for example the judicial discharge *onder handtastinge*, a discharge from prosecution whereby the defendant committed himself to appear at all times in court.[79] The still popular gesture of slapping hands to seal a business transaction is another example. The brokers at the Amsterdam stock exchange were even notorious for their 'manic display of wild and speedy hand slapping', but the same gesture could probably be noticed at every market whether in the city or the countryside. We can still recognize such hand slapping in one of Sebastiaen Vrancx's paintings of Antwerp.[80] Turning to other pictorial evidence, we can also point to the famous emblem of the Beggars: two hands clasped together, hung with a beggar's cup, denoting the league made between those Dutch nobles who had adopted the term of abuse bestowed on them by vice-queen Margaretha of Parma as an honorary title.[81] We find another clasping of the hands in Van der

Helst's painting of the Amsterdam St George guard celebrating the Peace of Munster in 1648 (see figure 7.6). We recognize the captain, Cornelis Jansz. Witsen, holding the silver drinking horn of the guard and shaking hands with his lieutenant, Johan Oetgens van Waveren. As the poem tucked under the snare of the drum

**Figure 7.6** Bartholomeus van der Helst, *The Celebration of the Peace of Munster, 18 June 1648, in the Headquarters of the Crossbowmen's Civic Guard, (St George's Guard), Amsterdam* (detail), 1648. (© Rijksmuseum-Stichting, Amsterdam.)

suggests, the captain offers his lieutenant 'the horn of peace'.[82] Even more telling are the handshakes depicted in the sometimes stately, sometimes quite informal marriage portraits of the period. In his catalogue *Portretten van echt en trouw* De Jongh selected a number of paintings in which man and wife (as well as engaged couples) extend a hand to one another. Sometimes they offer the right hand and sometimes the left. The meaning of the gesture, especially of the *dextrarum iunctio* in the marriage portraits, is easy to interpret. Then, as now, the gesture was used in all wedding ceremonies as a sacral and legal sign (as it was in antiquity) of the *consensus ad idem* between man and wife.[83]

### HIERARCHY AND EQUALITY

It seems quite likely, then, that one of our most popular salutations was still unknown before 1800. The gesture itself was certainly known but it had a different meaning from the present one. Indeed it was only in the nineteenth century, for example in a French manual of 1858, that the handshake was finally included in the official etiquette of the elite though the gesture was still deemed improper, at least outside the sphere of friendship. As its author, the Baronesse de Fresne, makes clear, 'Ne donnez votre main qu'à vos amis, et ne l'offrez jamais a un supérieur'. Such a gesture 'est de bien mauvais ton et peut vous exposer à recevoir un affront.'[84]

The baronesse's observation is interesting because two centuries earlier the Quakers had made a comparable distinction between friendship and the rules of civility. In his famous history of the sect, William Sewell explained that the Quakers declined the 'common fashion of greeting' such as baring their heads and other gestures of deference. Instead, they deemed it 'more agreeable with Christian simplicity to greet one another by giving their hand'. In the Quakers' view these and other 'innocent' gestures were 'signs of friendship and respect, that may be shewed, without giving to man that which appertains to God . . .'. For the Quakers this particular gesture connoted friendship and brotherhood, just as they addressed each other as 'friends' thereby eliminating all hierarchy and class distinctions among themselves.[85]

What these two examples seem to suggest is that the handshake as a salutation somehow originated with the Quakers and then spread from this highly closed and egalitarian community to other sections of society as a popular way to greet one's equals or friends. But we must be careful here. More than in any other field, that of the study of gesture is one in which the historian has to make the most of only a few clues. Still it is probably safe to say that our modern handshake first became known in England before it spread itself to other countries. The developments in England and France were certainly different. To the French in the first half of the nineteenth century the handshake was something new, a gesture that recently had come across the Channel. For example, when Leon Dupuis pays his farewell visit to Emma Bovary and then merely shakes hands with her, she exclaims 'A l'anglaise donc'.[86] Again, in Eugène Sue's *Mystères de Paris* Madame de Lucenay only receives a 'shake-hands' from a young cousin of hers, the Duke de Montbrison: 'Çelui-ci allait donner un shake-hands à sa cousine'.[87] Both ladies, expecting a kiss on the hand, were clearly surprised by this more informal gesture. To French and other continental travellers visiting England, the same, rather egalitarian gesture must have been construed as typically English. It was certainly so to Casanova who in his *Mémoires*, written in the last decade of the eighteenth century, chose the phrase 'shake-hand amical' in describing a meeting with one of his London acquaintances.[88] Part of the difference between England and France may have been caused by a steady process of informalization leading eventually to the rise of 'sentimentalism' with Laurence Sterne as its foremost exponent.[89] Much of his *Sentimental Journey* reads as a mockery of all French 'politesse'. In other words, if the sixteenth and seventeenth centuries saw a strengthening of social hierarchy resulting in a growing discipline over one's own body and an increasing formality in manners, then we should also reckon with the possibility of a subsequent softening of this very same process, in which the more informal gesture of shaking hands was spread.

Much later, Turgenev, in his *Fathers and Sons*, set in 1859, had the Anglophile Pavel Petrovich 'shake hands' in the European manner with his hero Bazarow. So, perhaps the gesture spread from England and France to Russia.[90] By 1919 the handshake had even reached the imperial court of China. Those who have seen Bertolucci's *The Last Emperor* will recall how the young emperor

178 *Herman Roodenburg*

responds to the ceremonial bow proffered by his first Western tutor, the Scotsman Reginald Fleming Johnston, by descending from the throne to shake hands. Later the significance of the gesture was noted both by the tutor and by the ex-emperor himself in his autobiography. To them it was clearly a gesture of equality and friendship.[91]

The hypothesis that the Quakers were the first to introduce our present handshake, that its history stems only from the seventeenth century, is more difficult to support. The history of the handshake is not as surprising as that. For example, in a manners book published in 1607, the English author James Cleland rejected all those 'French' and 'apish toies of bowing downe to everie mans shoe' in favour of 'our good olde Scottish shaking of the two right hands togither at meeting with an uncovered head'. He further added, 'I think that an handful of our old friendship is worth a whole armeful now.'[92] Indeed, it is not unlikely that the handshake as a salutation was widely known in Europe before the new fashions of bowing and other formal gestures spread from France, Italy, and Spain. Translating the scene where Frère Jean des Entommeures is received by Gargantua and his friends, Johann Schiffart (1540–90) wrote: 'da war nichts als alle frewd, viel tausent will-komm, viel hundert guter Tag, Säck voll Grüsz, ein solch Handgebens, Hänschlagens, Händeruckens'.[93] Surprisingly, the original did not mention anyone shaking hands at all: 'mille charesses, mille embrassemens, mille bons jours feurent donnez'.[94] If Schiffart adapted this passage to the customs and manners of his countrymen, as he did with so many other of Rabelais's passages, then the Germans, like the English, must have known the handshake long before the Quakers. In fact, Maria Bogucka's contribution to this volume (see pp. 192 and 195) suggests that the same gesture was also known in sixteenth-century Poland.

Shaking hands, then, has been rightly called a 'traditional' gesture; it clearly goes back to the sixteenth century at least. But its history is far from linear; from that century on an intriguing development ensured. The gesture was gradually displaced by more hierarchic ways of greeting or taking leave and even became a polemical instrument in the hands of the Quakers against all deference and worldly vanity. Then, as manners were relaxed, the handshake became popular again: first in England and probably also in the Dutch Republic, spreading later to France and later still to Russia. Viewed from that perspective, shaking hands and other 'nonsensical minutiae' were indeed as important as matters of state. In diplomatic circles they even *were* matters of state. More generally, we may conclude that the body reflected even in its smallest gestures the value that society, this other body, attached to matters of hierarchy or equality.

## NOTES

I would like to thank Rudolf Dekker, Wayne Franits and, especially, Eddy de Jongh for their helpful comments on an earlier draft of this article.

1 For example, in a general overview of 'hand and arm in greeting', the anthropologist Raymond Firth calls the handshake 'the traditional greeting of Western countries': Raymond Firth, *Symbols, Public and Private* (London, 1973), pp. 319–20.

2 G. Herman, *Ritualised Friendship and the Greek City* (Cambridge, 1987), pp. 41–72, esp. pp. 51–2. The connotations found by Herman are very similar to those discussed under 'Shaking hands' in this chapter, pp. 171–6.

3 See for example the observations by John Locke and Thomas Molyneux, mentioned in C.D. van Strien, *British Travellers in Holland during the Stuart Period: Edward Browne and John Locke as Tourists in the United Provinces* (Amsterdam, 1989), pp. 157 and 220 (Locke did not describe Dutch greeting and parting behaviour in general, but only that of the Labadists, a Protestant sect).

4 G. Brandt, *Historie der Reformatie en andere kerkelyke geschiedenissen* (4 vols, Amsterdam, 1674–1704), vol. II, p. 218.

5 For a very interesting analysis of the Quakers' language and gestures, see R. Bauman, *Let Your Words be Few: Symbolism of Speaking and Silence among Seventeenth-Century Quakers* (Cambridge, 1983), esp. pp. 43–62. Other sects, such as the diggers or the Fifth Monarchists, had similar ideas.

6 For a general, though incomplete, overview of Dutch manners books see Pieter Spierenburg, *Elites and Etiquette: Mentality and Social Structure in the Early Modern Northern Netherlands* (Rotterdam, 1981).

7 On this gesture, see J. Leite de Vasconcellos, *A figa: Estudo de etnografia comparativa* (Porto, 1925). The gesture is also mentioned by Erasmus, in a sermon from 1524. For a not completely correct translation, see *The Essential Erasmus*, ed. P. Dolan (New York, 1964), p. 228. I owe both references to Dr A. V. N. van Woerden. See also Driessen, p. 250 n. 5 of this volume.

8 The actual gesture is hard to detect from a reproduction. For this (much debated) observation see Peter C. Sutton, 'Masters of Dutch genre painting', in *Masters of Seventeenth-Century Dutch Genre Painting*, ed. J. Iandola Watkins (Wisbech, Cambs., 1984), p. xlv.

9 It is striking, for example, that sixteenth-century Dutch editions were published not in the northern Netherlands but in Antwerp. It was only in 1625 that Erasmus's manual, purged of its 'popish' passages, was declared compulsory reading at every Latin school, at least in the province of Holland. From 1626 onwards, when the expurgated text was finally published, it was used in the fifth form (our present first form) of these schools. In 1677 the booklet was still in use at Amsterdam, though now in the fourth form. However, as De la Fontaine Verwey concluded, it is not clear whether Erasmus's booklet was used at all the Latin schools in Holland. The number of copies extant is suspiciously low (the Rotterdam Public Library, which has one of the best collections of all Erasmus editions, mentions only editions of 1653, 1657, 1671, 1672 and 1703). Of course, schoolbooks seldom survive, but Erasmus's *Colloquia*, also declared compulsory subject matter, has survived in far greater numbers (this last conclusion based on an inventory which I drew up in 1982 of all books on the family and related themes, published in the northern Netherlands in the sixteenth and seventeenth centuries that are available in Dutch university libraries and the Koninklijke Bibliotheek at The Hague). Surprisingly, the first wholly Dutch translation of Erasmus's treatise was published as late as 1693. In 1678 it was preceded by a mixed edition, aimed at the pupils of Latin schools, containing both the Latin text and a Dutch translation. For these and further details, see H. de la Fontaine Verwey, 'The first "book of etiquette" for children: Erasmus's *De civilitate morum puerilium*', *Quaerendo*, 1 (1971), pp. 19–30, esp. 27–9, reprinted in his *Uit de wereld van het boek* (Amsterdam, 1975), vol. 1, pp. 41–50.

10 Stephano Guazzo, *Van den heuschen burgerlycken ommegangh: een seer sin-rijcke, lieflijcke, ende nuttighe t'samensprekinghe* (Alkmaar, 1603). This was followed by a Latin edition in 1650 and published at Leiden.

11 Baldassare Castiglione, *De volmaeckte hovelinck* (Amsterdam, 1662,

reprinted in 1675). Interestingly, the publisher dedicated the book to
Jan Six, the Amsterdam burgomaster who acted as Rembrandt's
patron for a long time. It seems that Six had recommended its
translation; he had mentioned his high opinion of the manual to the
publisher. He also had no fewer than three copies of the book. See
George Möller, 'Het album Pandora van Jan Six (1618–1700)',
*Jaarboek van het Genootschap Amstelodamum*, 77 (1984), p. 70.

12 (A. de Courtin), *Nieuwe verhandeling van de welgemanierdheidt,
welke in Vrankryk onder fraaye lieden gebruikelyk is* (Amsterdam,
1672). The title of the 1675 edition, reprinted in 1677, mentions the
'hoofsche wellevendheit, en loffelijcke welgemanierdheit, in Den
Haag aen het hof en voorts door geheel Nederland, by treffelijke
lieden gebruikelijk'.

13 Giovanni della Casa, *Galateus of welgemanierdheid* (Amsterdam,
1715).

14 *Het groot ceremonie-boeck der beschaafde zeeden, welleevendheid,
ceremonieel, en welvoegende hoffelykheden onderwyzende hoe ieder
een . . . zich behoorden te gedraagen, om zich zelven in deeze wereld,
bemind en gelukkig te maaken.* By C. v[an] L[aar]. Amsterdam, n.d.
[1735]. A second edition came out in 1755.

15 Cited after S. W. Bijl, *Erasmus in het Nederlands tot 1617* (Leiden,
1978), p. 250.

16 Jean de Parival, *Les délices de la Hollande: oeuvre panegirique*
(Leiden, 1651), p. 15.

17 Cited after J. G. C. A. Briels, 'Brabantse blaaskaak en Hollandse
botmuil. Cultuurontwikkelingen in het begin van de Gouden Eeuw',
*De Zeventiende Eeuw*, 1 (1985), no. 1, p. 14.

18 For the related problems of 'national character', see Driessen's
contribution to this volume, ch. 10, section on 'Gesture and national
stereotype'.

19 Bredero's comedy *De Spaensche Brabander* (The Spanish Brabanter),
published in 1614, and Visscher's *Brabbelingh*, published in 1599, are
the most telling examples of such scoffing. For these and related texts,
see Briels, 'Brabantse blaaskaak en Hollandse botmuil', passim, and
Willem Frijhoff, 'Verfransing? Franse taal en Nederlandse cultuur tot
in de revolutietijd', *Bijdragen en Mededelingen betreffende de
Geschiedenis der Nederlanden*, 104 (1989), 592–609, esp. pp. 594–6.
See also his contribution to this volume, ch. 9, section on 'The sacred
kiss'.

20 Herman Roodenburg, *Onder censuur: de kerkelijke tucht in de
gereformeerde gemeente van Amsterdam, 1578–1700* (Hilversum,
1990), p. 327.

21  Jacob Cats, *Al de werken* (Schiedam, n.d.), p. 146. His *Houwelijck* was first published in 1625.

22  On the Grand Tour and learning French, Italian or Spanish civility, see A. Frank-Van Westrienen, *De Groote Tour: Tekening van de educatiereis der Nederlanders in de zeventiende eeuw* (Amsterdam, 1983), esp. ch. 6. See also the observations on travelling by the famous humanist Justus Lipsius (1547–1606) in *Wegh-wyser, vertoonende de besonderste vremde vermaecklijckheden die in't reysen door Vranckryck en eenige aengrensende landen te sien zijn* (Amsterdam, 1647).

23  Little is known about the French schools in the Dutch Republic. However, in the beginning of the seventeenth century the Leiden poet and town clerk, Jan van Hout, sent his daughters to a French school, not to learn 'courtesan manners or to play the madam', he said when defending his decision, but to have a good education. Apparently, the school was offering more than this, cf. J. Prinsen, *De Nederlandsche Renaissance-dichter Jan van Hout* (Amsterdam, 1907), pp. 41–2. In 1761 a French school for girls in Maarssen provided lessons in French, orthography, geography, history 'and furthermore everything that belongs to mannerliness and a good education'; cf. E. P. de Booy, *Kweekhoven der wijsheid: Basis- en vervolgonderwijs in de steden van Utrecht van 1580 tot het begin der 19e eeuw* (Zutphen, 1980), p. 140. The role of tutors and dance-masters was well-known and often criticized.

24  See, for example, *Huygens herdacht: Catalogus bij de tentoonstelling in de Koninklijke Bibliotheek ter gelegenheid van de 300ste sterfdag van Constantijn Huygens*, ed. Arthur Eyffinger (The Hague, 1987), p. 140. Apparently, such considerations were often put forward, as they were contested by one of the leading Calvinist ministers, Gisbertus Voetius, as arguments that were only too popular. See Roodenburg, *Onder censuur*, p. 328.

25  James Boswell, *Life of Johnson*, ed. R. W. Chapman (London, 1970), p. 509.

26  N. Elias, *Über den Prozess der Zivilisation: Soziogenetische und psychogenetische Untersuchungen* (2 vols, Basel, 1939), vol. I, esp. pp. 174–230 on the essential activities.

27  The phrase is of course Erving Goffman's. See his *Relations in Public: Microstudies of the Public Order* (New York, 1971).

28  In his *Die höfische Gesellschaft* Elias sketches a picture of court life that comes much closer to the world of the manuals on civility, but there he hardly makes use of them, basing his case mostly on the memoirs of the Duke of St Simon and others. See Norbert Elias, *Die höfische Gesellschaft: Untersuchungen zur Soziologie des Königtums*

*und der höfischen Aristokratie* (Darmstadt and Neuwied, 1969), esp. pp. 120–77.

29 *Het boeckje van Erasmus aengaende de beleeftheidt der kinderlijcke zeden*, ed. H. de la Fontaine Verwey (Amsterdam, 1969), pp. 17–21, (hereafter, '*Boeckje*'). This is a reprint of the 1678 edition. For the arm akimbo, see Spicer, in this volume, ch. 5.

30 The differences seem even larger: Erasmus wrote his book for a young boy, whereas De Courtin intended his book to be read by boys and girls on the threshold of adulthood.

31 Honoré de Balzac, *Théorie de la démarche et autres textes*, 1st edn, 1833 (Paris, 1978), p. 52 (I owe this reference to Benjo Maso); Fr. Nietzsche, *Sämtliche Werke: Kritische Studienausgabe* (Munich and Berlin, 1980), vol. 11, p. 543.

32 *Nieuwe verhandeling*, pp. 231–3, 241–2.

33 *Officia Ciceronis, leerende wat yegelick in allen staten behoort te doen* (Leiden, 1589), p. 46. This translation, made by the well-known humanist Dirck Volckertsz. Coornhert, included one of Erasmus's letters praising Cicero's book. The translation itself was quite popular and went through three further editions. For the very similar rules in Greece and Rome, see Bremmer, this volume, ch. 1; Graf, this volume, ch. 2, note 18.

34 My own views on these depictions of lower-class life are close to those of Svetlana Alpers. See her 'Breugel's festive peasants', *Simiolus* 6 (1972/3), no. 3/4, pp. 163–76, and her 'Realism as a comic mode: low-life painting seen through Bredero's eyes', *Simiolus* 8 (1975/6), no. 3, pp. 115–44. See also Muchembled's contribution to this volume, ch. 6, section on 'The art of gesture', and his *L'invention de l'homme moderne: sensibilités, moeurs et comportements collectifs sous l'Ancien Régime* (Paris, 1988), ch. 2. Cf. Paul Vandenbroeck, *Beeld van de andere, vertoog over het zelf: over wilden en narren, boeren en bedelaars* (Antwerp, 1987); and idem, *Jheronimus Bosch: tussen volksleven en stadscultuur* (Berchem-Antwerp, 1987).

35 See Huygens's notes on the education of his children, published in *Huygens herdacht*, pp. 96–101. Cf. this passage with Samuel van Hoogstraten, *Inleyding tot de hooge schoole der schilderkonst: anders de zichtbaere werelt* (Rotterdam, 1678), p. 117. On the social meanings of an upright posture and also on early modern medical treatises how to avoid deformity in children by straightening and strengthening the joints, see Georges Vigarello, 'The upward training of the body from the age of chivalry to courtly civility', in *Fragments for a History of the Human Body* (3 vols, New York, 1989), vol. II, pp. 149–96; see also *Der aufrechte Gang: Zur Symbolik einer*

*Körperhaltung*, ed. J. J. Warneken (Tübingen, 1990).

36 *Groot ceremonie-boeck*, pp. 179, 181.

37 *Groot ceremonie-boeck*, pp. 68, 169, 171, 179.

38 (Fr. van Aerssen van Sommelsdijck), *Voyage d'Espagne, contenant entre plusiers particularitez de ce royaume, trois discours politiques sur les affaires du Protecteur d'Angleterre, de la Reine de Suède, et du Duc de Loraine* (Cologne, 1667), pp. 31, 34–5. For his travels through Italy and especially his remark on the elite at Genoa, see L. G. Pélissier, 'Sur quelques documents utiles pour l'histoire des rapports entre la France et l'Italie', in *Atti del Congresso Internazionale di Scienze Storiche (Roma, 1–9 Aprile 1903)*, vol. III (Rome, 1906), pp. 173–256, esp. p. 253.

39 G. A. Bredero, *The Spanish Brabanter: A Seventeenth-Century Dutch Social Satire in Five Acts*, ed. H. David Brumble (Binghamton N.Y., 1982). See esp. p. 78, where Robbeknol, Jerolimo's servant, comments upon his master: 'Now his pride is up again. / High words maintain his gravity – / He who hasn't yet a mussel shell to scrape his arse.' The character was grafted onto one of the figures in *Lazarillo de Tormes*. For other seventeenth-century references to Spanish 'gravity', see Aernout van Overbeke, *Anecdota sive historia jocosae*, ed. Rudolf Dekker and Herman Roodenburg (Amsterdam, 1991), nos. 783, 1726.

40 Around 1900 the expression was still known among the Dutch Sephardim. Cf. J. A. van Praag, 'Restos de los idiamos Hispanolusitanos entre los Sefardies de Amsterdam', *Boletin de la Academia Española* (1931), pp 177–201, esp. p. 195. I owe this reference to Tirtsah Levie-Bernfeld.

41 Cf. Burke, this volume, ch. 4, section on 'The gesticulating Italian'.

42 See for this distinction, E. Goffman, *The Presentation of Self in Everyday Life* (Harmondsworth, 1972), pp. 14 and 18.

43 Erasmus, *Boeckje*, p. 14.

44 De Courtin, *Nouveau traité de la civilité qui se pratique en France* (Amsterdam, 1671), pp. 24–5.

45 Erasmus, *Boeckje*, p. 19; *Groot ceremonie-boeck*, p. 204.

46 Cf. A. Mehrabian, *Nonverbal Communication* (Chicago and New York, 1972), esp. p. 153.

47 Giovanni Paolo Lomazzo, *Trattato dell'Arte de la Pittura* (Milan, 1584), p. 141.

48 I follow here the 'modalities of violation' suggested by Goffman, *Relations in Public*, pp. 44–9. The study of personal space when talking to each other has created an autonomous field of research called 'proxemics'. See for example, E. T. Hall, *Handbook for Proxemic Research* (Washington, 1974).

49 *Nieuwe verhandeling*, pp. 26, 59; *Groot ceremonie-boeck*, pp. 205–6, 371.

50 Erasmus, *Boeckje*, p. 8; *Nieuwe verhandeling*, pp. 21, 23; *Groot ceremonie-boeck*, pp. 180, 203–4.

51 *Nieuwe verhandeling*, pp. 33–4, 45; *Groot ceremonie-boeck*, p. 67.

52 *Nieuwe verhandeling*, pp. 34, 68; *Groot ceremonie-boeck*, pp. 204, 206.

53 *Nieuwe verhandeling*, pp. 16, 20, 23–4, 27, 185–6; *Groot ceremonie-boeck*, pp. 56–62.

54 Guazzo tells us how a couple of French courtiers were ridiculed because of such a 'gaffe'. Seeing an Italian duke standing with his hat in hand, they had taken him by the arm to urge him to cover his head. Guazzo's comment was clear: such rudeness would have demanded that the duke had put his hat on, letting the courtiers know that he had only bared his head because of the heat and certainly not to show any respect to his company: Guazzo, *Van den heuschen burgerlycken ommegangh*, p. 146.

55 E. Panofsky, *Meaning in the Visual Arts: Papers in and on art history* (New York, 1955), p. 26.

56 For one of the few exceptions, see Wayne Franits, 'The family saying grace: a theme in Dutch art of the seventeenth century', *Simiolus*, 16 (1986), pp. 36–49, esp. pp. 43 (n. 43) and 45, in which the author draws our attention to boys removing their hats at prayer. For an interesting historical study, see Penelope J. Corfield, 'Dress for deference and dissent: hat and the decline of hat honour', *Costume*, 23 (1989), pp. 64–79.

57 On the persons portrayed, see Gary Schwartz, *Rembrandt His Life, His Paintings* (New York, 1985), p. 336.

58 *Nieuwe verhandeling*, pp. 17–18; *Groot ceremonie-boeck*, pp. 64–5. On the masks, see also J. H. Der Kinderen-Besier, *Spelevaart der mode: de kledij onzer voorouders in de zeventiende eeuw* (Amsterdam, 1950), p. 68.

59 *Nieuwe verhandeling*, pp. 57–8; cf. De Courtin, *Nouveau traité*, pp. 61–4.

60 Peter Burke, *Dutch Popular Culture in the Seventeenth Century: A Reconnaissance* (Rotterdam, 1978); Simon Schama, *The Embarrassment of Riches: An Interpretation of Dutch Culture in the Golden Age* (London, 1987), p. 174.

61 Guazzo, *Van den heuschen burgerlycken ommegangh*, 'Voor-reden des oversetters tot den leser'.

62 (Justus van Effen), *De Hollandsche Spectator* (12 vols, Amsterdam, 1731–5), vol. VII, p. 10.

63 In a typical case the Quaker, Jacob van Buylaert, imprisoned in Leeuwarden, refused to bare his head when he was interrogated by one of the aldermen. The problem was solved when one of the sheriff's helpers just pulled the hat from his head. See C. B. Hylkema, *Reformateurs: geschiedkundige studiën over de godsdienstige bewegingen uit de nadagen onzer Gouden Eeuw* (2 vols, Haarlem, 1900), vol. II, pp. 68–9. It is possible that acts of deference were expected less within certain religious denominations. The Mennonite weaver Jan Stevensz. obviously annoyed his minister, Galenus Abrahamsz. de Haan, when he doffed his hat in front of him and the other members of the Mennonite consistory. In the weaver's eyes they had all acted not as brothers but as masters. (J(an) S(tevensz.), *Fondament-boeck, of grondigh bewijs van de kennisse Godts, en de christelijke godtsdienst* (Amsterdam, 1683), 'Eerste Aenhanghsel', p. 63.

64 J. Heringa, *De eer en hoogheid van de staat: over de plaats der Verenigde Nederlanden in het diplomatieke leven van de zeventiende eeuw* (Groningen, 1961), pp. 6, 154–5, 262–4. The author mentions many of the contemporary treatises on diplomacy.

65 Heringa, *De eer en hoogheid van de staat*, pp. 340–1.

66 Heringa, *De eer en hoogheid van de staat*, pp. 168–9.

67 Heringa, *De eer en hoogheid van de staat*, pp. 166–7.

68 This does not preclude, of course, that some members of the upper class were less refined in their manners. A lady-in-waiting of Elizabeth, Electress Palatine and Queen of Bohemia, was shocked to see the burgomaster of Alkmaar take leave of the queen by planting a big kiss squarely on her mouth. See *Adriaen van de Venne's Album in the Department of Prints and Drawings in the British Museum*, ed. Martin Royalton-Kisch (London, 1988), p. 349 (Appendix).

69 In the first half of the eighteenth century Justus van Effen poked fun at those of his countrymen who made fools of themselves in always demanding precedence, even from their superiors. See *De Hollandsche Spectator*, vol. VII, pp. 10–15. Anecdotes on diplomatic incidents in The Hague were equally popular, especially on the controversies between the French and the Spanish ambassadors who blocked the streets with their carriages as they refused to give each other right of way. The very Dutch and sober way in which Johan de Witt, the Grand Pensionary of Holland, settled these disputes was certainly part of the fun. See Van Overbeke, *Anecdota*, nos. 75, 749, 1979.

70 Pélissier, 'Sur quelques documents', pp. 221–2.

71 It is interesting that originally not only Tulp but also the surgeon Frans van Loenen had been depicted with a hat; cf. William

Schupbach, 'The paradox of Rembrandt's "Anatomy of Dr Tulp"', *Medical History*, 26 (1982), suppl. no. 2, pp. 29–30.

72 See note 3.

73 David Garrioch, *Neighbourhood and Community in Paris, 1740–1790* (Cambridge, 1986). Richard Cobb, *The Police and the People: French Popular Protest, 1789–1820* (Oxford, 1970), pp. 122, 198–200. For another stimulating study on neighbourhood life in Paris, see T. Brennan, *Public Drinking and Popular Culture in Eighteenth-Century Paris* (Princeton, 1988).

74 About the quarters, see esp. D. Haks, *Huwelijk en gezin in Holland in de 17de en 18de eeuw: processtukken en moralisten over aspecten van het laat 17de- en 18de-eeuwse gezinsleven* (Assen, 1982), pp. 62–4. See also Roodenburg, *Onder censuur*, esp. pp. 39–43 and 244–54.

75 Bruce Lenman and Geoffrey Parker, 'The state, the community and the criminal law in early modern Europe' in *Crime and the Law: The Social History of Crime in Western Europe since 1500*, eds V. A. C. Gatrell, B. Lenman and G. Parker (London, 1980), pp. 11–48.

76 De Parival, *Les délices de la Hollande*, pp. 17–19.

77 W. Aglionby, *The Present State of the United Provinces of the Low Countries* (London, 1669), p. 226.

78 Examples taken from Roodenburg, *Onder censuur*, esp. pp. 207–8, 248–9, 352–3, 359. In the criminal archives of sixteenth-century Artois the handshake equally figured not as a salutation but as a sign of confidence and appeasement. Robert Muchembled, *La violence au village: Sociabilité et comportements populaires en Artois du XVe au XVIIe siècle* (Turnhout, 1989), pp. 250–1.

79 Hans Bontemantel, *De regeeringe van Amsterdam soo in 't civiel als crimineel en militaire*, ed. G. W. Kernkamp (2 vols, The Hague, 1897), vol. I, p. 55.

80 Schama, *The Embarrassment of Riches*, p. 349.

81 On the remarkable ritual of inversion behind this confederation see Henk van Nierop, 'Beggars' banquet: the confederation of the nobility and the politics of inversion', *European History Quarterly*, 21 (1991).

82 The gesture may have had several meanings. It probably pointed to the ideals of peace and fraternity that were still cherished by the civic guards, but it also referred to the peace treaty and, more concretely, to a new alliance between two important factions within the Amsterdam goverment – those led by Witsen and Van Waveren. Cf. Schwartz, *Rembrandt*, p. 258.

83 E. de Jongh, *Portretten van echt en trouw: huwelijk en gezin in de Nederlandse kunst van de zeventiende eeuw* (Zwolle and Haarlem,

1986), esp. pp. 154–5. See also Erwin Panofsky, 'Jan van Eyck's Arnolfini portrait', *The Burlington Magazine*, 64 (1934), pp. 117–27. For an interesting critique of Panofsky, see Jan Baptist Bedaux, 'The reality of symbols: the question of disguised symbolism in Jan van Eyck's "Arnolfini portrait"', *Simiolus*, 16 (1986), pp. 5–28, repr. in his *The Reality of Symbols: Studies in the Iconology of Netherlandish Art 1400–1800* (The Hague and Maarssen, 1990), pp. 21–69.

84 Mme la Baronesse de Fresne, *De l'usage et de la politesse dans le monde* (Paris, 1858), p. 35.

85 William Sewell, *The History of the Rise, Increase and Progress of the Christian People Called Quakers, intermixed with several remarkable occurrences* (London, 1722), p. 690. The book was originally published in Dutch in 1717.

86 Gustave Flaubert, *Madame Bovary: Moeurs de province* (Paris, 1857), p. 131.

87 Eugène Sue, *Les mystères de Paris* (3 vols, Paris, 1977–8), vol. III, p. 249.

88 J. Casanova de Seingalt, *Mémoires* (8 vols, Paris, n.d.), vol. VII, p. 47.

89 In 1711 Joseph Addison observed a greater formality in the country, an adherence to 'the Manners of the last Age', to 'those Refinements which formerly reigned in the Court . . . .' Indeed, 'A Polite Country Squire shall make you as many bows in half an hour as would serve a courtier for a Week.' See Joseph Addison, *The Spectator* (4 vols, London 1907 edn), vol. I, 135–6. The remarks made by Justus van Effen (see note 62) suggest a similar process of informalization.

90 I. S. Turgenev, *Otcy i deti*, 2nd edn (Leipzig, 1880), p. 29. The author referred to the gesture, not in Russian but in English, using not the Cyrillic but the Roman alphabet. It should be added that Pavel Petrovich's handshake was considered quite old-fashioned by the young Bazarow.

91 Johnston described the event as follows: 'The little emperor Hsüan-T'ung had passed out of his mythological stage when he stepped down from his chair and shook hands with me on that cold March morning in 1919.' See R. F. Johnston, *Twilight in the Forbidden City* (London, 1934), p. 179. In the seventeenth century the Chinese were amazed at finding the Dutch shake hands with them at official welcome ceremonies. See Qu Dajun, *Guangdong xinyu* (Peking, 1985 edn), p. 481, quoted in K. Ruitenbeek, 'Westerlingen in de achttiende-eeuwse Chinese kunst', *Aziatische kunst*, 20 (1990), no. 4, pp. 10–22, esp. p. 12.

92 James Cleland, *The Institution of a Young Noble Man* (Oxford, 1607), Book V, ch. 5, pp. 176–8. I owe this reference to Keith Thomas and a further exploration of the passage to Robert Parker.

93 (Fr. Rabelais), *Affentheurliche, naupengeheurliche Geschichtklitterung von Thaten und Rahte der . . . Gorgellantua und . . . Pantagruel durch Huldrich Elloposeleron* (Grenflug im Gänsserich, 1590) ch. 42.

94 Fr. Rabelais, *Gargantua*, ed. Pierre Michel (Paris, 1969), ch. xxxix, p. 313.

# 8

# Gesture, ritual, and social order in sixteenth- to eighteenth-century Poland

## MARIA BOGUCKA

From the sixteenth to the eighteenth century a well developed ritual of gestures was an important part of the culture of the Polish gentry,[1] exhibiting a preference for oral creativity and a need to display social status by particular characteristics of behaviour.[2] Polish noblemen, who in the sixteenth century had just constructed their state, wanted to secure political power and social supremacy by clearly marking the distance between themselves and other groups. This resulted in an increasing taste for luxury and pomp in public as well as in private life. Sumptuousness became a requirement not only in dressing or the arrangement of homes, but also in manners which were codified in a complicated ritual of gestures. This ritual exhibited typical Polish traits despite being founded on a common European practice which derived from ancient Greek and Roman tradition, later enriched by Roman Catholic liturgy and the ceremonies displayed in the courts of feudal monarchs throughout medieval Europe.[3]

A knowledge of gestures was obligatory for every member of the noble class and served as proof of having been born and raised a noble. The lack of this knowledge would inevitably unmask a plebeian.[4] Foreigners visiting Poland in early modern times often described the manners of the gentry as 'theatrical' and noted that demonstrative gestures were used in abundance on every occasion. This phenomenon became evident especially in the seventeenth century. It is possible that the typically Baroque love for theatre and other shows inspired such artificial behaviour. Contemporaries were well aware of this extravagance. 'Human life is like a show', wrote a Polish writer in the second half of the seventeenth century, 'with people the actors and God the creator and manager of the stage . . . in short, *vita est scenae similis*' ('life is like a stage').[5]

Knowledge of how to move according to circumstances and position in society was indispensable for a noble. To this end, young men were trained within the family and in schools, especially in those of the Jesuits who enjoyed a reputation as great experts in 'gestural' *savoir vivre* which they used eagerly in their performances as preachers and leaders of religious ceremonies. A Polish writer of the eighteenth century recalls that young Jesuits were instructed 'how to make gestures, how to move, how to walk, in each body movement they were given special training.'[6]

## BODILY COMPORTMENT

Both manners and bodily comportment of a nobleman should be grave and full of dignity. Mikołaj Rej, a famous writer of noble origin, wrote in the middle of the seventeenth century:

You can tell the attitudes and inclinations of people from their comportment . . . Because when a rustic or cowardly person wants to say something seriously, what do you see? He squirms, picks his fingers, strokes his beard, pulls faces, makes eyes and splits every word in three. A noble man, on the contrary, has a clear mind and a gentle posture; he has nothing to be ashamed of. Therefore, in appearance, in his words, and in comportment he is like an eagle which without any fear looks straight at the sun, or like a commander-in-chief who by his noble posture and proud bearing inspires his soldiers and subordinates to courageous acts.[7]

Indeed, the posture of a Polish nobleman, especially in Renaissance times, was full of pride and gravity. 'They walk majestically, with a baton in one hand and a sword hanging from the belt,' observed a traveller in the seventeenth century.[8] This manner of walking, slow and full of dignity, gave birth to a dance peculiar to the Polish gentry, variously called 'Polish dance', 'walking dance', or 'great dance', and often admired by foreign visitors. 'Old gentlemen and respectable ladies open this dance. At the beginning it seems to be a religious procession, and only later do the steps become quicker and more vivacious', wrote a Frenchman in the middle of the same century. Another Frenchman describing the Polish manner of dancing said:

The dance was led in a circle, executed mostly by two women and two men in pairs. After a first sweep around, composed of curtsying, the dancers advanced with fluent and rhythmical steps. From time to time the ladies leading the procession would leap ahead, pretending to flee from the gentlemen . . . I had never seen a dance more majestic, more moderate, yet at the same time more full of dignity.[9]

Such preference for gravity, even in amusements, resulted in contempt for vigorous sports, especially the ball games popular in Western countries: in Poland only horse riding and hunting were regarded as proper pastimes for the nobility. King Sigismund III Vasa was ridiculed by the gentry because of his fondness for football – judged childish for a man and a ruler.

The dignity and gentle behaviour of a nobleman resulted from his pride in being a member of the noble group. But within this group – in spite of the official principle of equality – some differences existed and were reflected in behaviour. Everyone was obliged to know his proper place according to gender, age, and rank. It was a duty to give way to older or more important persons – passing through doors, dancing, at table, or in processions. It was connected with the ceremonial bowings, curtsying and inviting gestures, which constituted an inevitable ritual for each meeting.

Saying welcome and goodbye in the sixteenth century had already turned into a ritual of ceremonies with a very large and complicated protocol of activities. Among these were several kinds of bowing, handshaking, kissing, knee-bending, and hand-kissing – even hugging the knees or legs of aged persons or persons of higher social rank (parents, patrons, dignitaries). Welcome greetings were organized with special care. In many manors a servant would sit on the roof or in a large tree constantly watching the road; his duty was to announce the approaching visitors well in advance to enable the whole household to be prepared for such a happy occasion. The welcome ritual consisted of deep bowings and mutual embraces in front of the doors. Later the guests were ushered into the house; the host ceremoniously leading the male visitor, his wife the female. Crossing thresholds and taking seats in the room gave occasion to more fussing and mutual ceding of the best places. As a diarist noted, 'it was not without paying compliments, without ceremonies at the door or while taking seats. Next the host would rise asking the guest to give up his sword, which after long teasing would be done and the weapon would be placed carefully in a corner of the room. At this moment a servant would enter with several bottles and a glass on a tray; the glass . . . was emptied amidst more hugging and kissing.'[10] A visit was regarded as a very happy event and the entire household would be occupied with entertaining the guest, according to his age and social position, at banquets or hunts for many weeks. It was easy to come for a visit, but very difficult to leave. The host would protest and try to delay his visitor's departure, sometimes detaining the visitor's horses or taking the wheels off his carriage in order to prolong the visit. Such exaggerated hospitality, typical of the provincial gentry, may be explained by the deadly boredom of living in a small manor, with plenty of time to spare and almost no distractions except visits.

The use of headgear was connected with special rituals, both in public and private life. Cordial greetings, or those due to a person placed higher on the social ladder, were accentuated by doffing the hat or cap and by bowings just deep enough to sweep the floor with the hat. On several occasions, however, the hat would be only slightly touched or tipped. Taking off the hat was regarded as a sign of special respect with the first to doff the hat being either a younger person, someone of lower standing or a person obliged in some way to those whose presence he was in. Two gentlemen of the same social standing would be expected to take off their hats simultaneously. The hat would also be doffed while reading a letter from a person of high social standing or even when a well respected

name – of the King or the Pope – was mentioned.[11] When
Bonifacius Vanozzi described his meeting with the famous Polish
magnate Hetman, the Great Chancellor Jan Zamoyski in 1596, he
recorded that Zamoyski doffed his hat while reading Vanozzi's
credentials; he also doffed his hat at every mention of the Polish
king or of the Pope. Another Italian diplomat, Giovanni Paulo
Mucante, wrote in the same year that the Pope's envoy to Poland,
whilst attending a royal banquet in Warsaw, doffed his cap every
time King Sigismund Vasa drank to somebody's health; this
behaviour, however, was criticized by the clergymen present.[12]

Renaissance manners, so full of pride and dignity, began to
change towards the end of the sixteenth century. The Baroque
inclination to exaggerate soon resulted in the gentry affecting an
even more effusive demeanour which, however, was always subject
to constant fluctuations of fashion. 'What I do remember of
different fashions of garments, of hats, of boots, of swords, of
saddles, of weapons, of home arrangements, even of hairdress, of
gestures, of gait, of greetings – good Lord, I am not able to
describe it all,' wrote Jan Chryzostom Pasek in his diary in the
seventeenth century.[13] Along with the growing dependence of the
Polish gentry on magnates, gestures of adulation became more
frequent and more drastic. Not only would the hand of a powerful
patron be kissed on every occasion, but also his chest, his stomach,
his knees, and his feet. 'Two people of the same social standing
would embrace and kiss each other on the shoulders; subordinates
are expected to kiss the knees, calves or feet of their superiors,'
wrote a Frenchman visiting Poland in the second half of the seventeenth century.[14] A client's prostration on the floor before the
patron became commonplace – a custom unheard of in the sixteenth
century.[15] Also growing in importance was the custom of kissing
publicly, which in the sixteenth century had still been regarded as a
plebeian habit, peculiar to the eastern parts of the country and
connected with bad taste. 'Today to kiss is not a Polish habit. /
Only in plebeian Ruthenia / Do they like to greet each other by
embraces',[16] wrote the poet Jan Protasowicz.[17]

With the growth of eastern influences on Polish culture as well
as with the establishment of demonstrative Baroque ways of
behaviour, a kiss became an indispensable element of social
contacts. 'Usually Poles are accustomed to greet each other with

embraces, something which is not the practice in other countries even among relatives and family members. It is in this superficial manner that they try to show each other their mutual friendly affection,' wrote S. Starowolski around 1650 in his book *The Reformation of the Polish Customs.*[18] At the meeting of two equals, however, it was usually a kiss on the shoulder. A very popular gesture among equals was also to kiss one's own figures and to throw the kiss in the air. Such a symbolic kiss allowed the show of affection without really touching. Venozzi, who visited Jan Zamoyski in 1596 recalls how the Great Chancellor introduced him to his wife and other Polish ladies. The wife of the Chancellor shook hands with the Italian visitor, her female companions curtsyed and kissed their own fingers by way of greeting. It is worth noting that Vanozzi himself used such gestures while greeting Zamoyski's courtiers.[19]

From the end of the sixteenth century the hand-kiss became an obligatory gesture towards every older or more important person. Peasants kissed the hands of their lords and of members of their lords' families, children included. A petty noble in the seventeenth and eighteenth centuries customarily kissed a magnate's hand – a gesture unheard of a century earlier. Women's hands were also kissed on each social occasion – the hands of young unmarried girls as well as those of matrons. Girls were trained on how to extend the hand for a kiss. The gauntlet should be removed first – it was regarded as impolite to present the hand covered – and then the hand should be extended just high enough to give a man the possibility to raise it slightly to his lips. Albrycht St. Radziwiłł recalls that in 1644 King Ladislaus IV Vasa, displeased with Cracow's burghers when they came to greet him, extended a covered hand for their welcome kiss. One of the representatives of the city, very much confused by the pose of the King, bent his knee three times in front of the throne, thinking the King's gesture a mistake. Finally, he gave up and decided to kiss the gloved hand, but the King removed the gauntlet at the last moment. A similar small incident happened at the beginning of 1646, when a Pomeranian dignitary, Gerhard Denhoff, met Queen Louise Mary Gonzaga at the Polish border. She extended her gloved hand to be kissed from inside the carriage; Denhoff, very much confused and unhappy, was obliged to kiss her glove.[20] The habit of kissing

women's hands, rather amazing to foreigners, was preserved in
Poland well into this century. The last traces of the old ceremonies
still live on today among older gentlemen who greet a lady with: 'I
kiss your hands', or even 'I fall at your feet'.

Not only were gestures used as expressions of respect in social
life, they also served to indicate contempt in a variety of ways: the
refusal to shake hands, the thumbing of one's nose, the slap in the
face, or striking with the flat of one's sword. Anger would be
shown by gnashing the teeth, rolling the eyes, biting one's
moustache, or hurling one's cap on the floor. When pleased, a
noble would twirl up his moustache and/or rub his hands.[21]

Feasts and banquets – a significant part of the Polish gentry's
social life – had their own ritual of gestures. The diners were seated
around the table according to their age and social rank.[22] At the
royal court, as late as the middle of the seventeenth century, the
sexes were not mixed during feasts – the only exception being the
Queen. Women were usually seated around a special table.
Albrycht St. Radziwiłł notes in his diary that before the banquet,
on the occasion of the coronation ceremony of Ladislaus IV in
February 1633, 'it was considered whether the sister of the King
should be invited. Finally the King summoned her. At once a table
was arranged for the ladies of the court as well as for dignitaries'
and royal clerks' wives.' The King's sister, however, sat at the royal
table. One year later (September 1637), on the occasion of the
King's marriage to Cécile Renate Habsburg, the table for the
women happened to be too small and some ladies had to be seated
at the table of the King's officials; this broke the taboo on mixing
the sexes.[23]

Anyone not satisfied with his place at the table or with his
neighbours would immediately show his dissatisfaction by leaving
the room or cutting the tablecloth in front of him.[24] It was in this
way that the symbolic community of the table was destroyed. The
reaction of the Papal envoy, who left the royal castle in Warsaw in
July 1633 through dissatisfaction with his place at the table, shows
the importance of the place given at the table.[25]

Headgear was removed only whilst drinking someone's health.
There also was a custom of standing up while proposing a toast,
according to the old saying: 'the host at the head of table gives the
sign – everybody who is drinking someone's health should stand

up and remove his cap'.[26] Foreigners attending Polish banquets usually felt very much annoyed by this custom and complained that such a constant jumping up and sitting down was a great nuisance during a meal.[27]

The most important toasts were each drunk from a different cup – therefore the host usually had a whole collection of cups and glasses in different sizes, shapes, and colours.[28] After proposing a toast he would let the selected cup circulate round the table. The women were only allowed to put the glass to their lips and had to pass it on without drinking. Very often, after the toast had been drunk, the empty glass would be thrown to the floor and broken in pieces in order to prevent future use. From time to time an over-eager or drunk noble would break the glass on his own head to show a special respect for the toasted person. A feast held in the town of Tolloczyn in 1611 became very famous after just such an event. The commander-in-chief Chodkiewicz broke the cup given to him by King Sigismund III on his head. 'When I smashed the cup on my skull,' Chodkiewicz wrote later to his wife, 'the King said: "My dear lord, don't hurt your precious brain, we have great need of it"'.[29]

In general, however, comportment at the table had to be polite and civilized. Before the meal, water and towels were distributed to wash and dry the hands. The table had to be covered with a clean white cloth, often embroidered or even trimmed with pearls. The inventories of magnates' and burghers' households mention silver or even gold forks by the end of the sixteenth century, but the petty noble, on the other hand, used only spoons and knives well into the next century. The difference in table manners, more than anything else, reflected the scale of social degree in Polish society. The general trend among nobles and burghers, however, was to distinguish themselves from peasants by using their fingers less, by not eating from the common bowl, and by forbidding spitting, spilling beer, or taking too much food into one's mouth. Several books on good table manners were popular among the gentry as well as among burghers. Only peasants were supposed not to be able to control themselves when eating and they were despised because of their 'animal-like' habits. Foreigners, as well as some Polish writers, complain about disorders arising during feasts and banquets: insolent servants, messy tables, and the quarrelling of drunken diners. The gap between theoretical requirements and daily practice in this sphere of life was especially large.

Gestures in the small family group reflected gestures used at a higher level of social life. Every family event, such as courting, proposing, marrying, burying, saying farewell to parents or guardians by young noblemen leaving for school, going abroad or to war, was accompanied by the sacred ritual of bending one's knee, hugging, and kissing. A very popular farewell gesture was to hug the head of the departing person as he kneeled before his parents or guardians. Such a hug was also popular outside the family, and on many social occasions it was given as a sign of special affection by a person of higher social standing to one of lower standing; the King used to hug the head of his beloved courtier; a bishop or monk would hug the head of a lay person.[30] Kissing parents' feet was regarded as the duty of children on such occasions as leaving or returning home; so was asking permission in vital questions such as marrying, choosing monastic life, or undertaking a pilgrimage. It was common practice to bend the knee to one's parents: 'One knee the son, both the daughter / bend down to their mother,' the Polish poet J. Kochowski wrote in the seventeenth century.[31]

The existence of scores of formulas concerning behaviour on such occasions as funerals, weddings, or even simply calling on neighbours proves the fact that Polish family life was highly ritualized during the period from the sixteenth to the eighteenth century. In many manors, family books (the so-called *silva rerum*, a kind of memory book with carefully copied prescriptions, copies of letters, public orations, poems, anecdotes, etc.) displayed large compilations of letters received on different occasions: invitations to a dance or a hunt, condolences on someone's death, congratulations on the birth of a son or a daughter, on a happy marriage, or a safe return home. It seems that a formula was prepared for each family and social occasion, and a gentleman or lady had only to follow the patterns of established behaviour. To follow this code was proof of noble origin, good manners, and of belonging to the refined group of well-bred gentry. Such attitudes, however, did not mean stiffness or coldness in contacts between people. On the contrary, outbreaks of temperament seem to be included in the general pattern of comportment thought to be proper for a gentleman.

M. Matuszewicz presents a juicy example of this kind in his diary when he pictures the farewell ceremony in a Mazovian manor in 1740. A certain Miss Szamowska saying goodbye to a young gentleman called Tollohub offered him, as was customary, a glass of wine. Tollohub was already sitting on his horse, ready to ride off. He drank the wine, put the empty glass between the ears of his horse, broke it with one shot of his pistol, dismounted, prostrated himself, and asked the girl to marry him.[32]

Polish people were emotional and felt no need to hide their feelings. Indeed, gesticulating served to display one's honour and noble attitudes. It was deemed proper even for adult males to shed tears in public, to show their patriotism, their grief at someone's death, or their joy on a happy occasion. The Great Chancellor Jan Zamoyski wept openly on many occasions to express his grief.[33] A little later Pasek writes that King John Casimir burst into tears at hearing the news of a military victory: 'And tears as big as peas poured down his cheeks.'[34] Radziwiłł relates that after the King's son had died he 'wept and sighed loudly'.[35] In his diary he mentions numerous instances of the King, dignitaries, or noblemen shedding tears. A squire could cry in public without being called weak or effeminate. According to custom one had to weep, even if one did not feel too much pain. In 1570 Stanisław Czarnkowski wrote, perhaps sarcastically, to Sofia Jagiellon, the Duchess of Braunschweig, that King Sigismund August had managed to weep hot tears at the death of his wife, Catharina of Habsburg, though she had been sent away by him and had died in exile.[36]

## GESTURES AND OFFICIAL OCCASIONS

It was not only at private but also at public occasions that gestures were important. Here we can also distinguish a change of meaning in some seventeenth- and eighteenth-century gestures compared to those of the previous century. In the middle of the sixteenth century it was still thought highly unusual that the members of the Seym beseeched King Sigismund August on their knees to give up his unpopular marriage to the beautiful widow Barbara Radziwiłł.[37] A century and a half later nobody would have been surprised at such a sight: to kneel or even prostrate oneself on the floor had become a common habit in Polish public life.[38] Every official event was now marked by ceremony and a whole ritual of gestures.

The opening and closing ceremonies of the General Diet were particularly imposing performances with the procession of deputies coming to kiss the King's hand.[39] To be excluded from this ceremony meant banishment from the symbolic community of the Polish gentry. This was the fate of the Polish Arians who in 1658, just before they were expelled from the country, were not allowed to kiss the King's hand. Each public speech in the Diet had to be accompanied by theatrical movements of the hands and the whole body; the Swedish envoy to Poland, who in 1632 spoke to the deputies *plicatisque brachiis*, was judged a boor.[40] The relationship between the Polish Commonwealth and Sweden was rather unfriendly at this time so it is quite likely that this gesture of folding the arms was interpreted as being particularly impolite and arrogant.

During parliamentary sessions deputies did not remove their headgear or their weapons. Discontent was very often shown by waving swords and banging batons. Enthusiastic support would be demonstrated by throwing hats and caps into the air. On the other hand, deputies sometimes physically trampled on or chopped up unpopular bills.[41] With the disintegration of the parliamentary system from the middle of the seventeenth century onwards the extensive use of gestures became a necessity for understanding speakers in the general turmoil. The reforms of the eighteenth century put an end to this riotous behaviour, but the tragic years of 1772–95 again witnessed dramatic gestures in the Diet. In 1772 a deputy from the Novogrod district, a certain Tadeusz Rejtan, protested against the legalization of the first partition of Poland by throwing himself on the floor and baring his chest, asking to be killed first. Almost twenty years later, in 1791, a deputy from the Kalisz district, Jan Suchorzewski, who had tried to fight the reform of the Polish state, prostrated himself on the floor, begging the Seym to postpone voting on the famous Constitution of 3 May.

Gestures were especially important on diplomatic missions, as the dignity of the King and the whole nation depended on them. In the royal instruction to Polish diplomats issued in 1601 we read:

Your gestures should be manly and solemn according to the occasion – not womanly, not childish, not fearful, not shameful, not irritable, not frivolous . . . Being received in audience you should stand solidly like a tree, keeping a straight face, looking straight ahead. Look at the person to whom you are sent, without any movement, without looking sideways, without shaking the head. Hands should be quiet, without any trembling, not tugging at the beard. You should abstain from coughing, spitting, blowing the nose, and scratching the head or other parts of the body. Do not pick your nose or teeth or bite your lips.

The King's instruction of 30 May 1667 to Polish diplomats sent to Moscovy told them 'to behave according to ancient custom without removing headgear' as well as 'to bow to the Czar according to Polish habit', meaning without knocking their heads on the floor as was Russian custom. The long dispute which followed in Moscow was only ended when the Poles were permitted to enter the room where the Czar was sitting with their heads covered; subsequently they had to remove their hats and caps, 'in conspectum of the Czar sitting in maiestate', for a short while because, it was explained, to remain bareheaded would be against both the dignity of the Polish king and the Polish-Lithuanian Commonwealth. Yet it did not hurt the Polish envoy's sense of pride to kiss the hands of the Czar and his son.[42]

In the Saxon period (the end of the seventeenth and the beginning of the eighteenth century) the courtiers of the king, dressed by now according to German fashion, hastily covered their great wigs when a Turkish envoy wearing a turban was received in audience.[43] Indeed, Polish noblemen were most touchy on the subject of doffing or tipping the hat. After the famous battle near Vienna in 1683, King John III Sobieski and his men were deeply hurt when the Emperor Leopold did not doff his hat either before Sobieski's son or his colonels.[44] The Emperor soon learned that he had made a mistake. In order to make amends 'he not only doffed his hat but almost threw it before our soldiers at every meeting' a Polish diarist observed.[45]

Here we touch upon the vital question of military gesture. It is worth noting that the old Polish army did not have a special military drill for the nobles, who considered it beneath their dignity to be dressed and trained as common soldiers. Only foreign mercenary troops and private armies of magnates had their own uniforms and special training. Nevertheless, on some military occasions a particular ritual had developed which was patterned upon general European models. For example, it was obligatory to take off hats before military banners. After a victory it was normal to throw the captured insignia and banners on the floor before the commander-in-chief or the King – a custom observed not only in Poland but also in the rest of Europe and connected with ancient Roman tradition. Polish parades were also modelled on common European military usage. According to Pasek, in the middle of the seventeenth century the famous Czarniecki's troops observed 'German manners': when passing a city or during a parade officers would ride ahead of their corps with lifted swords, noblemen with lifted pistols, and common soldiers with lifted guns.[46] The so-called 'round circle', a meeting of military troops usually summoned by the commander-in-chief to discuss important matters and to appoint the military deputies for the Seym, was another ceremony peculiar to the Poles. Participants stood around a roped circle which they were forbidden to enter; before the meeting Holy Mass was celebrated, the ceremony being concluded by a military parade with a banquet following to which the ladies were invited.[47]

The importance of gesture in religious life is well-known to historians. In Poland the expressivity of the Baroque Catholic Church was increased by strong orthodox and Greek Catholic influences, the latter being an important denomination within the Polish-Lithuanian Commonwealth. Foreign visitors were amazed at the exotic practices of the local church, especially during prayer. Charles Ogier, writing in 1636, gives us an insight into the nature of these practices:

Everywhere there was sighing and crying for the Poles are very tender-hearted. When listening to the sermon, they start to groan audibly at the mention of the name of Christ, of the Blessed Virgin or at any other pious word or sentence. During Mass, when the Body of the Lord is elevated, they violently beat their faces, foreheads, cheeks and chests, and bang their heads against the earth.

On Good Friday, in the city of Gdańsk, Ogier witnessed a procession of flagellants behaving according to medieval custom now forgotten in Western countries:

Towards the evening, when we had returned to our Dominicans, I witnessed a spectacle which I had not seen before. Around seven o'clock a procession of penitents dressed in red garments assembled and after walking round the church while singing in Polish they prostrated themselves before the Body of the Lord; there they beat themselves with whips. I had thought that they did this very gently for outward appearances, but they whipped themselves so cruelly that it could have been the skin of an enemy. When after 100 strokes or more their prefect . . . gave a nod, they stopped and remained prostrated. I thought that it had ended. But immediately when the prefect began to beat the measure they renewed most violently the bloody game . . . Many of the prominent Polish nobles are said to chastise themselves in this way . . . during Holy Week publicly or privately. The penitents have covered their faces and cannot be recognized, unless by chance from their gait or posture.[48]

A century later Kitowicz described the same custom in detail; it must therefore be authentically Polish and not a foreign invention.[49]

In Polish churches dramatic gestures were in common usage: prostration to show penitence, lifting a sword to show one's readiness to defend the faith against the Turks, standing for hours with arms spread in the shape of a crucifix, or attending Holy Mass in full armour.[50] Gesture also played an extremely important role in Corpus Christi processions and in services dedicated to the Birth and Passion of Christ as they were accompanied by mimes performed by actors playing the roles of Jesus, Mary, Joseph, Roman soldiers, and King Herod. 'The actor playing Christ', wrote Kitowicz, 'would fall under the weight of his wooden cross; the soldiers would beat him and rattle his chains.'[51] Such shows, eagerly attended by all layers of society, contributed to a uniform piety and a reduction of the gap between the elite and popular culture. From the sixteenth to the eighteenth century the Polish church became a sort of national stage, with performers being both clergy and laity. Its significance was not purely religious. The

Polish-Lithuanian Commonwealth was tormented by heretics and pagans, just as Christ was by his persecutors: that was the message conveyed to both the gentry and the common people in the gestures of the archimimes. Messianic ideas – an important part of the gentry's culture – were thus spread among the lower classes.

The theatrical character of Polish mourning was regarded with astonishment by foreign visitors. A noble of moderate wealth would do his utmost to provide his parents with the kind of funeral accorded in Western countries only to princes of royal blood. The mourning chapel (*Castrum Doloris*), which was decorated with heraldic and symbolic signs and emblems, was built by the best architects available. The beginning of the funeral ceremony was announced by the ringing of church-bells and the firing of guns. At the funerals of kings, magnates, and other dignitaries the archimimus rode into the church on horseback and let himself fall next to the catafalque, thus symbolically representing the fate of the deceased. According to social rank, weapons and batons were broken with a loud clatter and seals and flag-staffs were smashed.[52] Hundreds of priests and monks prayed for days around the catafalque. A Frenchman visiting Poland in the middle of the seventeenth century wrote:

In Poland funerals are celebrated with great pomp, as festivities for the living rather than the dead. The corpse in the highly ornate coffin is put on a bier, drawn by six horses in black cloth. The coffin is covered by a large velvet pall adorned with a cross of red satin. Six or more servants, dressed in deep mourning, hold the edges of the pall. The bier is preceded by priests, monks, and other people carrying burning wax candles. Three riders on large black horses carry the weapons of the deceased: his sword, his lance, his spear. The procession proceeds very slowly and arrives at the church only after many hours. After the liturgical ceremony the horsemen ride into the church to break the weapons of the deceased on his coffin. Afterwards the participants at the funeral are invited to a rich banquet at which wine flows freely; as a result, even the clergy become drunk.[53]

## Conclusion

All our examples indicate the importance of gesture in the culture of the Polish gentry, the use of which clearly increased during the seventeenth and eighteenth centuries. On the one hand this process was a consequence of oriental influences on Polish noble society and the establishment of a Baroque style of life; on the other hand, of the gradual decline and disintegration of Polish political and social life, the predominance of magnates, the demoralization of much of the nobility, and the decline of the parliamentary system. This elaborate ritual of gestures, with its 'sacred' order and repetitions, saved the nobility from any encroachment and helped to strengthen their self-confidence and pride rather than maintain the Polish social order. By this specific ritual of gestures the gentry demonstrated their superior position at every public and private occasion. The life of a nobleman, from birth to death, was established with the help of this special code of behaviour. The gestures symbolized, and at the same time guarded, the dignity of noblemen, dignitaries, the King, and even the whole Polish-Lithuanian Commonwealth. It was also the most convenient way of expressing one's emotional state, both in public and private.

To what extent was the ritual of gestures as elaborated by the gentry also adopted by members of other social groups? – or did these rather develop their own language of gesture? Recent studies have shown that noble culture was very attractive to those rich burghers who wanted to diminish the gap between themselves and the more privileged layers of society.[54] 'Ennoblement', by adopting the comportment, gait, and manners of a gentleman, was very common in the Polish Commonwealth. Even rich peasants tried to imitate, when possible, the gestures and behaviour of their lords. The gentry struggled to prevent such dangerous encroachment by unmasking impostors. After many years of studying the genealogy of hundreds of families from Great and Little Poland, Walerian Trepka published his famous book *Liber chamorum* in the first decades of the seventeenth century.[55] Trepka, a typical member of the Polish gentry, was convinced that virtue and good manners resulted exclusively from noble birth. He analysed in detail th comportment of hundreds of persons, which led him to infer t

plebeian origin. A rustic will always betray himself, according to
Trepka, by his posture, speech, gait, and gestures. For example, a
certain Walenty Szymborski was 'plebeus, because both his looks
and his manners are not becoming to a nobleman'. A certain Storc
from Silesia was said to be a peasant because of his manners and
was thus spurned by a noble girl whom he was courting. Another
young man was said to be a rustic because of his coarse behaviour.
The members of Zarczynski's family 'were giving away their
plebeian, boorish background by hiding in corners and by being
unable to make polite gestures or to converse with noblemen.'[56]
Trepka mentions thousands of such examples and his book
confirms our assumption that to belong to the Polish gentry from
the sixteenth to the eighteenth centuries meant behaving in
accordance with a special code. Posture, gait, indeed every
movement of the body, was full of social significance.

The members of other social groups tried to adopt the behaviour
of the gentry in order to enhance their social standing. Such
attitudes were popular among the richer strata of society, the
wealthy burghers and, exceptionally, rich peasants who could hope
for upward social mobility. The members of the lower classes had
no such hopes. As a result they rejected the imitative attitudes
which were typical of the rich and ambitious 'plebeians' and
created their own, autonomous world of gestures. How autonomous,
however, is a subject for further research.

## NOTES

1  See P. Mrozowski, 'Klęczenie w kulturze Zachodu średniowiecznego:
   gest ekspiacji-postawa modlitewna (Kneeling in medieval western
   European culture: expiatory gesture–prayer gesture)', *Kwartalnik
   Historyczny*, 40 (1968), pp. 37–60; M. Bogucka, 'Le geste dans la vie
   religieuse, familiale, sociale, publique et politique de la noblesse
   polonaise aux XVIe, XVIIe et XVIIIe siècles', *Revue d'histoire
   moderne et contemporaine*, 30 (1983), pp. 4–19
2  See H. Dziechcinska (ed.), *Kultura żywego słowa w dawnej Polsce
   [Oral Culture in Old Poland]* (Warsaw, 1989), passim.
3  See R. Brilliant, *Gesture and Rank in Roman Art* (New Haven, 1963);

A. Alföldi, *Die monarchische Repräsentation im römischen Kaiserreich* (Darmstadt, 1970); J. le Goff, *Pour un autre Moyen Age* (Paris, 1977), pp. 349–420; R. Schmidt-Wiegand, 'Gebärdensprache im mittelalterlichen Recht', *Frühmittelalterliche Studien*, 16 (1982), pp. 363–79.

4 For characteristic examples see the Polish nobleman Walerian Nekanda Trepka who at the beginning of the seventeenth century collected evidence on false nobility in his *Liber Chamorum*, ed. W. Dworzaczek et al. (Wrocław, 1958), especially vol. I, no. 8, 101, 151, 181, 336, 468, 567, 641, 1144, 1874, 2098, 2327, 2465. See also pp. 205–6 in this chapter.

5 K. J. Wojsznarowicz, *Orator polityczny [The Political Orator]* (Cracow, 1677), p. 61.

6 J. Kitowicz, *Opis obyczajów za panowania Augusta III [Customs under the Rule of King August III]*, ed. R. Pollak (Wrocław, 1970), p. 110.

7 M. Rej. *Zwierciadło [The Mirror]*, eds J. C. Czubek and J. Los (Cracow, 1913), vol. I, pp. 75–6.

8 Bogucka, 'Le geste', p. 7.

9 *Cudzoziemcy o Polsce. Relacje i opinie [Foreign Visitors on Poland. Reports and Opinions]*, ed. J. Gintel (Cracow, 1971), vol. I, pp. 257, 325.

10 Cited after J. Bystron, *Dzieje obyczajów w dawnej Polsce [A History of Customs in Old Poland]* (Warsaw, 1976), vol. II, p. 162.

11 Bogucka, 'Le geste', p. 9.

12 *Cudzoziemcy o Polsce*, vol. I, p. 202 (Vanozzi), 195 (Mucante).

13 J. Ch. Pasek, *Pamiętnik [Memoirs]*, ed. W. Czaplinski (Wrocław, 1968), p. 93.

14 *Cudzoziemcy o Polsce*, vol. I, p. 297.

15 Bogucka, 'Le geste', p. 9.

16 In those times Ruthenia was part of the Polish Commonwealth.

17 Cited after Bystron *Dzieje obyczajów dawnej Polsce*, vol. II, p. 166.

18 Cited after Bystron, *Dzieje obyczajów w dawnej Polsce*, vol. II, pp. 166–8.

19 *Cudzoziemcy o Polsce*, vol. I, p. 205.

20 A. S. Radziwiłł, *Pamiętnik [Memoirs]*, eds. A. Przybos and R. Zelewski (Warsaw, 1980), vol. II, pp. 409 (1644) and 472 (1646).

21 Bogucka, 'Le geste', pp. 10–11.

22 See Pasek, *Pamiętnik*, p. 15, and J. Ossolinski, *Pamiętnik [Memoirs]*, ed. W. Czaplinksi (Warsaw, 1976), p. 48.

23 Radziwiłł, *Pamiętnik*, vol. II, pp. 48, 282, (1636); vol. I, p. 321 (1637).

24 Bystron, *Dzieje obyczajów w dawnej Polsce*, vol. II, pp. 180–1.

208    *Maria Bogucka*

25  Radziwiłł, *Pamiętnik*, vol. I, p. 321.
26  W. Lozinski, *Zycie polskie w dawnych wiekach [Polish Life in Old Times]* (Cracow, 1958), p. 209.
27  *Cudzoziemcy o Polsce*, vol. I, p. 92.
28  See Z. Wojcik (ed.), *Eryka Lassoty i Wilhelma Beauplana opisy Ukrainy [The Descriptions of the Ukraine by Eric Lassota and Willem Beauplan]* (Warsaw, 1972), p. 174.
29  H. Malewska (ed.), *Listy staropolskie z epoki Wazów [Old Polish Letters from the Time of the Vasas]* (Warsaw, 1959), p. 110.
30  See Pasek, *Pamiętnik*, pp. 25, 103, 243f, 251, 297; *Cudzoziemcy o Polsce*, vol. I, p. 201.
31  Cited after Bystron, *Dzieje obyczajów w dawnej Polsce*, vol. II, p. 168.
32  M. Matuszewicz, *Diariusz życia mego [Diary of My Life]*, ed. B. Królikowski (Warsaw, 1986), vol. I, p. 148.
33  See J. Piotrowski, *Dziennik wyprawy St. Batorego pod Psków [Diary of King Stephen Batory's Campaign at Psków]*, ed. A. Czuczyński (Cracow, 1894), p. 36; A. Śliwiński, *Jan Zamoyski, kanclerz i hetman wielki koronny [Jan Zamoyski, Great Chancellor and Commander-in-Chief]* (Warsaw, 1947), p. 96.
34  Pasek, *Pamiętnik*, pp 25, 366.
35  Radziwiłł, *Pamiętnik*, vol. I, p. 400.
36  Cited after Bogucka, *Anna Jagiellonka* (Warsaw, 1964), p. 100.
37  J. Szujski (ed.), *Diariusz sejmu piotrkowskiego w r. 1548 [Diary of the Seym held in the City of Piotrków in the year 1548]* (Cracow, 1872), pp. 178–207.
38  See Bogucka, 'Le geste', p. 9.
39  See J. Michalski (ed.), *Historia sejmu polskiego [History of the Polish Seym]* (2 vols, Warsaw, 1984), vol. I, pp. 258–9.
40  W. Czaplinski (ed.), *Caroli Ogerii Ephemerides sive iter Danicum, Sueccicum, Polonicum* (Gdansk, 1950), vol. II, pp. 127–9.
41  See *Historia sejmu polskiego*, pp. 250ff; Radziwiłł, *Pamiętnik*, vol. II, p. 358.
42  Cited after A. Przybos and R. Żelewski (eds), *Dyplomaci w dawnych czasach. Relacje staropolskie z 16–18 w. [Diplomats in Ancient Times. Old Polish Reports from the 16th–18th Century]* (Cracow, 1958), pp. 170–1, (1601), 339–40 (1667), 345 (Polish envoy).
43  Bystron, *Dzieje obyczajów w dawnej Polsce*, vol. II, pp. 165–6.
44  See J. Sobieski, *Listy do Marysieńki [Letters of Jan Sobieski to his wife 'Marysieńka']*, ed. L. Kukulski (Warsaw, 1962), p. 527.
45  Cited after Bystron, *Dzieje obyczajów w dawnej Polsce*, vol. II, p. 165.
46  Pasek, *Pamiętnik*, p. 14.

47 For an exhaustive description see Matuszewicz, *Diariusz życia mego*, vol. I, pp. 691ff.
48 *Caroli Ogierii Ephemerides* vol. II, pp. 74, 70 respectively.
49 Kitowicz, *Opis obyczajów za panowania Augusta III*, pp. 43ff.
50 See Bogucka, *Obyczaje staropolskie [Old Polish Customs]*, forthcoming.
51 Kitowicz, *Opis obyczajów za panowania Augusta III*, p. 45.
52 J. Chróścicki, *Pompa funebris* (Warsaw, 1974), passim.
53 *Cudzoziemcy o Polsce*, vol. I, p. 326.
54 See Bogucka, 'L'attrait de la culture nobilaire? Sarmatisation de la bourgeoisie polonaise au XVIIe siècle', *Acta Poloniae Historica*, 33 (1976), pp. 23–42.
55 See note 4.
56 For these examples see the *Liber Chamorum*, vol. I, pp. 472, 514, 645, respectively.

# 9

# The kiss sacred and profane: reflections on a cross-cultural confrontation

## WILLEM FRIJHOFF

### THE KISS: BODILY GESTURE AND CULTURAL PRACTICE

Though apparently a universal gesture in the history of mankind, kissing is also one of the most difficult to study. As an intimate token of love it usually escapes formal recording or public observation which are the main sources of historical knowledge. Besides, written celebrations and depictions of the kiss often seem to reflect literary and aesthetical standards rather than actual practice. Studying the kiss of love is like violating another person's private life. It makes the historian uneasy about the limits of decency and therefore about his personal involvement in his work. Being unable to overlook the historical practice of kissing in its whole range and its full depth, he may feel tempted to rely upon his own experience. In doing so, he would imperceptibly introduce universal, unhistorical categories into his interpretation of a practice which is culture-dependent and therefore subject to changing historical conditions. So the historian should be disturbed not only by questions of ethics, but also by questions of methodology.

Unlike many other gestures, kissing is at the same time a gesture and a ritual.[1] It is a simple but complete gesture, a bodily expression of social interaction which is a cultural practice in itself. As a cultural practice, it involves both a language of gestures and a range of meanings. As such the gesture of kissing is accomplished, within each culture, in a diverse but always limited number of situations and relationships. The kiss does not forcibly remain confined to the sphere of intimacy or express passion, love, or affection. It is charged with a variety of meanings corresponding to the precise social and cultural context in which it is given. That is why Roman grammarians distinguished between three kinds of kisses: *oscula* (kisses of friendship and affection), *basia* (kisses of love) and *suavia* (passionate kisses) even though the distinction is not borne out in usage.[2]

Besides its symbolic meanings such as greeting, respect, friendship or veneration,[3] the kiss may be an instrument of peace (like the holy kiss in St Paul's Epistles or the ritual kiss of peace during the Holy Mass),[4] the public seal of an alliance (the feudal kiss), or an instrument of reconciliation – such as the famous, but somewhat treacherous *baiser Lamourette* given to each other by all the deputies of the French Legislative Assembly on 7 July 1792.[5] And naturally, the ritual of kissing that confers and confirms fullness of life may be perverted, just like all rituals, into a ritual of death: the kiss of betrayal by the apostle Judas, or the kiss of death by a member of the Mafia. Mostly, however, positive meanings prevail. Some kisses are a supreme expression of worship or, as in the blasphemous rite of kissing the devil's ass,[6] of counter-worship. The story of Saint Martin healing a Parisian leper by his kiss shows that the kiss of a saintly person has curative power. And the old noble family of the counts of Habsburg was reputed to heal stammering children by a mouth-kiss. The kiss may even serve magical or counter-magical aims: kissing an artificial phallus once served the fertility of nature; as a true rite of passage, the kiss is able to change a man into an animal, and vice versa; by kissing the Sleeping Beauty, the prince breaks the spell that struck the enchanted castle more than a lifetime before.[7]

It is scarcely difficult to draw up such an inventory of virtual meanings of the kiss, but it would be an error to believe that they can be found simultaneously in each culture or that a similarity of forms would entail similar meaning. In fact, each culture creates its own configuration of forms and meanings. Even very close cultures may differ considerably in their use of the kiss because of the particular configuration of the variables involved:

- the object of the kiss: human persons, man-like figures, or things;
- the social sphere where the interaction ritual of kissing is permitted: public or private;
- its extent: social networks, friends, family, personal intimacy;
- the relation of the rite to age: babies, children, adults, or elderly people;
- social status: unauthorized kissing of a higher-placed person can be an injury, if not a crime;
- gender: is kissing gender-specific (only man to man, or woman to woman), mixed or indifferent, and in which situation?;
- the form of the kiss and the parts of the human body involved: the hand-kiss, the mouth-kiss (mouth-to-mouth, mouth-to-cheek, mouth-to-front, etc.), the nose-kiss, the foot-kiss, and so on;
- its cultural domain: sacred or profane;
- but also its meanings: love, attachment, affection, deference, submission, etc.

Besides, the gesture of kissing is often incorporated into more elaborate and complex rites called 'kissing' only by extension or analogy: giving an accolade, embracing each other, or ritual acting in connection with the gestures or posture of prostration as kissing the earth, the King's feet, the Pope's mules.[8] Even there, the meaning of the ritual is not fixed. Prostration, for example, may express unconditional submission, worship, or penance, but also demand, prayer, or veneration. In the case of Pope John Paul's ritual of prostration and kissing the earth on his arrival in the countries he is visiting, the respect and humility symbolized by the Pope's prostration seem counter-balanced by his taking possession of the community, symbolically expressed in the aggregation rite of kissing the soil.[9]

All this accounts for the diversity of kissing practices even within relatively small areas. Mediterranean cultures which permit effusive forms of public kissing of sacred bodies or things may remain reluctant towards public kisses in purely profane situations, even in the personal sphere. They replace them with more complex and less unambiguous rites of embracing, preferably by persons of the same sex. Present-day northern Europe offers the reverse picture on virtually every point, though even there history shows huge variations in what a quantitative historian would surely call the kissing cycles: after the kissing-eager Middle Ages all kinds of public kissing have been gradually banished, to be readmitted only recently – but exclusively in the profane area; the taboo that actually remains attached to the sacred kiss is so strong that most northern Europeans cannot imagine that the rules of conduct of their cultural systems once resembled those of the present-day Mediterranean nations.

In spite of Western influences, certain African cultures and still more the great Asiatic cultures (e.g. those of the Indian, the Indo-Chinese, and the Chinese peoples), still predominantly consider as disgusting or immoral all the public or semi-public manifestations of the mouth-kiss performed by mutual bodily contact and consign them exclusively to the sphere of intimacy. The act of greeting involves the use of the nose (the 'sniff-kiss') or, more frequently, a bow of the body or a gesture of the hands. This does not mean that those cultures are wholly unfamiliar with mouth-kissing. They simply do not recognize this act as a legitimate public rite or even as a decent public gesture. Public expressions of love should not be physical but symbolic, even if this symbolic language can be extraordinarily crude to Western eyes. Although it might be enlightening to study the substitute gestures which express similar meanings, it will be clear that in this context the mouth-kiss itself largely eludes our historical knowledge.

## THE SACRED KISS

It was for this sort of reason that I wanted to organize my reflection around a personal experience. Indeed, the conscious involvement of one's own experience in historical and anthropological analysis seems to me the only way to avoid reductionism in a field of study that still remains full of cultural prejudices and more or less unconscious taboos, and where scholarly imagination has to be challenged by a personal interest. My case centres on a visit to Rome, where I observed the public rite of kissing the feet of St Peter's statue in his own basilica. An old, simple and customary rite, mentioned as such in every visitor's guide, barely spoiled by religious ideology, and apparently performed without much thinking. But on closer investigation my search for meaning led me to some substantial reflections embedded in my own experience.

As a matter of fact, nowhere in Europe is the cultural variety of the gestures of deference, devotion, and respect so strikingly displayed as in Rome. And perhaps nowhere else are conditions so ideal for a cross-cultural study of ritual gestures in the sphere of the sacred. Other famous shrines and places of pilgrimage with an international attendance, such as Lourdes, Santiago, or Fatima suffer from polemics surrounding the cult of the saints and especially the Holy Virgin. Sometimes sacred rites are so deeply embedded in local codes of cultural expression that visitors quite visibly can be divided into two categories: those involved in the ritual and the outsiders, the latter being curious about what happens but unable to join the ritual, not only mentally but even physically. In what we may call the kinesics of such religious cults – i.e. the study of the dynamics of religious expression from the beginning of the act of pilgrimage to the end – insiders do not behave in the same way as outsiders. The difference lies not so much in the emotional involvement as in body-language.[10]

In some major shrines pilgrims (the insiders) perform unusual body-acts.[11] At Locronan in French Britanny they pass underneath St Renan's tomb. Early on Whit Monday (the second Monday after Easter Sunday) the pilgrims rush into the Church of the Madonna dell'Arco at Naples and scramble for the moisture that covers the marble key-stone of the niche containing Our Lady's image.[12] The pilgrims' practices at Lough Derg and at Croach Patrick (Ireland) combine asceticism or physical exhaustion with a ritual of repeated *circumambulationes* around the holy places.[13] At Fatima (Portugal) and Tinos (Greece) pilgrims crawl on their stomachs, hands firmly crossed, over holy ground which they are eager to lick with their tongues or to kiss with their mouths. Images of such prostration rites may easily communicate to us some of the emotion involved in the pilgrim's experience – as in the superb photographs of Spanish rituals by Cristina García Rodero,[14] and as in the marvellous reports some years ago of the Dutch photographer Marrie Bot on penitential practices at Fatima, Lourdes, and other Christian shrines (see figure 9.1).[15]

Of course, pilgrimage embodies the pilgrim's own need for penance. His kissing of the earth is an expression of self-abasement and personal mortification.[16] Therefore his emotion is different from that of observers, although even at a distance we may recognize some of his personal involvement and feel an outburst of sympathy, pity, or anger. But few outsiders share the gestures themselves with the pilgrims. The reason is not that those gestures would be extravagant as such. Anyone really familiar with pilgrimages in those Catholic regions of Europe where religious expression sometimes seems to be too exuberant to outsiders and physically unrestrained, knows that this is only appearance. In fact, the kinesics of pilgrimage correspond in each case to a customary sequence of bodily expressions, mostly executed in a quite routine way – something like a religious *habitus*, as the French sociologist Pierre Bourdieu would call it.

More than sixty years ago, Robert Hertz was one of the first anthropologists to analyse in such terms the pilgrimage to the Chapel of St Besse at Cogne in the Alps, on the frontier between France and Italy. His description establishes a basic structure which still fits most forms of collective pilgrimage: the faithful ascend in a group to the chapel on the mountain, where Holy Mass is said and a sermon preached; then a procession goes clockwise round the mountain with the statue of the saint carried by an even number of male adolescents, the girls being somehow disguised; finally, having returned to the chapel, each of the faithful kneels down or prostrates himself before the holy image and devotely kisses its feet. This individual kiss marks the end of the collective ritual. Then the pilgrimage is over and the *agape* or village fair begins.[17] The apparently routine progress of the pilgrimage makes some outsiders speak of superficial forms of popular religion, as opposed to true religion with a heavy personal involvement of man's intelligence and feelings. A closer look shows that this cannot be correct.[18]

In holy places of more than local importance, such as Lourdes or Fatima, and today perhaps even Medzugorje in Yugoslavia, the

**Figure 9.1** Untitled photograph, Tinos, Greece, 1980 by Marrie Bot.

customary religious routines are transmitted orally by former pilgrims, by printed pilgrim's manuals or by the organizers of the pilgrimage. Carefully respected by all, they form the matrix for sudden individual experiences of strong religious emotions, expressed in extraordinary behaviour – extraordinary for the outsider, but not for the regular pilgrim. In May 1984, an Italian research team went to the Madonna dell'Arco, the famous shrine near the city of Naples, in order to make a video-film of this cult for an analysis of the kinesics of the pilgrimage.[19] By chance, three days earlier, on 17 May, a miracle had occurred: the statue of the Holy Virgin began to shed tears of blood. The film clearly shows how the miracle transformed the pilgrimage: not by changing the customary ritual of the collectivity, but by intensifying, in the context of a receptive crowd, the emotional charge of individual experience until a limit was crossed and individual pilgrims went into trance, one after another, still mechanically fulfilling the customary ritual.

However, the extraordinary gestures provoked by the trances did not arouse a particular emotion among the participants – nor do they at Fatima, where pilgrims crawl and kiss the soil seeking their way amidst a barely interested crowd of people turned in upon their own form of religious experience. They never become a spectacle, unless for the outsiders. The crossing of the emotional border by individual pilgrims is immediately integrated in the customary ceremony: helpful attendants take care of the people in trance and bring them down to earth or transfer them immediately to an ambulance. But even such plain everyday solutions remain within the boundaries of the ritual. There is no amusement amongst the bystanders. All those who participate in the ritual form a single undifferentiated crowd, held together by an initial rite: kissing the earth of the holy place on arrival at the shrine. That kiss, ritual mark of deference, is the sign of recognition which effects the reception of the individual into the society of pilgrims. It is a rite of aggregation.

The difference between such shrines, even when attracting huge numbers, and St Peter's Basilica in Rome is that there are virtually no outsiders in Rome. Everyone seems somehow involved. That is why I went to St Peter's for a bit of participatory observation with the theme of the history of gestures in mind. It was a day of prayer for the Lebanon (3 October 1989), and there were thousands of pilgrims on the esplanade, But what interested me was a particular rite. Indeed, the most repeated sacred kiss in Western Christianity is perhaps the kiss given to the feet of St Peter's bronze statue which probably dates back to the early Middle Ages.[20] One of the feet has been polished by the millions of kisses and other forms of touching.[21] As this part of the statue is quite shiny, it immediately attracts the attention of passers-by. Non-Catholics who want to have a close look at the famous statue must approach it and, in busy periods (as was the case on that particular day of prayer), join the kissing queue. The statue itself is placed on the right side of the nave just before Maderna's *Confessio*. Nobody can avoid seeing it, and as a matter of fact nobody does avoid it. The scene is therefore perfect for the student of ritual acting and body-language.

But there is a problem with the kissing ritual. From some distance I observed hundreds of visitors – not all of them pilgrims in the ecclesiastical sense of the word – all clearly involved in the multidimensional experience of visiting the central holy place of the Old and the New Rome: the tomb of the apostle of all the Christians with its architectural space effusing aesthetic and mystic perfection. Everyone wanted to pass close to the statue and in fact there was a queue, barely interrupted and continuously lengthened by newcomers who obviously did not all know what exactly they were expected to do at the statue except 'kiss' it – whatever that might be in their own cultural practice. But because everybody looked at the statue, they saw the ritual executed by those ahead of them. As the queue relentlessly advanced, the moment came for each person to make up his mind. Would he actually kiss St Peter's feet or not? And if so, in what way?

Here the cultural codes come in. They show how a single ritual, unofficially codified and adopted by Roman Catholics all over the world, namely, the kissing of the statue's feet, may assume very different forms and undoubtedly be invested with very different meanings according to the cultural code which the pilgrim or visitor brings with him. Once in a queue, as newcomers press behind him, the surprised visitor does not have enough time to elaborate a well-considered code of conduct. He has to proceed by customary rites, i.e. customary in his own ritual language, as close as possible to what is expected from him *hic et nunc*. The first question that arises is whether to kiss or not. Actually, very few refused to make a gesture, but it was not always a plain kiss. Those who remained reluctant either simply crossed themselves, thus marking their provenance from those areas with a Roman Catholic culture where plain kissing does not belong to religious body-language (as is the case in most parts of northern Europe), or they somehow touched the statue with their hand. As a matter of fact, few of them seemed to touch the actual foot of the statue which perhaps was too brilliantly polished. Most of the 'not-kissing' visitors avoided the toes, a nude part of the body, but stroked some part of the apostle's long garment with the fingers of one hand.

Involuntarily, the historian is here reminded of similar touching procedures in history which, though not always involving direct bodily contact, have the same healing or revivifying meaning as the kiss of life through mouth-to-mouth resuscitation, already practised by the prophet Elisha (2 Kings 4:34–5) and now legitimized by medical knowledge. There are of course several biblical examples of healing by a sacred touch (Luke 8:45–6; Acts 5:15 and 19:12). But the most famous rite in history is certainly the 'royal touch'. This rite, notably analysed by Marc Bloch, was performed for some centuries by the English and French kings as a true mark of the sacred character of their function: the King laid his hands on the assembled infirm suffering from the 'King's Evil' or scrofula.[22] The King's healing power was not limited to the territory of his monarchy, but attached to his public body. It accompanied him wherever he went. Thus Charles II of England could perform a ceremony of the 'royal touch' at the Court Chapel of The Hague in 1660 under the troubled, but still not altogether incredulous eye of the Dutch upper class.[23] William of Orange (William III of England), who was a Dutchman himself, called it 'a silly superstition', but his wife and co-regent Mary continued it, as did her successor Queen Anne until her death in 1714.

Some decades later, the touch of the garment of a sacred person caused a new miracle in Holland. In 1727, after the Jansenist schism of the Church of Utrecht, Agatha Stouthandel, a 45-year old dropsical woman, was instantly cured when she deliberately touched the *rochet* of the new schismatic archbishop of Utrecht, whose legitimacy was thus proved by Heaven itself.[24] This miracle presents a striking resemblance with the touching of St Peter's

garment by present-day visitors to Rome. In both cases, it is the
bishop, sacred either by martyrdom or by formal consecration,
who uses the robe representing his office to communicate his
'virtue' – in the strong, archaic sense of the word – to those who
touch it.

Most of the visitors of St Peter's Basilica, however, performed
some form of kissing. Here again two main rites can be
distinguished. A majority – at least at the moment when I observed
the ritual[25] – bowed their body forward and touched St Peter's
worn toes with their lips. Others stroked the toes with their hand,
then touched their own mouth with it and finished the rite by
crossing themselves. Specialists in proxemics would have noted
that the gesture of kissing with the mouth required that there be a
greater distance between the trunk of the kisser's body and the
statue than was the case when the simple touch with the fingers
was employed, this allowing closer bodily proximity of man and
saint. This second method was obviously more common among
those whom I assumed to be of Mediterranean stock – as far as it is
possible to recognize geographical origins *de visu* without falling
victim to grotesque clichés[26] – and certainly among visitors who
were regular users of the basilica. There were even some lay
visitors using this form of the rite who seemed to have entered the
basilica specifically to touch the statue and who left immediately
having done so.

If these observations are correct, the most intimate form of
bodily contact, by kissing the toes with the lips, was not the one
most frequently used – in Rome – by Christians of Mediterranean
cultures. Generally speaking it is true that they are more
accustomed to rituals of kissing sacred places or artefacts[27] – to
name only some of the most famous: the kissing of the phial that
contains the blood of San Gennaro at Naples, or of a ribbon
attached to the statue of the Black Madonna in the national shrine
of Catalonia at Montserrat, or of the tomb of Pope John XXIII in
St Peter's itself. Perhaps the habit of kissing sacred things makes it
emotionally less urgent that a kissing gesture should be strictly
mimetic, either for a good performance or for the communication
of the saint's virtue.

*A contrario*, I could observe this in my own behaviour. Until
then, I had been an observer, not a participant. But I think

historians have to share other people's experiences in order to discover some of their depth. Having a Catholic background, I am not unacquainted with ritual kisses in liturgy. But then, liturgy offers the emotional safeguard of ceremony – that is, of a strictly prescribed ritual with a fixed set of meanings. There is not enough room for personal emotion in liturgy to cause concern when going to a service. As I had observed at length many people behaving in different ways at the statue, the ritual had gained an objectified status in my mind: mentally it was difficult for me to join the queue. It was only when the statue was free of visitors for a while that I could bring myself to raise towards it to perform my ritual hurriedly. As a matter of fact, I found myself kissing the toes of St Peter – just as my present analysis would have predicted.

### The profane kiss

At first sight, this conclusion appears to corroborate the common stereotype of heavily gesticulating southern European crowds versus northern Europeans who remain more sober in their gestures. Even when kissing, the northern European seems to be more direct. But he prefers not to kiss at all, at least not in the sphere of the sacred. However, further examination of historical evidence makes the historian more circumspect. As I said earlier, kissing is an extremely difficult subject for historical study. The hypothesis that the frequency of the kiss in historical sources, either written or artistic, is not a function of reality but of collective representation is probably correct. In medieval sculpture, where the expressiveness of the human face plays an important role, representations of kissing seem much more frequent than in later centuries when other gestures prevail.[28] In his study on the kiss in Western literature, Nicholas James Perella concludes that kissing becomes rarer in literary sources after the Renaissance.[29] Naturally the evolutionary vision of Norbert Elias (cf. Thomas, p. 4 of this volume) on the rise of self-restraint in public life provides an obvious explanation. Kissing is represented less in this hypothesis because, as an act of intimacy, it is more and more the exclusive privilege of the private sphere.

Though this remains a stimulating hypothesis, I am not sure that things are that simple. Several lines of evolution cross at this point, for historically the kiss has many meanings. The first line is chiefly concerned with literature and art. It represents what Perella calls the 'soul-in-the-kiss conceit' – that is, the Platonic (and Neoplatonic) idea that through the mouth-to-mouth kiss the couple intermingle their life-forces or souls. In the fairy-tale of the Sleeping Beauty, kissed back to life by a foreign prince, this motive finds its supreme expression. Linked with Christian themes, this kiss conceit – with its powerful background of sacred practice – develops into several amatory conceits of a more profane nature: in the Middle Ages, the kiss is mainly a kiss of love, but love at the same times means living. 'The most important of these [amatory conceits],' writes Perella, 'are the migration and exchange of the souls or hearts of lovers; the union and transformation of lovers into one another; the metaphorical "death" and subsequent resuscitation (or "new life") of lovers in the beloved; the oneness of lovers unto and beyond the grave, that is, the love-death.'[30] In Renaissance poetry these images come to a climax. John Donne, for example, assimilates the amatory kiss to life, but hence – in another, more sacred, sense – also to death. Love is as strong as death, and the kiss achieves what otherwise only death can – the union of the soul with God.[31]

After the Renaissance, the spread of court etiquette all over Europe makes kisses less frequent in literature until Romantic love brings them back. But there are still some Neoplatonic accents, as in the theme of the *éducation sentimentale*, announced by Rousseau, lavishly described by Stendhal and Balzac, and finally celebrated by Flaubert: young male adolescents come to life and to love through kisses (*ces terribles baisers*) furtively received from a mature woman.[32] As an expert in love, that woman embodies the fullness of life. She is the supreme mediatrix. The important point is not just the transformation of the sacred theme of the soul-kiss into a more profane version, the love/life-kiss, but the fact that centuries-old conceptions are still echoed in modern models of behaviour. The soul-in-the kiss conceit even makes a glorious comeback on a panel by the painter W. J. Martens (1839–95) showing young Eros inspiring true love in a woman by a mouth-to-mouth kiss.[33] But at the same time Rodin's *Kiss* (1886), and still more that of Brancusi (1908), definitively mark the secularization of the vital union of the couple through the kiss and the embrace. As far as Western civilization is concerned, one may perhaps speak of the timeless gesture of the loving kiss. But through its change from the sacred sphere to the profane, the kiss of love has acquired a fundamentally different meaning. or should we say 'meanings', each corresponding to a specific cultural system?

There are other lines of evolution too. The kiss, a body technique as Marcel Mauss has called it,[34] is one of those gestures which, though cultural products like others, are not necessarily used for the public expression of human relations, still less for the public presentation of the self.[35] It may express public values – a welcome, reverence or affection – but at the same time it expresses an intimacy that wants to be preserved. The kiss of love, for example, is simultaneously – to use the terminology of the French ethnologist Arnold Van Gennep[36] – a rite of aggregation and of appropriation, implying a separation from others. It is the more general relationship between the public and the private sphere in a given society that decides whether the kiss as a ritual of aggregation belongs to the public world of those from whom one separates oneself or to the private world of the person who appropriates. In the second case, kissing may be usual, even ritual, but is not shown in public and is therefore not necessarily an object of public knowledge.

This ambiguity is quite clear in Van Gennep's own description of marriage rituals in France before the Second World War.[37] He analyses the public part of these rituals: embracing each other fraternally, arms around shoulders, and touching each others' cheeks in a cheek-to-cheek kiss or at most a mouth-to-cheek kiss. The kiss of love (the mouth-to-mouth kiss) belonged to the private sphere, or perhaps was not practised at all. It is hard to know which conclusion is right, because the ethnologist Van Gennep closed his eyes at the threshold of the bedroom and indeed to private life in general. Hence a strange distortion in his analysis: peasants (because the world he describes is essentially a rural world) embrace each other at virtually every stage of the marriage ceremony, but there is never really any question of a loving kiss between bride and bridegroom.

This surely reflects in some way the reality of the public ceremony. The kiss between the newly married couple recalls old laws and customs which considered it a formal promise of marriage, or even, as in Roman law, a legal bond making the future bride a *quasi uxor*. Indeed, for St Ambrose the bridal kiss was 'the pledge of marriage and the privilege of wedlock'. This wedding kiss as the public seal upon the new bond still exists in present-day marriage ceremonies. Hence perhaps, as Perella suggests for an earlier period, there lingers on a fear of some quasi-magical effect of the mutual kiss.[38] The public kiss between bride and bridegroom had therefore to wait for the very end of the ceremony, inaugurating the consummation of the contracted marriage. And then it naturally hides itself from the ethnologists's view. At least from the ethnologist of half a century ago.

Van Gennep's presentation of public life in France does not leave any space for kissing in the most intimate sense of the word, i.e. the mouth-to-mouth kiss. However, he describes perfectly the aggregation rite of the cheek-to-cheek kiss, the public gesture of embracing which at present is spreading rapidly from France over several European countries, including the Netherlands.[39] Every Dutch observer knows that this new ritual gesture of greeting and saying goodbye sometimes causes horrible misunderstandings about the number of cheek-kisses to be given: people seem either to make this number proportional to a personal scale of affection rates, or to be convinced that some hidden rule about the number exists in etiquette books. Uncertainty about the number causes visible confusion and raises doubts both about one's public self-presentation and the real value of the affective bonds.

As a matter of fact, the gesture of embracing each other by means of holding the shoulders and kissing the cheeks seems to be – at least in France – an example of an original peasant custom adopted by urban culture, probably through migration, but with one important change: in the countryside, the affection shown by the gesture could be measured by the sound of the kisses on the cheeks; in urban culture, body sounds are reprehensible. Hence, perhaps, the reinvestment of affection in the number of the kisses. Van Gennep wrote in 1943:

Embracing in the sense of 'giving one or more kisses' [*baisers*] is rather new. In the countryside, this kiss is given on the cheeks, never on the mouth as in Russia. In most cases, it is simulated. A person with rural *savoir-vivre* touches another man's cheeks only very slightly, although a real kiss is given between mother and daughter, and between sisters or close cousins. The more such a kiss sounds, the stronger is its manifestation of friendship. This friendly kiss is given two times, rarely three.[40]

Elsewhere, as in Flanders, one single cheek-kiss could suffice, whereas the Walloons distinguished themselves from other Belgians by embracing three times.[41]

Although it remains unclear to what extent embracing rituals have been gender-specific in history, there is a curious parallel between this new embracing rage in the kissing-shy Netherlands and one of five centuries ago. In 1499 Erasmus wrote about it from England to his friend Faustus Andrelinus:

Nevertheless, did you but know the blessings of Britain, you would clap your wings to your feet, and run hither . . . To take one attraction out of many; there are nymphs here with divine features, so gentle and kind that you may well prefer them to your Camenae. Besides, there is a fashion which cannot be commended enough. Wherever you go, you are received on all hands with kisses; when you take leave, you are dismissed with kisses. If you go back, your salutes are returned to you. When a visit is paid, the first act of hospitality is a kiss, and when guests depart, the same entertainment is repeated; wherever a meeting takes place, there is kissing in abundance; in fact, whatever way you turn, you are never without it. Oh Faustus, if you had once tasted how sweet and fragrant those kisses are, you would indeed wish to be a traveller, not for ten years, like Solon, but for your whole life in England.[42]

According to the amazed Erasmus, English people seem to have passed their lifetime kissing each other. Clearly, something has happened since 1499 in the kingdom of England. In his contribution to the conference on which this book is based, Keith Thomas mentioned the English movement in the direction of greater bodily reserve. As a matter of fact, the examples given by Erasmus do not give an exhaustive picture of the realm of kissing. He is only concerned by the rite of fraternal, public salutation, i.e. aggregation.

There is nothing in his text about the love-kiss, nor about the sacred kiss.

Conversely, such a text makes us wonder how, just across the North Sea, Dutch people behaved in public. Erasmus of Rotterdam was a Dutchman by birth and very well acquainted with public customs in the Netherlands as his perceptive dialogues and other works show perfectly. Yet he wonders about an apparently striking difference between the English culture and his own. In his manners book *De civilitate morum puerilium* he mainly speaks of postures, much less of gestures. The salutation ritual he defines is meant to honour a person (*praestare honorem*), therefore Erasmus prescribes to *reverenter aperire caput*, i.e. to take off the cap, the hat or something similar.[43] There is nothing in his booklet about any form of bodily contact during the act of greeting, let alone about kissing. But Erasmus wrote in order to define a standard for children's manners, and even then in the children's world acts of embracing or kissing may have had functions and meanings different from those in the adult world.

Besides, Dutch people deliberately presented themselves as blunt and obtuse. Whereas Erasmus still blames Dutch bluntness, Dutch authors such as the playwright Bredero (1585–1618) or the poet Roemer Visscher (1547–1620), both from Amsterdam, exalt it a century later.[44] Ever since Erasmus's own time Dutch lack of refinement was not so much a residue of unrefined manners as a trade mark of the original inhabitants of Holland. As such, Dutch lack of sensitivity and the lack of refinement of the gestures is consciously upheld as a positive value by an author like Roemer Visscher: he uses it to define a strategic position for the protection of the ancient Dutch culture against the threat of assimilation by the apparently more refined manners of the immigrants who came, at the turn of the sixteenth century, in huge numbers from the southern Netherlands.

Does that opposition explain the difference of opinion between two scholars from the Netherlands, Adriaen Hereboord (1614–61) and Erycius Puteanus (1574–1646)? Hereboord, a professor of philosophy at Leiden University and born in the northern provinces, agreed, in a Latin treatise, that male visitors were allowed to kiss the women present, both young and old: kisses demanded by mere politeness can be given without any *arrière-*

*pensée*. But Puteanus, his elderly colleague at Louvain University in the southern Netherlands, underlined the danger of that custom to more sensually-disposed temperaments.[45] Apparently, Hereboord tried to justify a precept of the new etiquette coming from the south, whereas Puteanus opposed himself to the excesses of a widespread practice. But the difference of opinion points equally to another difference: in the northern Netherlands of that time public practice seems less pervaded by private affection.

Such reflections are important for our theme, because the general orientation of a system of values can help us to reconstruct hidden gestures. Did Dutch people kiss or embrace each other as a rite of aggregation before their cultural elites adopted the French *civilité* style, restricting public bodily contact to the kissing of a lady's hand – as represented by Johannes Vermeer in a painting of 1662 (*Women and Two Men*)?[46] It is hard to say, but there is some evidence that bodily contact was less inhibited before the breakthrough of the court style in the seventeenth century. There is much Neoplatonic kissing in Dutch neo-Latin poetry of the sixteenth century. In his famous and influential work *Basia* ('Kisses'), first published in Lyons in 1539, Erasmus's contemporary and fellow-countryman Janus Secundus (1511–36), the gifted but short-lived son of the president of the Supreme Court of the Netherlands, sings his physical love for a courtesan.[47] This collection of nineteen poems, corresponding to as many sensual kisses beautifully described, was the main source of inspiration for generations of love poets, including Ronsard and the Dutch author Janus Dousa the Elder.[48]

But the kiss remains virtually confined to the context of love. Kissing scenes and other forms of close bodily proximity in Dutch genre painting concern plain love affairs (without marital implications) or take place in bawdy-houses.[49] And ever since the seventeenth century a profuse erotic literature naturally abounds with all sorts of embraces and kisses.[50] As a rule, public kissing was characteristic of situations outside marriage, particularly in pre-marital courtship or love-games in youth-groups where there was abundant kissing but within strictly codified rules.[51] The wedding kiss itself appears as a rite of separation: it closes the period during which public kissing is permitted and transfers the kiss of love to the private sphere where it escapes our investigation. Outside the context of love, the kiss apparently remained gender-specific. Thus in the flush of liberty during the Batavian Revolution (1795) women 'embrace and kiss each other on the streets in the name of liberty and equality', whereas men 'shake the hands of brotherhood'.[52] And in an old aggregation ritual of new neighbours to the existing population, once practised in the district of Nijmegen, there was much kissing, but never between men.[53]

On the other hand, the sacred kiss was certainly not unknown in the Netherlands, even outside liturgy or official devotion. In his *Dialogue on Pilgrimage*, Erasmus himself ridicules the kissing of the sacred phial containing some solidified milk from the breast of the Holy Virgin, exposed to public veneration in the Cathedral of Antwerp. And there exists a 1630 painting by Gerrit de Jongh with a scene of the by then forbidden devotion practised by Roman Catholic pilgrims around the ruined chapel of Our Lady of Runxputte, near Heiloo in the northern district of Holland. In the middle of the painting a man is shown prostrated on the ground, obviously kissing it as a sign of reverence or penance, like modern pilgrims at Fatima or Tinos (see figure 9.2).[54]

This painting and other representations of pilgrims' practices there suggest another clue. The kissing man is lying in the middle of a circle of male and female pilgrims walking devoutly or progressing on their knees on a circular pathway around the chapel. This reminds us that the sacred kiss is only a specific manifestation of a more universal need for bodily contact between man and the sacred sphere, which the French historian and anthropologist of religious experience Alphonse Dupront has called the need for sensory nourishment.[55] In a given cultural system the precise practice which will be adopted for the satisfaction of that need depends largely on the valuation of each of the human senses in the system. Sometimes, as in Locronan in Britanny, passing underneath the tomb of the saint will suffice. In other cultural circumstances more direct contact will be required, going as far as a plain kiss on the sacred object (as on the Black Stone at Mecca), or even a copulation at the holy place.

**Figure 9.2** Gerrit Pietersz de Jongh, *De capel van Ons Lieve Vrouwe te Runxputte te Heyloe in Oesdom* (The Chapel of Our Lady at Runxputte, Oesdom, near Heiloo), 1630.
(Rijksmuseum Het Catharijneconvent, Utrecht.)

## Concluding remarks

It is now time to sum up the argument. Why did I, and many other visitors, spontaneously kiss St Peter's statue in his basilica with my mouth and not by using some composite gesture of lips and hand? That was the question which arose from my participating observation. In trying to answer that question, we saw that the distinction between the sacred kiss and the profane kiss does not really matter. Another distinction seems more important – that between the public and the private sphere. Public rites of kissing and embracing – rituals which express a welcome or a goodbye, reverence, or an encouraging sign of fraternity – are mainly aggregation rites. As such, they obey cultural standards of public expression: people have to be sure that the message of union and association will be understood by the outsiders. That does not imply that such rites are pure convention. The public message does not exclude a private meaning.[56]

In the private sphere, even when performed in public (such as a penitential kissing of a holy space or a kiss of love), kissing and embracing are rites of appropriation and therefore of separation from the public sphere. In this sense, the public kiss might even be considered as the most basic liminal ritual, the very gesture separating the public sphere from the private: the pilgrim kissing the ground nourishes himself – and only himself – with sensory experience of a sacred meaning; the young couple practising a mouth-to-mouth kiss build a wall around their intimacy, deny momentarily the existence of the public sphere and thus cause public scandal – as in Georges Brassens's wonderfully sensitive *chanson* 'Les amoureux qui se bécotent sur les bancs publics . . . '

If this is true, the individual decision to touch, embrace, or kiss a sacred object depends on two conditions. The first is the affective (and eventually gender-related) value of each of those gestures related to the scale of affection which is operative in a given cultural system.[57] The other is the answer to the question whether, for the subject who wants to kiss, the sacred belongs to the public or the private sphere. These two conditions direct the action of the subject, consciously or not. In my individual case the sacred seems to have withdrawn from the public sphere and become a private affair, but one requiring a highly affective investment. Hence my plain kiss of St Peter's toes.

## NOTES

1  The main general works on the kiss are the very delightful little book of Christopher Nyrop, *The Kiss and its History*, trans. William Frederick Harvey (London, 1901; repr. Detroit, 1968), and the important literary study by Nicholas James Perella, *The Kiss Sacred and Profane: An Interpretative History of Kiss Symbolism and Related Religio-Erotic Themes* (Berkeley/Los Angeles, 1969), with further references. More specialized studies include: August Wünsche, *Der Kuss in Bibel, Talmud und Midrasch* (Breslau, 1911), and F. Cabrol, 'Baiser', in *Dictionnaire d'archéologie chrétienne et de liturgie*, 2nd edn (Paris, 1925), vol. II, pt 1, cols 117–30. Rather strangely, both the inventory of gestures and the extensive bibliography given by Desmond Morris et al., *Gestures, Their Origins and Distribution* (New York, 1979) virtually ignore the gesture of the kiss. Indeed, the fingertips kiss which their book begins with (pp. 1–14) is more a composite practice than a simple gesture.

2  See most recently Ph. Moreau, '*Osculum, basium, suavium*', *Revue de Philologie*, 52 (1978), pp. 87–97; P. Flury, '*Osculum* und *osculari*'. Beobachtungen zum Vocabular des Kusses im Lateinischen', in S. Krämer and M. Bernhard (eds), *Scire litteras. Forschungen zum mittelalterlichen Geistesleben* (Munich, 1988), pp. 149–57.

3  On the kiss of greeting and its various forms, see Raymond Firth, *Symbols, Public and Private* (London, 1973), pp. 314–18.

4  Rom. 16:16; 1 Cor 16:20; 2 Cor. 13:12; 1 Thess. 5:26. Also 1 Petr. 5:14. Cf. E. Lengeling, 'Kuss', in *Lexikon für Theologie und Kirche* (Freiburg, 1961), vol. VI, cols. 696–8. However, Perella, *The Kiss Sacred and Profane*, pp. 13–27, rightly points out that with St Paul's pneumatology in mind we may well suppose a mystical background to the kiss of peace mentioned in the New Testament. It refers to the 'breath' of the Holy Spirit, to communion, union, and new life. As a matter of fact, that was exactly the Gnostic idea of a sacred kiss.

5  See the article 'Baiser Lamourette' in *La Grande Encyclopédie* (Paris, 1885), vol. I, p. 71. See also Robert Darnton, 'The Kiss of Lamourette', in *The New York Review of Books* (19 January 1909), pp. 2–10.

6  Nyrop, *The Kiss and its History*, pp. 126–30. Cf. the French word *lèche-cul* and the German expression 'Leck mich am Arsch!', both with a very pejorative or contemptuous meaning, exactly like the English expression 'kiss my arse!' (American: 'kiss my ass!').

7  See B. Karle, 'Kuss, küssen', in *Handwörterbuch des deutschen Aberglaubens*, ed. H. Bachtold-Stäubli (10 vols, Berlin and Leipzig, 1927–42), vol. V, cols 841–63.

8  Cf. Frederick M. Denny, 'Postures and gestures', in *The Encyclopedia of Religion*, ed. M. Eliade (16 vols, New York and London, 1987), vol. XI, pp. 461–4. I am also indebted to Marijke Jalink (Amsterdam) who let me discuss her cross-cultural research project on *proskunesis*, i.e. greeting rituals by prostration. For the history of such rites in oriental cultures, see J. Oestrup, *Orientalische Höflichkeit: Formen und Formeln im Islam. Eine kulturgeschichtliche Studie* (Leipzig, 1929).

9  See also on this rite: F. Lot, 'Le baiser à la terre: continuation d'un rite antique', in *Annuaire de l'Institut de philologie et d'histoire orientales*, 9 (1949), pp. 435–41.

10  For general considerations on touching, embracing, and kissing as religious practices, see Geoffrey Parrinder, 'Touching', in *The Encyclopedia of Religion*, vol. XIV, pp. 578–83.

11  For body-language in pilgrims' rituals see various contributions to *Wallfahrt kennt keine Grenzen: Themen zu einer Ausstellung des Bayerischen Nationalmuseums*, ed. Lenz Kriss-Rettenbeck and Gerda Möhler (Munich and Zurich, 1984), with an extensive bibliography.

12  Paolo Toschi and R. Penna, *Le tavolette votive della Madonna dell'Arco* (Naples, 1971), p. 64.

13  Margit Wagner, 'Tradition der Askese bei Wallfahrten in Irland', in *Wallfahrt kennt keine Grenzen*, pp. 45–54.

14  Cristina García Rodero, *España oculta*, ed. Julio Caro Baroja (Barcelona and Madrid, 1989). See also *Photographies des pratiques religieuses en pays méditerranées*, ed. Pedro Provencio (Montpellier, 1985).

15  Marrie Bot, *Miserere: De grote boetebedevaarten in Europa* (Rotterdam, 1984); German edn: *Miserere: Die groszen Buszwallfahrten in Europa* (Rotterdam, 1985); French edn: *Miserere: Les grands pèlerinages de pénitence en Europe* (Rotterdam, 1985).

16  On the historical depth of this penitential kiss, see L. Gougaud, 'Baiser', in *Dictionnaire de spiritualité ascétique et mystique* (Paris, 1937), vol. I, cols 1203–4.

17  Robert Hertz, 'Saint Besse, étude d'un culte alpestre' [written in 1913], in his *Mélanges de sociologie religieuse et folklore* (Paris, 1928),

pp. 131–94; repr. in R. Hertz, *Sociologie religieuse et folklore*, ed. Marcel Mauss (Paris, 1928; repr. 1970), pp. 110–60.

18 This is not the right place to deal with the current debate on popular religion. The reader is referred to my extensive international bibliography on this subject in *Religieuze volkscultuur: de spanning tussen de voorgeschreven orde en de geleefde praktijk*, ed. Gerard Rooijakkers and Theo Van der Zee (Nijmegen, 1986), pp. 137–71.

19 For what follows, I rely upon Mrs Mara Rengo's presentation of this event and the video film at the research seminar of Prof. Alphonse Dupront, École des Hautes Études en Sciences Sociales, Paris, on 5 June 1984.

20 Cf. Nyrop, *The Kiss and its History*, pp. 115–20. Firth, *Symbols, Public and Private*, p. 318, considers this kiss a simple mark of respect similar to kissing a bishop's ring. I think that this is a reduction of its full meaning, at least in historical perspective. Kissing the statue of a saint is a rite of veneration, even of worship, and sometimes involves a magical intent.

21 Cicero (Act. II *In Verrem*, 4,94 informs us of a similar effect of the rite: the lips and beard of the statue of Hercules at Agrigentum were worn away by the kisses of the devotees. Continuous touching by countless hands performing the customary money-spending rite (which involves the insertion of a coin into the animal's snout) has given a similar aspect to the bronze muzzle of *Il Porcellino* at the Mercato Nuovo in Florence.

22 Marc Bloch, *The Royal Touch. Sacred Monarchy and Scrofula in England and France*, trans. J. E. Anderson (London, 1973). Original French edn: *Les rois thaumaturges* (Paris, 1924).

23 Abraham de Wicquefort, *Verhael in forme van journael, van de reys en 't vertoeven van den seer Doorluchtige ende Machtige Prins Carel de II. koning van Groot Britannien* (The Hague, 1660). Cf. W. Frijhoff, 'The emancipation of the Dutch elites from the magic universe', in *The World of William and Mary*, eds Dale Hoak and Mordechai Feingold (Berkeley/Los Angeles and London, 1991), forthcoming.

24 See W. Frijhoff, 'La fonction du miracle dans une minorité catholique: les Provinces-Unies au XVIIe siècle', *Revue d'histoire de la spiritualité*, 48 (1972), pp. 175–6.

25 It is, of course, quite possible that the day of prayer for the Lebanon attracted a particular group of Christians, difficult to identify visually.

26 Yet such a recognition is less arbitrary than it may seem at first sight. Catholics from Mediterranean countries use the space of the church in a different way: their churches are void of pews but full of statues and

altars, which determines a particular way of visiting a church, less straightforward and more immediately attentive to the riches in the margin than northern Europeans, Catholic or not.

27 See for example the suggestive film *Der Himmel auf Erden* made by Alois Kolb (1974) on processions and pilgrimages in Southern Italy. And on the same region: Annabella Rossi, *Le feste dei poveri* (Bari, 1969), with a series of very perceptive photographs.

28 Cf. François Garnier, *Le language de l'image au Moyen Age: Signification et symbolique* (2 vols, Paris, 1982–9), vol. I. There seems, however, to be little attention paid to kissing in the written records analysed by Jean-Claude Schmitt, *La raison des gestes dans l'Occident médiéval* (Paris, 1990).

29 Perella, *The Kiss Sacred and Profane*, passim.

30 Perella, *The Kiss Sacred and Profane*, p. 9.

31 Perella, *The Kiss Sacred and Profane*, p. 243.

32 Laurence Viglieno, 'Le thème de l'éducation sentimentale de Rousseau à Balzac', in *Aimer en France 1760–1860: Actes du Colloque international de Clermont-Ferrand*, eds P. Viallaneix and J. Ehrard (2 vols, Clermont-Ferrand, 1980), vol. I. pp. 131–40.

33 Reproduced in *Romantische liefde, een droombeeld vereeuwigd*, ed. Marjan Rinkleff (Nijmegen, 1985), pp. 97–8.

34 Marcel Mauss, *Sociologie et anthropologie* (Paris, 1950, repr. 1966), p. 383.

35 That might well be the reason why Erving Goffman in his numerous studies on public presentation of the self remains so remarkably reserved towards kissing rituals. See, for example, E. Goffman, *The Presentation of Self in Everyday Life* (Edinburgh, 1956; revised edn: New York, 1959) and *Interaction Ritual: Essays on Face-to-face Behavior* (New York, 1967).

36 Arnold Van Gennep, *Les rites de passage* (Paris, 1909), pp. 5–18 and 188. English trans. by M.B. Vizedom and G.L. Caffee: *The Rites of Passage* (Chicago, 1960).

37 Arnold Van Gennep, *Manuel de folklore français contemporain* (4 vols, Paris, 1943), vol. I, pp. 375–7, 475, 494–5, 513–14.

38 Perella, *The Kiss Sacred and Profane*, pp. 40–5.

39 Cf. Marie van Dijk, ' "Er wordt gekust bij het leven!" ', *Mededelingen van het P. J. Meertens-Instituut*, 37 (December 1985), pp. 12–14. This article presents a short synthesis of the results of a nation-wide inquiry on greeting customs in the Netherlands held by the P. J. Meertens-Instituut in 1984.

40 Van Gennep, *Manuel*, vol. I, p. 376.

41 André Goosse, 'Géographie du baiser', in *Enquêtes du Musée de la vie*

*wallonne*, 46–8 (1969–71), pp. 205–10; idem, 'Le nombre des baisers dans les embrassades', ibid., 50 (1973), pp. 235–6; A. Harou, 'Notes et enquêtes', *Revue des traditions populaires*, 24 (1909), p. 448.

42  *The Epistles of Erasmus from His Earliest Letters to His Fiftieth Year*, trans. Francis Morgan Nichols (New York, 1962), vol. I, p. 203, Epistle 98.

43  *Het Boeckje van Erasmus aengaende de beleeftheidt der kinderlijcke zeden* (edn of 1678, repr. Amsterdam, 1969), p. 45. In his contribution to this volume (see pp. 28–9), Jan Bremmer rightly points to Erasmus's dependence on the codes of behaviour of the Classics.

44  Cf. J. G. C. A. Briels, 'Brabantse blaaskaak en Hollandse botmuil. Cultuurontwikkelingen in Holland in het begin van de Gouden Eeuw', *De Zeventiende Eeuw* 1 (1985), pp. 12–36; W. Frijhoff, 'Verfransing? Franse taal en Nederlandse cultuur tot in de Revolutietijd', *Bijdragen en mededelingen betreffende de geschiedenis der Nederlanden* 104 (1989), pp. 592–609; Herman Roodenburg, this volume, ch. 7.

45  Nyrop, *The Kiss and its History*, pp. 156–7.

46  See Peter C. Sutton, *Masters of Seventeenth-Century Dutch Genre Painting* (Philadelphia, 1984), pp. 338–9.

47  *The Love Poems of Janus Secundus: A Revised Latin Text with an English Verse Translation*, ed. and trans. F. A. Wright (London, 1930). Cf. G. Schoolfield, *Janus Secundus* (Boston, 1980); Cl. Endres, *Janus Secundus. The Latin Love Elegy in the Renaissance* (Hamden, Conn. 1981); M. de Schepper and R. De Smedt (eds), *Symposium Janus Secundus, 1511–1536 [Handelingen van de Koninklijke Kring voor Oudheidkunde, Letteren en Kunst van Mechelen, 90, part 2]* (Malines, 1987), especially the contribution of C. L. Heesakkers, 'Secundusverering in Nederland', pp. 25–37.

48  Perella, *The Kiss Sacred and Profane*, pp. 194–6, 217–22, 331, 333.

49  Cf. Lotte C. van de Pol, 'Beeld en werkelijkheid van de prostitutie in de zeventiende eeuw', in *Soete minne en helsche boosheit: Seksuele voorstellingen in Nederland 1300–1850*, eds G. Hekma and H. Roodenburg (Nijmegen, 1988), pp. 109–44; and Sutton, *Masters of Seventeenth-Century Dutch Genre Painting*, plates 10 (Dirck van Baburen), 90 (Cornelis Saftleven), and p. 193 (Jacob Duck), p. 321 (Gillis van Breen), pp. 350–1.

50  D. Haks, 'Libertinisme en Nederlands verhalend proza', in *Soete minne*, pp. 85–108; for further reading see the bibliography at the end of that book.

51  Seventeenth-century portraits of married couples virtually show no kissing scenes according to E. de Jongh, *Portretten van echt en trouw: huwelijk en gezin in de Nederlandse kunst van de zeventiende eeuw*

(Zwolle and Haarlem, 1986); see also P. van Boheemen et al. (eds), *Kent, en versint Eer dat je mint: Vrijen en trouwen 1500–1800* (Zwolle, 1989). Examples of kissing rites in games of courtship: Jan ter Gouw, *De volksvermaken* (Haarlem, 1871; repr. Arnhem, 1969), pp. 408, 577, 621–2, 667; H. W. Heuvel, *Oud-Achterhoeksch boerenleven het geheele jaar rond* (Zutphen, 1927), p. 90; Waling Dykstra, *Uit Friesland's volksleven van vroeger en later* (Leeuwarden, 1892; repr. 1967), vol. I, p. 287; J. Roelant, 'Het kussen', in *Volkskunde* 12 (1899–1900), pp. 81–7, 247–8.

52 *Extra Nationale Courant*, 20 June 1795, quoted by Ter Gouw, *De volksvermaken*, p. 433. In the Netherlands, shaking hands formerly had a legal meaning, as Herman Roodenburg points out in his contribution to this volume (see ch. 7, pp. 171–6), but later it developed into a gesture of greeting. In 1793, however, an anonymous Dutch engraver represented a male French revolutionary embracing a Dutchman – perhaps because the Frenchman was supposed to have taken the initiative? See M. Jongedijk, 'Nederlandse spotprenten en de Franse Revolutie', in *Het Nederlandse beeld van de Franse Revolutie in prent en film*, ed. E. O. G. Haitsma Mulier and A. M. J. T. Leyten (eds), (Amsterdam, 1989), p. 45, fig. 51.

53 Ter Gouw, *De volksvermaken*, p. 533.

54 The painting is reproduced in Joan Bertrand, *De Runxputte en Onze Lieve Vrouw ter Nood, een bekend bedevaartsoord te Heiloo* (Schoorl, 1980), p. 12, and also in De Jongh, *Portretten van echt en trouw*, pp. 212–14, neither of whom noticed this particular sacred act.

55 Alphonse Dupront, *Du Sacré: Croisades et pèlerinages. Images et langages* (Paris, 1987), pp. 452–61.

56 Cf. on this point the classic study of Edmund Leach, 'Magical hair', *Journal of the Royal Anthropological Institute*, 88 (1958), pp. 147–64.

57 It goes without saying that the construction of such a scale will not only have to take account of social hierarchy, but perhaps even more account of the changing public discourse on expressions of affection – for example, the medical discourse (medical theory was as important in the history of gestures as it is nowadays when defining the limits of bodily approach in relation to the AIDS-problem) or the theories of the social hygienists, not to speak of gender-related changes in cultural codes. See, for example, J. A. Mangan and James Walvin (eds), *Manliness and Morality: Middle Class Masculinity in Britain and America 1800–1940* (Manchester, 1987).

# 10

# Gestured masculinity: body and sociability in rural Andalusia

## HENK DRIESSEN

In the previous chapters the contributors to this volume have mainly studied gestures in the past. As an anthropologist, specializing in Mediterranean cultures, I want to present a case study of male gesturing in contemporary rural Andalusia.[1] My point of departure will be that the study of gestures should be firmly grounded in an analysis of networks and social relationships, and in sets of cultural notions that govern and maintain these relationships and provide identity to the actors involved. Given the wide range of gestic behaviour, some disclaimers have to be made. I concentrate on one specific setting – the drinking establishment – and on a small number of gestures. These are emblematic or iconic in the sense that they represent cultural notions independently of speech, although they may also be used to add emphasis to verbal expression.[2] I will discuss their role in male sociability. Given the extreme paucity of reliable historical sources covering different periods, I leave aside the question of the origin, diffusion, and the eclipse of specific gestures.[3]

Mediterranean people, probably like most peoples, make extensive use of a vast range of gestures and body movements to convey

messages silently. In travel accounts as well as scholarly writings, Mediterranean gesticulation has been frequently misrepresented as spontaneous and even instinctive behaviour expressing the emotions of the actors. Many of the gestures I observed in Andalusian cafés, have nothing spontaneous about them nor are they a mirror of temperament. They are, in fact, to a greater or lesser degree, formalized. The messages they convey are predictable. This holds particularly true for the obscene gestures which are almost exclusively executed in jest as part of ritualized competitive interaction among drinking companions. Such gestures are staged, evocative, ordered, stylized, and carry a message.[4] They articulate the dominant notion of masculinity. But before going into the details of description and argument, let me first review how Spanish gestures have been represented in popular and scholarly literature.

## GESTURE AND NATIONAL STEREOTYPE

Northern travellers have frequently observed Spanish gesticulation with affection, but they have also deprecated and ridiculed it. They have stressed its range and intensity in contrast to the control and rigidity of the body in English or German interaction. On the basis of such 'observations' extreme conclusions have been drawn concerning the Spanish 'character'. Let us consider some paradigmatic examples.

Richard Ford, who wrote one of the best nineteenth-century travel books, provides a list of seven common gestures as an appendix to his discussion of the Spanish language and its dialects. He concludes his list with the following reflection:

To speak Spanish well [a man must] suit his action to his words; especially in Andalucia and southern countries, where bodily excitement keeps pace with mental imagination. It is no *still* life, and, although a pantomime, is anything but a dumb show: gesticulation is a safety-valve of the superabundant energy and caloric of the South . . . As far as power over, stress, intonation, and modulation (forgive the word) of the voice is concerned, even a Parisian might take a lesson on gesticulation . . . The Spaniards, in this respect perfectly Oriental, are formal and ceremonious, *etiqueteros*, sensitive and touchy . . . As they have nothing to do, the grand object is to kill time, and practice has made them perfect . . . all this is very natural and excusable in a self-loving, proud, decayed, semi-Oriental people, and it is quite distinct from the disposition to take affront which characterises the Anglo-Americans . . . Excess of ceremony is considered a high manner in the East, although among more western nations it is one indication of low breeding.[5]

Of special interest is his remark that 'most of the finger-talk . . . is confined to the lower classes'.[6] This may have been true for the Spanish cities but probably not for the rural towns. Also note how Ford, apart from airing the usual prejudices toward southerners, implicitly relates a presumed excess of gesturing and etiquette to a decline of civilization. At the same time there is a hint of cultural relativism in his observations on ceremonious behaviour.

Preoccupation with national character and civilization also marks the work on Spanish gesticulation published in the 1930s by two German linguists. Both have been strongly influenced by Wilhelm Wundt's *Völkerpsychologie*, in particular by the popular idea that primordial speech was a gesture and that gesticulation is a mirror of the soul. In his study of colloquial Spanish, entirely based on literary sources, Beinhauer deals with a small number of gestures that accompany speech. He maintains that gesticulation, intonation, and mimicry play a more prominent role in Spanish than in the 'more abstract northern languages', a contrast explained with reference to the 'strong imagination, talent for improvisation and enjoyment of theatricality' on the part of the Spaniards.[7] Flachskampf, who wrote the first catalogue of Spanish gestures, amplified such statements. Following Wundt, he claims that gestures are 'manifestations of a pre-logical and emotional substratum'. Consequently, a systematic study of gesturing will yield access to the 'soul of a race'.[8] Like a collector of butterflies, he gathered approximately one hundred gestures which he treated as isolates neatly classified under various headings. The two main categories are *gestos cultos*, confined to the upper classes, and 'affective' or 'irrational' gestures. The latter serve as a vehicle for the expression of unbridled emotion and make up the larger part of his catalogue. They are divided among seven subclasses: surprise and admiration, approval and disapproval, beckoning, disappointment, mockery and insult, refusal, magic and obscenity. Apart from the arbitrariness of such classifications, the ethnographic value of his inventory is further restricted by the dissociation of gestures from performers and context.

A more recent gesture inventory, published for the benefit of teaching Spanish, suffers from the same flaws. Green, an American linguist, describes the performance of 120 different gestures in narrative form, many of them illustrated by drawings. Gestures that function as a replacement for speech are excluded, as are erotic and obscene gestures because 'their pedagogical value is naturally limited'.[9] Regional and class differences are simply assumed to be non-significant. Since observations were almost exclusively conducted in an academic setting in Madrid, the selection and interpretation of gestures are strongly biased. Many of the depictions of individual gestures are shallow and incomplete. One example will suffice to illustrate these points. Embracing among men is described as follows:

The Spanish embrace is a gesture of greeting which is often, but not always, accompanied by verbal behavior. It is a distinctively masculine gestural phenomenon, and is executed only by close friends. It often serves to conclude or seal a business agreement. An example of the latter context from a Spanish novel: 'Se dieron un abrazo sellando lo acordado' (Zunzunegui, *La vida como es*, p. 76). American movers would rarely be observed in such a display of affection. In normal social interaction, Spanish men use the familiar handshake, but it should be noted that the handshake is observed much more frequently in contemporary Spain than in the United States. Handshaking between men and women is likewise more common in Spanish culture.[10]

Green does not include the postures and gestures preceding the actual embrace nor does he describe the accompanying verbal greeting. Two men who are equals, relatives, or close friends and have been separated for some time, meet and walk towards each other with extended arms, exclaiming before or during the embrace: 'Hombre, cómo estás? Tanto tiempo sin verte, coño!' If pronounced during the embrace, the words are emphasized with firm pats on the shoulder. The form, duration, and intensity of the embrace depend on many factors, including age, class, social distance, lapse of time since last meeting, and setting (arranged or casual meeting, agreement, festivity, burial, etc.). The specific combination of these factors determines variations in the form and sequence of actions. Men who are friends but not very close may perform a semi-embrace which consists of handshaking with the left hand gripping or patting the shoulder at the same time. Intimate friends and relatives may kiss each other on the cheeks while embracing. Similar specifications can be made with regard to the handshake. In Spain, members of a face-to-face community rarely use the handshake as a gesture when meeting each other. They prefer other body-contact movements. Handshaking between men and women is less common in towns and villages than in cities. Strangers usually shake hands briefly, while a businessman may grip the right hand of his business partner with both hands. Degree of social proximity or distance generally determines the extent of spatial distance and the intensity and duration of the physical performance. Differences in the degree of physical performance of both parties are often an index of status differentials, the superior party moving less than the inferior. A description of the Spanish embrace should also contrast masculine and feminine body movements. The female equivalent of the male embrace is typically more restrained and involves less physical performance when executed in public: the hands are placed slightly on the shoulders while the lips brush the cheeks. It is wrong to assume, as Green does, that the male embrace is a 'display of affection'. In Andalusia, male embraces are often quite formal. Here men have other gestures at their disposal to show their affection. I hope these marginal notes, which could be expanded at length, suffice to show that gestures of greeting are ethnographically complex phenomena. Decontextualized descriptions of bare physical movement yield caricatures of gestures.

The stereotype of the excessively gesticulating Spaniard, linked to his spontaneous, emotional, quick-tempered and high-spirited disposition, looms large in the accounts so far discussed. It persists in the images of Spain created by the tourist industry but also surfaces in recent ethnographies.[11] This cliché should be seen in relation to Western attitudes towards gesticulation. In the course of the civilizing process the upper classes of western Europe consciously suppressed the use of gestures and body movements, employing a less obvious and more subtle repertoire of gestic behaviour.[12] Civilized behaviour, control of emotion, and body movements were equated and became important markers of social class and status. This mechanism of creating and maintaining power differentials not only plays an important role in the relationships between elites and masses but also among nations. The stereotype of the gesticulating Spaniard fits well into the overall symbolic ordering of the north–south divide which roughly seems to follow the anatomy of the human body.[13] The gesticulating south is associated with emotion and spontaneity, and the more rigid north with rational (verbal) and control functions.

## MALE SOCIABILITY IN AGRO-TOWNS

The agro-town is the dominant habitat of southern Spain and its population ranges from 700 to 60,000 inhabitants. It prevails statistically as the home for the majority of landowners, farmers, peasants, and agricultural workers and it is superior to the countryside in terms of power and civilization.[14] This compact settlement is overwhelmingly rural in its basis of subsistence yet urban in size, townscape, and orientation. In Andalusia the opposition between town (*pueblo*) and country (*campo*) is fundamental. The agro-town, where houses are huddled on narrow streets, is the realm of *cultura* and *ambiente*, whereas the country is the non-social space of fields, animals, isolated farmsteads and hamlets. The people who live there are considered slow, ignorant, and uncouth.

The tavern, bar, or café is the focal institution of public life in these urbanesque settlements. The drinking establishment is more than a recreational centre where men gather for daily rounds of sociability and exchange. It is a social context for the creation and maintenance of friendship and for the celebration of masculinity.[15] Andalusian men distinguish between three different degrees of friendship. The first is ordinary friendship which is casual and takes place in cafés, social clubs, and other public places. Men who congregate in bars constitute fluid groups of companions. This kind of friendship rarely goes beyond the reciprocation of drinks, cigarettes, snacks, and information. Out of daily sociability may arise a second degree of friendship, called *amistad de compromiso* (committed friendship), which involves exchanging all kinds of services implicating members of the respective nuclear families of both parties. The most intimate type of friendship is *amistad de confianza*, a tie of mutual trust and affection which should go beyond mere self-interest.[16] Although the first degree of friendship is rather superficial, it is very important in the sense of serving male identity functions.

Andalusian men of all ages and classes spend much of their leisure time in bars. When a man gets up in the morning he immediately leaves his house to visit a café and have a glass of coffee, anisette, or cognac. If he works in the town or its vicinity, he will have some glasses of wine between one and two before going home for lunch. After the summer siesta he will have another coffee between four and five. The high time of bar attendance is in the evening between seven and ten when the cafés fill up with men busily talking and gesticulating. Alcohol, cigarettes, snacks, gestures, tall stories, horseplay, discussions of work, politics, sex, and football are the recurrent ingredients of bar sociability. Bar attendance is in fact a highly patterned social activity regulated by a strict etiquette.[17]

A wide variety of bars is felt to be a necessary condition for the *ambiente* of agro-towns. Attending them on a regular basis is considered imperative for a real man (*to' un hombre*). The bar is the place to show off masculinity and commit oneself to the game of power and domination. The essence of manliness is to 'have balls' (*tener cojones, un hombre de cojones*). Apart from sexually aggressive behaviour, it implies the will-power and ability to defend one's interest. A true man does not allow others to boss him around. Masculinity is by definition competitive. It is won or lost in confrontations with other men and with women. It entails comparison, challenge, defence, and offence and hinges upon honour. The ultimate proof of honour lies in the use of physical violence.[18] It has been argued that in Andalusia the emphasis in manliness is entirely on sexual aggression rather than on physical toughness.[19] It is true that the actual use of violence is rare in

Andalusian agro-towns. Violent behaviour is considered ugly (*feo*) and strongly condemned. However, this does not mean that physical strength and aggression are entirely absent in masculine behaviour. It is my contention that it is ritualized in many of the gestures performed in drinking establishments.

GESTURING MALE IDENTITY

Physical performance in bar sociability is direct and obtrusive. Men display their potential for physical aggression, proving their virility to their companions.[20] This is apparent from the amount of force when they smite each other on the back or shoulder, hit their coins on the counter, knock their dominoes on the table, or order drinks with a sharp and loud clapping of their hands. Men perform a large number of body-contact gestures when greeting each other or taking leave. These include striking the back of the head, the back of the neck, the chest, or stomach. Such slaps of 'affection' among equals and drinking partners are usually executed with considerable force. They communicate a man's strength and test the other man's toughness, how much he can take, and whether he is able to control himself.

In Andalusia, as elsewhere in Spain, virility is thought to reside in the testicles. Hence they play an important part in the body language of men in bars. Men frequently touch their testicles, lifting them up with one hand, for instance, upon entering a bar, taking a position at the counter, or while driving a point home during a debate. These are all situations in which they have to assert themselves. There are also iconic gestures specifically related to the *cojones* as in the case of the superlative *cojonudo* (*cojones* and *nudos* are 'balls'), meaning huge, powerful, and enormous: the gesticulator extends his arms a short distance at the level of the chest, fingers slightly curled, hollow palms facing upward, and alternately moving the hands up and down as if weighing something or juggling with balls. Testicles are also targets in pranking. A man stealthily approaches a friend, who is involved in a conversation at the counter, surprising him by grabbing his testicles from behind to the amusement of his drinking partners.

Another part of the male body which represents masculinity,

honour, and shame is the face. It is a man's visible self, embodying his identity and integrity before the community. If a man possesses a good face, he has shame. If he has a 'hard' face, he is insensitive, immoral, without shame. There is a standard gesture in the repertoire of male sociability indicating that a man has a hard face (*cara dura*): the gesticulator slaps his right cheek two or three times with the right hand; the mouth corners are lowered. This gesture is usually performed independently of speech, for instance to point out a man present in the bar. A variant of this gesture may be performed on a friend as part of horseplay. It consists of pinching a man's cheek to imply that he is a hard-faced one.

The eyes are a source of power and knowledge, instruments of domination. They figure in several iconic gestures. One of the most widespread is the eyelid pull. The gesticulator pulls down the loose skin below the lower lid of his right eye with the extended index finger of his right hand. This is a classic example of a gesture, sufficient by itself, which may be used in many different ways, according to the context. It is a polyvalent gesture. Morris lists two common meanings of the eyelid pull: alertness on the part of the gesturer himself or on the part of a companion.[21] In Andalusia, as elsewhere in Spain and southern Europe, its dominant meaning is *ojo!*, a friendly warning to be alert. In Andalusian bars I have observed the same gesture in yet other important ways. It is performed to indicate to a companion that a third man is a *tio prepara'o*, a guy to count on. But it may also be executed to point out a shrewd man. And, finally, it may be used to communicate that the gesturer sees through the hidden intentions of another man. In the latter case it is accompanied by a grinning mouth distension.

Another group of gestures, in which face and finger movements are combined to send out a message, relates to the law of hospitality in bar exchanges. Elsewhere I have dealt with the etiquette governing social drinking in Andalusia.[22] Generosity and reciprocity are sacred values which are tied to the ethos of equality. A man who frequently accepts drinks without reciprocating not only offends the law of hospitality but also the code of masculinity. If he persists in his anti-social and anti-masculine behaviour, he will be stigmatized for being a sponger (*gañote*, literally a gullet). There is a silent way of pointing out such men:

the gesturer moves his thumb and index finger fork-wise up and down the Adam's apple, his head thrust upward and face in deprecating grimace. This gesture is sometimes directed at solitary drinkers.

Obscene, derisive, and abusive gestures constitute a special category in the gestic repertoire of Andalusian men. Some general remarks are appropriate before going into details. Rude gestures are directly linked to notions of sexuality, masculinity, and femininity. In the context of agro-towns they are performed in exclusively male gatherings, regardless of class, education and occupation, although they may be observed more frequently among working-class men than among the elite. They are not executed in the presence of women. Obscene gestures challenge and threaten the masculinity of the male at whom they are addressed. In a face-to-face community they are rarely used to offend. If performed with serious intention they would trigger off violence. However, they may be directed at outsiders, for instance boys and men from neighbouring towns who visit the annual fair. Strangers in a city context may also exchange them, for instance in traffic situations. But within the *pueblo* their use is generally confined to male joking in bars. Rude gestures are the gist of *cachondeo*.[23]

Competitive joking is very popular among drinking companions in Andalusian cafés. *Cachondeo* is a playful yet aggressive type of joking in the sense that the initiator tries to get a rise out of his victim. Since it capitalizes so strongly upon male sensibilities, *cachondeo* means a challenge to a man's dignity and self-control (*formalidad*). Self-control is another important ingredient of the masculinity code. The victim must keep his face, withstand the jest, and strike back in a cool manner. A man who loses his temper is scorned by the audience. In sum, *cachondeo* is a test of manliness.

Intimate and easy-going body contact among men in homosocial gatherings sharply contrasts with the generally professed disgust of homosexuality. Several iconic gestures imply homosexuality and when directed at heterosexual men they become serious insults. A homosexual man and an effeminate man are conceptually identical in Andalusia. Not all men are cut for the macho role. The opposite of being a real man is being weak (*flojo*). A weak man spends too much time at home and is perceived as being dominated by females. The following gestures indicate homosexuality or effeminacy and are common throughout Andalusia. The most graphic one is to kiss the raised and extended forefinger, place it into the opening of the left fist, and move it in and out of the opening. The symbolism of this gesture is simple and direct. Less obvious is a second gesture: the left lower arm rests in the palm of the right hand and is moved upward until the extended forefinger presses against the left cheek. The forearm cum extended index finger is a phallic gesture, the cheek being converted into buttocks. The third gesture is similar: the extended index finger of the left hand is 'screwed' into the centre of the left cheek.[24] Whatever the origin of these gestures, it is obvious that they directly challenge a man's virility. In the context of the agro-town they are used in a variety of ways. They are sometimes applied to particular men who are assumed homosexuals or to persons mentioned in a conversation. They may be made to heterosexual men as an intended insult. Usually, however, they are used among friends in order to tease. It has been noted that Andalusian men have an obsessive fear of playing the passive role in a homosexual encounter, of 'being converted symbolically into a woman'.[25] A standard expression, *tomar por culo* (to take by the ass), voices this fear of subordination by anal penetration. It means making a fool of a man by taking his honour away. Many of the rude jokes men play upon each other in bars capitalize on this fear of being turned into a woman.

The same mechanism of dishonouring underlies gestures implying cuckoldry.[26] A man whose wife has been seduced by another man is deprived of his virility and converted symbolically into a woman. In Andalusia there are two basic versions of the *cornudo* gesture. The right or left hand is raised, the two middle fingers are doubled down by the thumb, leaving the index and little fingers standing out in a vertical position like a pair of horns. In the second version the hand is pointed forward with the index and little fingers extended horizontally. Both variants are common throughout Spain. In the bar context the vertical horn gesture is more often used in jest than meant seriously. In *cachondeo* it is performed behind the victim's head. This prank can be played over and over again and still provoke hilarious laughter. A mock fight may ensue between the victim and aggressor. It has been observed that in some parts of the Mediterranean area the horizontal horn gesture may be used as a device to ward off danger, especially the evil eye.[27] While there are some indications that this usage was known in Spain in former times, I have never observed or heard of this use in Andalusia.[28]

One of the most current obscene gestures to be observed in Andalusian bars is the so-called *puñeta* which means masturbation (*hacer la puñeta*, to masturbate). This gesture is a graphic representation of the masturbating hand. The right or left hand is held out in a diagonal position in front of the chest or somewhat lower, fingers slightly bent towards the palm as to leave an opening, the hand being pumped vigorously a number of times. This gesture carries at least three different meanings depending on the context. It may be used as a gross rejection *vis-à-vis* outsiders. It also conveys a sexual insult or threat by forcing the person to whom the *puñeta* is made into an inferior sexual position. When used among drinking companions in the bar setting it may carry an opposite meaning, i.e. a laudatory comment on sexual vigour, or, more generally, praise with regard to something powerful and pleasurable like the act of sexual penetration and intercourse as seen from the Andalusian male point of view.

There are many ways to insult a man. The most serious and powerful ones all involve gestured phallic obscenities. Two of the familiar offensive gestures are the stiff middle or index finger extended from the right fist with the back of the hand turned toward the person offended, and what has been called the forearm jerk.[29] They may also be combined. In Spain the forearm jerk is known as *el corte de mangas*, the cut of the sleeves. It is a very hostile gesture challenging the virility of another man. In the café context it is performed as a gesture of rage, scorn, or contempt towards a person or event discussed in a conversation. In Andalusia I have never seen the forearm jerk being performed in the sense of a praise of sexual vigour and strength.

Sexual differentiation in terms of dominance and submission is thus a pervasive theme in male social drinking behaviour. Some bodily performances in *cachondeo* graphically reproduce the physical act of intercourse, such as placing the elbows on both hips and moving the abdomen back and forth in rapid motions. At one of the revels I attended a landowner forced one of his labourers into playing the female part in a burlesque of the coitus, being taken from behind. This is an instance in which social and sexual submission coincide. The worker was feminized by his employer and had to suffer this humiliation, probably for fear of being sacked. To be sure, this is one of the crudest obscene performances I witnessed in Andalusia. Much of the horseplay in bars consists of less offensive bodily performances. Yet, as I noted above, approaching a man from behind is frequently part of it.

## CONCLUSION

Gesticulation is a highly articulated and meaningful form of communication. Contrary to the received wisdom on Spanish gesturing, I have argued that iconic gesture is not emotion expressed freely but, rather, an ordered representation of basic cultural notions. Most of the gestures discussed in this chapter hinge upon the theme of power. We have seen that Andalusians use icons of male physical form, in particular icons of sexual penetration, to sustain their notion of masculine domination. Sexual inequality is revealed in the nature and extent of gestic behaviour in public. Women, especially those who are sexually active and married, are not only restricted in the use of public space, they are also less visible than men when they do appear in public.[30] They refrain from performing gestures that direct too much attention to their bodies. Constrained behaviour is inherent in the female modesty code. Men, on the other hand, are expected to move and gesticulate in highly visible ways.

Male body movements and gestures in the bar setting are to a large extent controlled and even formalized. Iconic gestures are repeated over and over again so that the messages they convey become fixed and predictable. They are an integral part of what one might call the choreography of male sociability. This is particularly evident in the cultural genre of *cachondeo* in which gestures and postures figure prominently. This ritualized form of male competition captivates the men who are involved in it to the extent that they believe in what they perform. In a paradoxical way, contentious gesticulation enhances male companionship and helps to sustain the notion of masculine superiority.

## NOTES

I should like to express my gratitude to Anton Blok for his comments on a first draft of this paper.

1 Fieldwork in Andalusia was conducted in the summer of 1974, one year during 1977/8, followed by brief visits in 1979, 1984, and 1986.

2 It should scarcely need to be stressed that the boundary between gestures, postures, and manners is uncertain. Strictly speaking, verbal and non-verbal behaviour are not separable. In this chapter I use the word gesture rather loosely. The concept of emblematic gesture was coined by D. Efron, *Gesture, Race and Culture*, 1st edn 1941 (The Hague, 1972). It denotes standard gestures that are learned like a vocabulary with more or less fixed meanings.

3 See F. Poyatos, 'The morphological and functional approach to kinesics in the context of interaction and culture', *Semiotica*, 20 (1977), p. 209, for a superficial speculation about the historical development of the male deep squat: 'The male deep squat observed among the working class in southern Spain closer to Morocco (a home culture of such a posture), is obviously a vestigial trait from the eight-century occupation of the area by the Moslems.' It is impossible to document or prove what is assumed to be 'obvious'. Moreover, there are significant differences between the Andalusian and Moroccan deep squat. In the latter both feet are firmly on the ground, the haunches lowered so that they barely touch the heels. The knees are pointed up at a slight angle and are held closely in front of the chest. Arms rest on the knees. With trousers on, this posture is difficult to make. Consequently, the Andalusian squat is less deep. The position of haunches, feet, and heels differ. Also see D. Morris et al., *Gestures: Their Origins and Distribution* (New York and London, 1979), for many wild guesses concerning the origin of gestures.

4 For a useful definition of ritual, see S. F. Moore and B. G. Myerhoff, 'Introduction. Secular ritual: forms and meanings', in S. F. Moore and B. G. Myerhoff (eds), *Secular Ritual* (Assen, 1977), pp. 7–8. Also see E. Goffman, *Interaction Ritual. Essays on Face-to-Face Behavior* (New York, 1967). The vignette of the winker in Clifford Geertz's essay on thick description shows how to move from a 'thin' description of physical movements to a 'thick' description of meaningful behaviour; *The Interpretation of Cultures* (New York, 1973), pp. 3–31.

5 R. Ford, *A Hand-Book for Travellers in Spain, and Readers at Home* (3 vols, London, 1966). This superb travel book was first published in 1845. The seven standard gestures are described in vol. 1, pp. 127–8. Five of these gestures are also included in Morris, *Gestures*: the

forearm jerk, beckoning, the finger-tips kiss, the fig, and the vertical horn-sign.

6  Ford, *A Hand-Book for Travellers in Spain*, p. 128.

7  W. Beinhauer, *Spanische Umgangssprache* (Berlin, 1930), p. 191. He attributes these faculties to the 'subjective and passionate character of the Spanish people, a disposition common to all southerners' (p. 112).

8  L. Flachskampf, 'Spanische Gebärdensprache', *Romanische Forschungen*, 52 (1939), pp. 205–58. In spite of obvious regional differences, this author postulates 'a strong unity of the Spanish nation, a common psychic structure' (p. 209). The four cardinal sins of national character studies are essentialism, reification of traits, projection and stereotyping. See H. C. J. Duijker and N. H. Frijda, *National Character and National Stereotypes* (Amsterdam, 1960).

9  J. R. Green, *A Gesture Inventory for the Teaching of Spanish* (Philadelphia, 1968), p. 9.

10  Green, *A Gesture Inventory*, p. 34.

11  See D. D. Gilmore, *Aggression and Community: Paradoxes of Andalusian Culture* (New Haven, 1987): 'Andalusians do not hesitate to express their feelings, and they do so volubly and eloquently in spontaneous song, art, and sunny poetry as well as in the mundane rituals of their daily lives', p. 3.

12  The connection between civilization and bodily control has been explored in a wide range of influential studies. See M. Mauss, 'Body techniques' (first published in 1935), in his *Sociology and Psychology: Essays* (London, 1979), pp. 97–123; N. Elias, *Über den Prozess der Zivilisation* (2 vols,Basel, 1939); M. Douglas, *Purity and Danger: An Analysis of Concepts of Pollution and Taboo* (London, 1966); R. Firth, *Symbols, Public and Private* (London, 1973); J. Blacking (ed.), *The Anthropology of the Body* (London, 1977); B. S. Turner, *The Body and Society: Explorations in Social Theory* (Oxford, 1984). The work of Foucault is almost entirely devoted to this fascinating problem. See also the bibliography at the end of this volume.

13  See J. Fernandez, 'Consciousness and class in southern Spain' (review article), *American Ethnologist*, 10 (1983), pp. 165–73.

14  See A. Blok and H. Driessen, 'Mediterranean agro-towns as a form of cultural dominance. With special reference to Sicily and Andalusia', *Ethnologia Europaea*, 14 (1984), pp. 111–24.

15  For a general discussion of the drinking establishment in Andalusia see H. Driessen, 'Male sociability and rituals of masculinity in rural Andalusia', *Anthropological Quarterly*, 56 (1983), pp. 125–34; D. D. Gilmore, 'The role of the bar in Andalusian society: observations on political culture under Franco', *Journal of Anthropological Research*, 41 (1985), pp. 263–76.

16  For a discussion of friendship see D. D. Gilmore, *The People of the*

*Plain: Class and Community in Lower Andalusia* (New York, 1980).

17 I have elaborated this point in Driessen, 'Male sociability and rituals of masculinity'. Also see S. H. Brandes, *Metaphors of Masculinity: Sex and Status in Andalusian Folklore* (Philadelphia, 1980).

18 See J. Pitt-Rivers, *The Fate of Shechem or the Politics of Sex: Essays in the Anthropology of the Mediterranean* (Cambridge, 1977), p. 8.

19 Cf. M. Gilmore and D. D. Gilmore, ' "Machismo": A psychodynamic approach (Spain)', *The Journal of Psychological Anthropology*, 2 (1979), pp. 281–300.

20 Brandes, *Metaphors of Masculinity*, p. 126.

21 Morris, *Gestures*, pp. 71–3.

22 Driessen, 'Male sociability and rituals of masculinity', p. 128.

23 See for a general discussion of *cachondeo*, H. Berger, M. Hessler, B. Kaveman, *"Brot für Heute, Hunger für Morgen": Landarbeiter in Südspanien* (Frankfurt am Main, 1978), pp. 224ff.; Brandes, *Metaphors of Masculinity*, pp. 122–3; Driessen, 'Male sociability and rituals of masculinity', p. 130.

24 Interestingly enough, Morris (*Gestures*, p. 62) lists what he calls the cheek screw as a typical Italian gesture of praise. His team also discovered the entirely different meaning attached to this gesture in southern Spain (p. 67). He attributes this meaning to an Arab influence. In Arab countries this gesture is a way of commenting on a beautiful woman. Says Morris: 'Such an Arab gesture, deliberately applied to a male in southern Spain (where there has been an Arab influence for centuries) would obviously become an immediate challenge to his masculinity and could quickly grow into a local insult.' This is, of course, pure speculation.

25 Also see Brandes, *Metaphors of Masculinity*, pp. 95–6.

26 For a general discussion of the horizontal and vertical horn signs, see Morris, *Gestures*, pp. 120–46. For an excellent contextual analysis of the horn symbolism in the Mediterranean area, see A. Blok, 'Rams and billy-goats: a key to the Mediterranean code of honour', *Man*, 16 (1981), pp. 427–40. Also see R. A. Barakat, 'Arabic gestures', *Journal of Popular Culture*, 6 (1973), pp. 749–87.

27 Morris, *Gestures*, pp. 138–43.

28 The same observation is true for the well-known fig gesture (*hacer la higa*).

29 Cf. Morris, *Gestures*, pp. 80–93.

30 See for a general study C. Mayo and N. M. Henly (eds), *Gender and Nonverbal Behavior* (New York, 1981), and for a case study W. Jansen, *Women Without Men: Gender and Marginality in an Algerian Town* (Leiden, 1987).

# Gestures in history:
# a select bibliography

JAN BREMMER AND HERMAN ROODENBURG

What follows is a personal sampling of the vast literature on gestures. The subject is, of course, endless and we have therefore concentrated on books and articles with a historical interpretation of gestures in Europe; for non-European gestures we refer to the excellent bibliography of Morris. We do mention, however, those studies of other disciplines, such as anthropology, kinesics, proxemics, and semiotics which are of great value to the historian. Naturally we have profited from previous bibliographies, in particular the one by Jean-Claude Schmitt. We thank Fritz Graf for various suggestions.

## BIBLIOGRAPHIES

Bäuml, B. J. and N. F. H., *A Dictionary of Gestures*, Metuchen, J., 1975, pp. xiii–xxxiii.
Davies, M. and Skupien, J. (eds), *Body Movement and Non-verbal Communication: An Annotated Bibliography 1971–1981*, (Bloomington, 1982.
Gadeau, P., 'Les domaines de la gestuelle italienne: orientation bibliographique', *Les Langues Néo-latines*, 80 (1986), pp. 109–26.

Hayes, F. C., 'Gestures: a working bibliography', *Southern Folklore Quarterly*, 21 (1957), pp. 218–317.

Morris, D., Collet, P., Marsh, P., and O'Shaughnessy, M., *Gestures: Their Origins and Distribution*, New York and London, 1979, pp. 275–92.

Schmitt, J.-C., 'Introduction and general bibliography', *History and Anthropology*, 1 (1984), pp. 1–28, esp. 18–23.

## HISTORIOGRAPHY AND METHODOLOGY

Cocchiara, G., *Il linguaggio del gesto*, Palermo, 1977.

Kendon, A. (ed.), *Nonverbal Communication, Interaction and Gesture: Selections from 'Semiotica'*, The Hague, Paris, and New York, 1981.

'Geography of gesture', *Semiotica*, 37 (1981), pp. 129–63.

'The study of gesture: some observations on its history', *Recherches Sémiotiques/Semotic Enquiry*, 2 (1982), pp. 45–62.

'Some reasons for studying gestures', *Semiotica*, 62 (1986), pp. 3–28.

Kriss-Rettenbeck, L., 'Probleme der volkskundlichen Gebärdenforschung', *Bayerisches Jahrbuch für Volkskunde* (1964–5), pp. 14–46.

Mauss, M., 'Les techniques du corps', *Journal de psychologie normale et pathologique*, 39 (1935), pp. 271–93, reprinted in his *Sociologie et anthropologie*, Paris, 1950, pp. 365–86 [*Sociology and Psychology*, London 1979, pp. 97–123].

Röhrich, L., 'Gebärdensprache und Sprachgebärde', in *Humaniora: Essays in Literature, Folklore, Bibliography. Honoring Archer Taylor on his Seventieth Birthday*, New York, 1960, pp. 121–49, reprinted in his *Gebärde – Metapher – Parodie*, Düsseldorf, 1967, pp. 7–36.

Schmitt, J.-C., 'Introduction and general bibliography', *History and Anthropology*, 1 (1984), pp. 1–28, esp. 1–18.

## HISTORY AND ART HISTORY

*Through the Ages*

Elias, N., *Über den Prozess der Zivilisation: Soziogenetische und psychogenetische Untersuchungen*, 2 vols, Basel, 1939.

*Gestes et paroles dans les diverses familles liturgiques*, Rome, 1978.

*Gestures*, ed. J.-C. Schmitt [*History and Anthropology*, 1 (1984)].

Nitschke, A., *Körper in Bewegung: Gesten, Tänze und Räume im Wandel der Geschichte*, Stuttgart, 1989.

Riemschneider-Hoerner, M., *Der Wandel der Gebärde in der Kunst*, Frankfurt, 1930.


*Antiquity*


Brilliant, R., *Gesture and Rank in Roman Art: The Use of Gestures to Denote Status in Roman Sculpture and Coinage*, New Haven, 1963.

Brown, P., *The Body and Society: Men, Women and Sexual Renunciation in Early Christianity*, New York, 1988.

Evans, E. C., 'Physiognomics in the ancient world', *Transactions of the American Philosophical Society*, New Series, 59, pt 5 (Philadelphia, 1969), pp. 3–101.

Fehr, B., *Bewegungsweisen und Verhaltensideale: Physiognomische Deutungsmöglichkeiten der Bewegungsdarstellung an griechischen Statuen des 5. und 4. Jh. v. Chr.*, Bad Bramstedt, 1979.

Foerster, R., *Scriptores physiognomicici*, 2 vols, Leipzig 1893.

Jorio, A. de, *La mimica degli antichi investigata nel gestire Napoletano*, Naples, 1832, repr. 1964.

Jucker, I., *Die Gestus des Aposkopeion*, Zurich, 1956.

Maguire, H., *Eloquence and Gestures in Byzantium*, Princeton, 1981.

Maier-Eichhorn, U., *Die Gestikulation in Quintilians Rhetorik*, Frankfurt and Bern, 1989.

Neumann, G., *Gesten und Gebärden in der griechischen Kunst*, Berlin, 1965.

Sittl, K., *Die Gebärden der Griechen und Römer*, Leipzig, 1890.

Taladoire, B.-A., *Commentaires sur la mimique et l'expression corporelle du comédien romain*, Montpellier, 1951.


*Middle Ages and Renaissance*


Amira, K. von, *Die Handgebärden in den Bilderhandschriften des Sachsenspiegels*, Munich, 1905.

Baaren, T. P. van, 'The significance of gestures in the paintings of Hieronymus Bosch', *Visible Religion*, 7 (1990), pp. 21–30.

Barasch, M., *Gestures of Despair in Medieval and Early Renaissance Art*, New York, 1976.

*Giotto and the Language of Gestures*, Cambridge, Mass., 1987.

Benson, R. G., *Medieval Body Language: A Study of the Use of Gesture in Chaucer's Poetry*, Copenhagen, 1980.

Frenzen, W., 'Klagebilder und Klagegebärden in der deutschen Dichtung des Höfischen Mittelalters', *Bonner Beiträge zur deutschen Philologie*, 1, Wurzburg, 1936, pp. 22–4.

Garnier, F., *Le langage de l'image au Moyen Age: Signification et Symbolique*, 2 vols, Paris, 1982–9.

Goedecke, A., *Die Darstellung der Gemütsbewegungen in der isländischen Familiensaga*, Hamburg, 1933.

Habicht, W., *Die Gebärde in englischen Dichtungen des Mittelalters*, Munich, 1959.

Harbison, C., 'Sexuality and social standing in Jan van Eyck's Arnolfini double portrait', *Renaissance Quarterly*, 43 (1990), 249–91.

Hood, W., 'Saint Dominic's manners of praying: gestures in Fra Angelico's cell frescoes at S. Marco', *Art Bulletin*, 68 (1986), pp. 195–206.

Jarecki, W., *Signa loquendi: Die cluniacensischen Signa-Listen*, Baden-Baden, 1981.

Kushner, E., 'Gesture in the work of Rabelais', *Renaissance and Reformation/Renaissance et Réforme*, 10 (1986), pp. 67–71.

Lommatsch, E., *System der Gebärden, dargestellt auf Grund der mittelalterlichen Literatur Frankreichs*, Berlin, 1910.

Manard, P., 'Les gestes et les expressions corporelles dans la *Chanson de Roland*', in *Guillaume d'Orange and the Chanson de Geste*, ed. W. van Emden et al., Reading, 1984, pp. 85–92.

Nitschke, A., *Bewegungen in Mittelalter und Renaissance: Kämpfe Spiele, Tänze, Zeremonielle und Umgangsformen*, Cologne, 1987.

Peil, D., *Die Gebärde bei Chrétien, Hartmann und Wolfram: Erec–Iwein–Parzival*, Munich, 1975.

Rijnberk, G. van, *Le langage par signes chez les moines*, Amsterdam, 1953.

Roeder, A., *Die Gebärde im Drama des Mittelalters: Osterfeiern, Osterspiele*, Munich, 1974.

Rothschild, J. R. 'Manipulative gestures and behaviors in the *Lais* of Marie de France', in *Spirit of the Court*, ed. G. S. Burgess et al., Dover N.H., 1985, pp. 283–8.

Russell Major, J., '"Bastard feudalism" and the kiss: changing social mores in late medieval and early modern France, *Journal of Interdisciplinary History*, 17 (1987), pp. 509–35.

Schmidt-Wiegand, R., 'Gebärdensprache im mittelalterlichen Recht', *Frühmittelalterliche Studien*, 16 (1982), pp. 363–79.

Schmitt, J.-C., *La raison des gestes dans l'Occident médiéval*, Paris, 1990. '*Gestus/Gesticulato*. Contribution à l'etude du vocabulaire latin médiéval des gestes', in *La lexicographie du latin médiéval et ses rapports avec les recherches actuelles sur la civilisation du Moyen Age*, Paris, 1981, pp. 377–90.

Suntrup, R., *Die Bedeutung der liturgischen Gebärden und Bewegungen in lateinischen und deutschen Auslegungen des 9. bis 13. Jahrhunderts*, Munich, 1978.

Umiker-Sebeok, J. and Sebeok, T., *Monastic Sign Languages*, Berlin, 1987.

Wandruszka, M., *Haltung und Gebärde der Romanen*, Tübingen, 1954.

Wells, D. A., 'Gesture in Hartmann's *Gregorius*', in T. McFarland and S. Ranawake (eds), *Hartmann von Aue: Changing Perspectives*, Göttingen, 1988, pp. 159–86.

Windeatt, B., 'Gesture in Chaucer', in *Medievalia et Humanistica*, 9 (1979), pp. 143–61.


*The Early Modern Period*

Barnett, D., *The Art of Gesture: The Practice and Principles of 18th Century Acting*, Heidelberg, 1987.

Bevington, D., *Action is eloquence: Shakespeare's Language of Gesture*, Cambridge, Mass., 1984.

Bogucka, M., 'Le geste dans la vie religieuse, familiale, sociale, publique de la noblesse polonaise aux XVIe, XVIIe et XVIIIe siècles', *Revue d'histoire moderne et contemporaine*, 30 (1983), pp. 4–19.

Bonfatti, E., 'Vorläufige Hinweise zu einem Handbuch der Gebärdensprache im deutschen Barock', in J. P. Strelka and J. Jungmayr (eds), *Virtus et Fortuna: zur deutschen Literatur zwischen 1400 und 1720*, Bern, 1983, pp. 393–405.

Bonifacio, G., *L'arte de' cenni*, Vicenza, 1616.

Bulwer, J., *Chirologia: or the Naturall Language of the Hand . . . Whereunto is added Chironomia: or the Art of Manuall Rhetoricke*, 2 vols, London, 1644.

Damisch, H., 'Charles le Brun: Conférence sur l'expression de Passions', *Nouvelle Revue de Psychanalyse*, 21 (1980), pp. 93–109.

Dumont, M., 'Le succès mondain d'une fausse science: la physiognomie de Johann Kaspar Lavater', *Actes de la recherche en sciences sociales*, 54 (1984), 2–30.

Engel, J.-J. *Ideen zu einer Mimik* Berlin, 1756–86.

Fischer-Lichte, E., 'Theatergeschichte oder Theatersemiotik: eine echte Alternative? Versuch einer semiotischen Rekonstruktion der Theater-

258  Jan Bremmer and Herman Roodenburg

geste auf dem deutschen Theater im 18. Jahrhundert', *Maske und Kothurn*, 28 (1982), pp. 163–94.

Kaüser, A., *Physiognomik und Roman im 18. Jahrhundert*, Frankfurt, 1989.

Knowlson, J. R., 'The idea of gesture as a universal language in the XVIIth and XVIIIth centuries, *Journal of the History of Ideas*, 26 (1965), pp. 495–508.

Knox, D., 'Ideas on gesture and universal language c.1550–1650', in J. Henry and S. Hutton (eds), *New Perspectives in Renaissance Thought. Studies in Intellectual History in Memory of Charles B. Schmidt*, London, 1990.

Lavater, J. C., *Physiognomische Fragmente* 4 vols, Leipzig and Winterthür, 1775–8.

Lebrun, C., *Conférence sur l'expression générale et particulière*, Amsterdam, 1698.

Muchembled, R., 'Pour une histoire des gestes (XVe–XVIIIe siècle)', *Revue d'histoire moderne et contemporaine*, 34 (1987), pp. 81–101.

*Rhetorique du geste et de la voix à l'age classique [XVIIe Siècle*, 33 (1981), pp. 235–355].

Porta, G. B. della, *Coelestis physiognomoniae libri sex*, Naples, 1603.

Sena, J. F., 'The language of gestures in *Gulliver's Travels*', *Papers on Language and Literature*, 19 (1983), pp. 145–66.

Siegel, J., 'The Enlightenment and the evolution of a language of signs in France and England', *Journal of the History of Ideas*, 30 (1969), pp. 96–115.

Smart, A., 'Dramatic gesture and expression in the age of Hogarth and Reynolds', *Apollo*, 82 (1965), 90–97.

Torrini, M., *Giovanni Battista della Porta nell'Europa del suo tempo*, Naples, 1990.


*Modern Times*


Calbris, G., *The Semiotics of French Gestures*, Bloomington, 1990.

and J. Montredon, *Des gestes et des mots pour le dire*, Paris, 1986.

Eason, A., 'Emotion and gesture in *Nicholas Nickelby*', *Dickens Quarterly*, 5 (1988), no. 34, pp. 136–51.

Efron, D., *Gesture and Environment*, New York, 1941, reprinted as *Gesture, Race and Culture*, The Hague, 1972.

Heine, T., 'The force of gestures: a new approach to the problem of communication in Hofmannsthal's *Der Schwierige*', *German Quarterly*, 56 (1983), pp. 408–18.

Meo-Zilio, G. and S. Mejía, *Diccionario de gestos: España e Hispanoamerica*, 2 vols, Bogotà, 1980–3.
Monahan, B., *A Dictionary of Russian Gesture*, Ann Arbor, 1983.
Ricci-Bitti, P. E., 'Communication by gestures in south and north Italians', *Italian Journal of Psychology*, 3 (1976), pp. 117–26.
Schwalbe, J., *Sprache und Gebärde im Werke Hugo von Hofmannsthals*, Freiburg, 1971.
Wylie, L. W., *Beaux Gestes: A Guide to French Body Talk*, Cambridge, Mass., 1977.


## LINGUISTICS, SEMIOTICS, NON-VERBAL COMMUNICATION, KINESICS


*Approaches to Gesture* [special issue: *Semiotica*], 62 (1982).
Bachmann-Medick, D., *Die Ästhetische ordnung des Handelns: Moral philosophie und Asthetik in der Popularphilosophie des 18. Jahrhunderts* (Stuttgart, 1989).
Birdwhistell, R., *Introduction to Kinesics*, Louisville, 1954.
    *Kinesics and Context: Essays on Body Motion Communication*, Philadelphia, 1970.
    'Kinesics: inter- and intra-channel communication research', in J. Kristeva et al. (eds), *Essays on Semiotics*, The Hague and Paris, 1971, pp. 527–47.
Henley, N. M., *Body Politics*, Englewood Cliffs, 1977.
Hinde, R.-A. (ed.), *Non-verbal Communication*, Cambridge, 1972.
Jakobson, R., *Aufsätze zur Linguistik und Poetik* Munich, 1974, pp. 150–224. [(abbreviated) *Selected Writings*, The Hague, 1971, vol. 2, pp. 655–96].
Key, M.-R., *The Relationship of Verbal and Nonverbal Communication*, The Hague, 1980.
Mayo, C. and Henley, N. C. (eds), *Gender and Nonverbal Behavior*, New York, 1981.
Mehrabian, A., *Nonverbal Communication* Chicago and New York, 1972.
Poyatos, F., *Man Beyond Words: Theory and Methodology of Nonverbal Communication*, New York, 1976.
    'The morphological and functional approach to kinesics in the context of interaction and culture', *Semiotica*, 20 (1977), pp. 197–229.
    (ed.), *Crosscultural Perspectives in Nonverbal Communiction*, Toronto, 1988.

Sacks, O., *Seeing Voices: A Journey into the World of the Deaf*, London, 1990.
Wundt, W., *The Language of Gestures: With an Introduction by A. L. Blumenthal and Additional Essays by G. H. Mead and K. Bühler*, The Hague and Paris, 1973; 1st German edition 1921.

## ANTHROPOLOGY, SOCIOLOGY, PROXEMICS

Blacking, J., *The Anthropology of the Body*, London, 1977.
Douglas, M. *Natural Symbols*, London, 1970.
Firth, R., *Symbols, Public and Private*, London, 1973.
Geertz, C., 'Thick description: Toward an Interpretive Theory of Culture', in: idem, *The Interpretation of Cultures: Selected Essays* (New York, 1973), pp. 3–32.
Goffman, E., *Encounters: Two Studies in the Sociology of Interaction*, Indianapolis and New York, 1961.
*Interaction Ritual: Essays on Face-to-Face Behavior*, New York, 1967.
*Gender Advertisements*, London, 1970.
*Relations in Public: Microstudies of the Public Order*, New York, 1971.
Hall, E. T., *The Silent Language*, New York, 1959.
*The Hidden Dimension*, New York, 1969.
'Proxemics', *Current Anthropology*, 9, no. 2/3 (1968), pp. 83–108.
*Handbook for Proxemic Research*, Washington, 1974.
Polhemus, T. (ed.), *Social Aspects of the Human Body*, Harmondsworth, 1978.
*Présentation et représentation du corps* [*Actes de la Recherche en Sciences Sociales*, 14 (1977)].
Turner, B. S., *The Body and Society: Explorations in Social Theory*, Oxford, 1984.
Watson, M., *Proxemic Behaviour*, The Hague, 1970.

## BIOLOGY AND ETHOLOGY

Darwin, C., *The Expression of Emotions in Man and Animals*, London, 1872.
Eibl-Eibesfeldt, I., *Ethology: The Biology of Behavior*, New York, 1970.
Ekman, P. (ed.), *Darwin and Facial Expression: A Century of Research in Review*, London, 1973.
Ekman, P. and Friesen, W., *Unmasking the Face*, Englewood Cliffs, 1975.
Morris, D., *Manwatching: A Field Guide to Human Behaviour*, London, 1977.

# Index of names

Bulwer, J.   2, 74, 95
Burke, P.   9, 161

Calbris, G.   4
Caravaggio, M.   86, 120
Caroso, F.   77
Carrière, J.-C.   129
Casa, G. della   75, 77
Casanova de Seingault, J. de   177
Cascudo, C.   71
Castiglione, B.   75–8, 93
Catharina of Habsburg   199
Cato   44
Cats, J.   157
Cattaneo, Flippo   112
Cattaneo, Marchesa   112
Cecile Renate of Habsburg   196
Champigne, Ph. de   142
Charlemagne   10, 63
Charles II, king of England   219
Charmides   18
Chodkiewicz   197
Christ   61, 88
Cicero   11, 29
Cleland, J.   178
Clement of Alexandria   28
Cleon   50
Cobb, R.   172
Cornazano, F.   75
Cortese, P.   76
Coryate, Th.   74, 80
Cosimo I de Medici   93
Courtin, A. de   74, 118
Crassus   39, 46
Croesus   18
Cuyp, A.   117
Czarnkowski, S.   199

Darrell, W.   7
Darwin, C.   2
David   67, 86
Davis, N. Zemon   129

Demetrios of Phaleron   37
Demosthenes   19, 48
Denhoff, G.   195
Denmark, king of   5
Descartes, R.   85
Dio Chrysostom   22
Diogenes   22
Dionysos   21, 48
Donne, J.   222
Doria, P. M.   78
Douglas, M.   4
Dousa the Elder, J.   227
Driessen, H.   8
Dupront, A.   228
Dürer, A.   86, 88
Dyck, A. van   90, 112

Effen, J. van   169
Efron, D.   3, 39
Eike von Repgow   64
Ekman, P.   39
Elias, N.   4, 11, 79
Elisha, prophet   219
Episcopius, S.   152, 153
Erasmus, D.   9, 11, 28
Euripides   21
Eve   110
Evelyn, J.   73, 74
Eyck, J. van   108

Fail, N. de   134
Félibien, A.   142
Flachskampf, L.   239
Flaubert, G.   222
Flinck, C.   104
Ford, R.   238
Foucault, M.   79
Francken II, F.   112
Fresne, Baronesse de   176
Freud, S.   72
Friesen, W. V.   39
Frijhoff, W.   11

Leonardo   85, 108
Lievens, J.   97
Locke, J.   171
Lomazzo, G. P.   162
Lotto, L.   90
Louis XIV, king of France   170
Louise Mary Gonzaga   195

Maderna, C.   218
Maecenas   45, 47
Maes, E. van der   95
Mander, K. van   85
Mars   48
Martens, W. J.   222
Master ES   110
Matuszewicz, M.   199
Maurits, prince of Orange   112, 115
Mauss, M.   3, 15, 21
Meeckenem   110
Melanchton, P.   52
Menelaus   16
Metsu, G.   90, 115
Molière   137, 142
Montaigne, M. de   74
Montredon, J.   4
Moore, J.   80
Morelli, G.   72
Morris, D.   4, 72, 245
Moryson, F.   156
Mucante, G. P.   194
Muchembled, R.   8

Nietzsche, F.   159
Nottingham, earl of   5

Odysseus   17
Ogier, C.   202–3
Ostade, A. van   159
Ottonelli, G. D.   75

Panaetius   29
Panofsky, E.   166
Paris   16
Parival, J. de   156
Parker, G.   173
Parmigianino   90
Pascal, B.   74
Pasek, J. C.   194, 199
Patroclus   26
Pedro de Toledo   78
Perella, N. J.   221–2
Pericles   19, 28
Perrucci, A.   75
Perugino   88
Peter the Chanter   68
Phrynichus   18
Plato   18, 19, 40
Plautus   49, 52
Plutarch   19, 28
Polemon   18
Polyphemus   17
Pontormo   93, 120
Porta, G. B. della   2, 77
Poussin, N.   74
Priam   26
Protasowicz, J.   194
Puteanus, E.   226–7

Quast, P.   100
Quintilian   10, 36–52

Rabelais, F.   146, 178
Radziwill, A. St   196, 199
Radziwill, B.   199
Raphael   108
Rej, M.   191
Rejtan, T.   200
Rembrandt   88, 97
Remigius of Auxerre   66
Restif de la Bretonne, N   135
Richelieu, Duke of   142
Rodin, G.   222

# Index of subjects